ENGLISH WORKSHOP

FIFTH COURSE

HOLT, RINEHART AND WINSTON

Harcourt Brace & Company

Austin • New York • Orlando • Chicago • Atlanta
San Francisco • Boston • Dallas • Toronto • London

ACKNOWLEDGMENTS

We wish to thank the following teachers who reviewed materials for *English Workshop*, either in manuscript or in field tests.

Loraine Hammack
Beachwood High School
Beachwood, OH 44122

Nancy Lewis Hankins
Socorro High School
El Paso, TX 79927

Jan McClure
Winter Park High School
Winter Park, FL 32792

Ronessa McDonald
Judson High School-Gray Campus
Converse, TX 78109

Judy Mullins
Westwood High School
Austin, TX 78750

Jeanne Provencher
Nashua Senior High School
Nashua, NH 03062

Dr. Ester Scott
Lincoln High School
Los Angeles, CA 90031

Dolores Sgambati
Burnt Hills High School
Burnt Hills, NY 12027

Executive Editor: Mescal Evler

Managing Editor: Robert R. Hoyt

Project Editor: Suzanne Thompson

Editorial Staff: Laura Britton, Tara Ellis, Karen Forrester, Karen Hoffman, Guy Holland, Christy McBride, Michael Neibergall, Marie Price, Patricia Saunders, Amy Simpson, Atietie Tonwe

Editorial Support Staff: Carla Beer, Stella Galvan, Margaret Guerrero, Ruth Hooker, Pat Stover

Editorial Permissions: Ann Farrar

Design, Photo Research, and Production: Pun Nio, *Senior Art Director;* Rebecca Byrd-Bretz, *Cover Design;* Debra Saleny, *Photo Research Manager;* Mavournea Hay, *Photo Researcher;* Beth Prevelige, *Production Manager;* Joan Eberhardt, *Production Assistant;* Linda Moyer, *Production Coordinator;* Carol Martin, *Electronic Publishing Manager;* David Hernandez, Mercedes Newman, *Electronic Publishing Staff*

Printed in the United States of America

ISBN 0-03-097178-0

14 15 16 17   095 – 07 06 05 04 03

TABLE OF CONTENTS

GRAMMAR, USAGE, AND MECHANICS

PREWRITING: FINDING IDEAS

Writing starts when you get an idea and collect information about it. Your experiences, observations, feelings, and opinions are rich sources of ideas for writing topics. The following prewriting techniques can help you to find and explore these ideas.

WRITER'S JOURNAL

Use a *writer's journal* to keep a daily record of your experiences, observations, feelings, opinions, original ideas, and unanswered questions. Your journal might be a notebook, a blank book, or a special folder. Add to it every day.

- Use your imagination. Be creative. Write original poems or song lyrics if you want. Jot down story ideas.

- Paste in newspaper or magazine articles, a quotation or a line from a song that struck you, pictures that have special meaning to you—anything that sparks your interest or brings thoughts to mind. Write a note next to each paste-in item to tell why the item means something to you.

- Don't worry about punctuation, grammar, or usage. Let your ideas flow from your mind to your journal as freely as possible.

FREEWRITING

When you *freewrite*, you jot down whatever pops into your head.

- Set a time limit of three to five minutes, and write until the time is up.
- Start with any topic or word, such as *freedom* or *dancing* or *courage*.
- Don't worry about complete sentences or correct punctuation. Just write!
- Every now and then, choose one key word from your freewriting, and use it as a starting point for more freewriting. This *focused freewriting*, or *looping*, allows you to explore your thoughts more deeply.

EXERCISE 1 **Journal Writing and Freewriting**

Think about experiences that have made you happy or places that have given you a feeling of peace or happiness. To find and develop your ideas, write a page for your writer's journal, or freewrite for three to five minutes.

BRAINSTORMING

Another way to find and develop ideas is to *brainstorm* or use free association. You can brainstorm alone or with others.

- Write a word, phrase, or topic at the top of a sheet of paper. Use what you've written as a starting point, and then list every idea you think of. If you are brainstorming with a partner or group, one person should record all the ideas.

- Don't stop to judge or evaluate any of the ideas. Let them flow freely.

- Keep brainstorming until you or everyone in your group runs out of ideas.

CLUSTERING

Clustering is another free-association technique. It is sometimes called *webbing* or *making connections*. This process helps you break a topic into smaller parts and show how those parts are related.

- Write your subject in the center of a sheet of paper. Circle it.

- All around the circle, write related ideas. Circle each one, and draw lines to connect them to the original subject.

- Create offshoots by adding and connecting "ideas about ideas." Connect each addition to the appropriate circle.

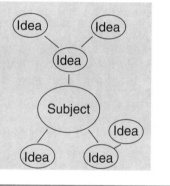

EXERCISE 2   Brainstorming and Clustering

With a partner or group, choose one of the subjects below. Work together to brainstorm a list of related ideas or subjects. Record everyone's ideas. Then, working alone, choose another of the listed subjects. Use it as the topic for a clustering diagram. When your clustering diagram is complete, meet with your partner or group to compare and contrast your individual diagrams.

courage	great actors	interesting careers	television violence
pride	teamwork	success	the environment

ASKING THE *5W-HOW?* QUESTIONS

News reporters often ask the *5W-How?* questions—*Who? What? Where? When? Why?* and *How?*—to gather information on a topic. Not every question applies to every situation, and, at times, you may use some of the questions more than once. But you will discover that asking the *5W-How?* questions will help you find and develop ideas. Here is an example of the way you might use the questions to gather information on Mitch Williams, the major-league relief pitcher, who has been given the nickname "Wild Thing."

- *Who?*   Who gave Mitch Williams that nickname?
- *What?*   What does Williams do while he is pitching that makes people think of him as funny or "wild"? What teams has he played for?
- *Where?*   Where did Williams train as a pitcher?
- *When?*   When did Williams break into the major leagues? When did he first become known as a great, but unpredictable, pitcher?
- *Why?*   Why do baseball fans like Williams so much? Why is he so much fun to watch? Why do so many reporters want to interview him?
- *How?*   How is Williams's behavior on the pitching mound different from that of most pitchers? How does his appeal add to his "wildness"?

EXERCISE 3   Using the *5W-How?* Questions

Choose one of the topics below. On the lines provided, make a list of the *5W-How?* questions you might use to explore the topic.

the U.S. Olympic Basketball Team   the Sahara   Geronimo

the U.S. Senate   the Nile River   the Gettysburg Address

_____

_____

_____

_____

_____

_____

OBSERVING

Recording your own observations or physical reactions to a scene or an event is an extremely useful way to recall important details. Jot down notes on everything you saw, heard, felt, tasted, and smelled. Here is an example of details recorded at a picnic on the bank of a river.

- Sight: green, grassy riverbank; clear water; plaid picnic blanket; straw basket brimming with sandwiches; apples; a jug of lemonade; wild ducks waddling up the bank
- Hearing: gurgling of the water flowing over the rocks; quacking ducks
- Smell: "green" smell of the grass; tuna sandwiches
- Taste: salty tuna; sweet apples; tart lemonade
- Touch: soft grass; cold river water; little peck from the duck when I fed it a scrap of bread; warmth of the sun

IMAGINING

Using your imagination will help you to stretch your mind as you explore your ideas for writing topics. Ask "What if?" questions to look at events and situations creatively.

- *What if my situation suddenly changed?* (What if I moved to a new city? What if I won a contest? What if I became famous? What if I won an athletic scholarship to college?)

- *What if world events took a new direction?* (What if all wars ended? What if everyone had enough food? What if a second sun suddenly appeared in the sky?)

EXERCISE 4   Observing and Imagining

Choose one of the topics below. Imagine the scene in your mind. On a separate sheet of paper, write down your observations about the scene. Use all your senses—sight, hearing, taste, smell, and touch. Then meet with a partner who has selected the same topic. Work together and use your imaginations. Write four "What if?" questions related to that topic.

a parade   an exciting game

a day at the beach   the filming of a movie scene

the food court at a mall   a gas station

PREWRITING: ARRANGING IDEAS

After you have gathered all your ideas, you need to arrange them in the order that you plan to present them. There are four usual ways to order ideas. Pick the method that makes the most sense, based on the type of writing you are doing and the purpose of your writing.

ARRANGING IDEAS		
Type of Order	**Definition**	**Examples**
Chronological	Narration: order that presents events as they happen in time	Story, narrative poem, explanation of a process, drama, history, biography
Spatial	Description: order that describes objects according to location	Descriptions (near to far, outside to inside, left to right, top to bottom)
Importance	Evaluation: order that gives details from least to most important, or the reverse	Persuasion, description, explanation, evaluation
Logical	Classification: order that relates items and groups	Definitions, classifications

EXERCISE 5 Arranging the Order of Details

Choose one of the topics listed below. First, on your own paper, brainstorm by listing all the details you can think of that are related to the experience. Then make two separate, numbered lists to arrange the details for two different paragraphs: (1) a paragraph that describes the scene (spatial order) and (2) a paragraph that relates the events (chronological order).

a performance by a popular singer
a visit to a museum
a tour of a famous building or ship

WRITING A FIRST DRAFT

At some point, you have to stop prewriting—gathering and organizing ideas—and get on with the business of writing. Here are some suggestions to help you with the drafting stage.

- Use your prewriting notes or outline as a guide.
- Write freely. Concentrate on expressing your ideas.
- Include new ideas that come to you as you write.
- Don't worry about errors in grammar, usage, or mechanics. You can fix them later.

Here is a first draft of a paragraph about a sculpture. Notice how the writer has inserted questions and notes. They will remind the writer to return to prewriting for more information before the final draft. Also, notice that the writing still needs more polishing. The polishing comes later.

> The sculptor Serena de la Hey has put a group of dancers [check--are there four or five of them?] on a grassy hillside in Dorset, England. The life-size figures, made of iron, ~~seems~~ seem to run and leap across the ridge of the hill. Their long, graceful [spelling correct?] arms seem to sway back and forth in the breeze, very much the way human arms might move during a dance. By day, cows graze near the dancers. But at sunset, the dancers take on a strange and almost spooky appearance. Against a pink sky, their long, thin shadows stretch down the hill, spreading [better word?] the dance almost to the village below.

EXERCISE 6   Writing a First Draft

Below are some notes about a long flight on an airplane. On your own paper, arrange or group the notes, and add to them if you like. Then use the details to write the first draft of a paragraph.

before boarding, I had to show my passport
plane left New York City at 5 P.M., landed in Amsterdam at 7:30 A.M.
dinner served at 7 P.M.
the flight attendant showed me to my seat—at the rear of the plane
after boarding, the flight attendant gave us a snack
after dinner we watched the movie *The Last of the Mohicans*
at around 6:30 P.M., I saw the coast of Nova Scotia out the window
during the movie, the flight attendant brought more snacks!
I saw the sun rise over England, many canals and a windmill when landing
breakfast served at 6:30 A.M.

EVALUATING AND REVISING

Evaluating and revising are like two half-steps joined together. When you *evaluate*, you decide what changes need to be made. When you *revise*, you make the needed changes.

EVALUATING

What seems good about your draft? What changes might make it even better? Ask the following questions when you evaluate a piece of writing.

- Is the writing interesting?
- Did the writing achieve the writer's purpose?
- Are there enough details?
- Are there any unrelated ideas or details that distract the reader?
- Are unfamiliar terms explained or defined?
- Are ideas and details arranged in the best possible order?
- Are the connections between ideas and sentences logical and clear?
- Is the meaning clear?

You can evaluate your paper yourself. Or you can exchange papers with a peer, or classmate, and the two of you can evaluate each other's writing. Peer evaluation can be helpful because being objective about your own writing is often difficult. Peers can offer valuable suggestions about improving your work.

Self-Evaluation	Peer Evaluation
1. Set your draft aside for a while to give yourself a rest. Then you'll be better able to find parts needing revision.	1. Be sure to tell the writer what's right as well as what's wrong. Be sensitive and helpful rather than critical.
2. Read your paper several times—first for content (what you say), next for organization (how you've arranged your ideas), then for style (how you've used words and sentences).	2. Make thoughtful suggestions. Help the writer by suggesting ways to improve the writing. Ask helpful questions, too.
3. Read your paper aloud. What looked all right on paper may sound awkward or unclear when you read it aloud.	3. Concentrate on content and organization. Don't worry about spelling and mechanics.

EXERCISE 7   Evaluating a Paragraph

Work with a partner to evaluate the paragraph below. On your own paper, complete the two parts of the exercise, as described below.

Part A: Answer the questions at the top of the previous page to decide what might need to be changed and improved.

Part B: Use the peer evaluation tips to write suggestions and questions as useful feedback to the writer.

1   About 20 percent of major-league baseball players in the United States

2   and Canada are Hispanic, and they have many fans in their native

3   countries [add examples here]. These fans do not all speak English, and so

4   the broadcasts of major-league games in English are difficult for them to

5   understand and enjoy. Television reporter Clemson Smith Muñiz

6   broadcasts in Spanish. Thanks to Clemson Smith Muñiz, Hispanic baseball

7   fans all over the world can share in the fun and excitement. Clemson

8   Smith Muñiz grew up in Puerto Rico. San Juan is the capital of that

9   country. As a boy, he learned and spoke both. After he graduated from

10   college, he worked as a newspaper reporter. A few years ago, he switched

11   to television reporting, with an emphasis on Hispanic culture and issues.

12   Today he broadcasts the play by play of major-league baseball games. His

13   broadcasts are seen in thirty Spanish-speaking countries.

REVISING

Revising, although difficult, is one of the most important parts of writing. Every problem you have uncovered in the evaluation stage can be corrected by using one or more of four basic revising techniques: **add, cut, replace,** and **reorder**.

GUIDELINES FOR EVALUATING AND REVISING	
Evaluation Guide	**Revision Technique**
Content	
1. Is the writing interesting?	**Add** examples, an anecdote, dialogue, or additional details. **Cut** repetitious or boring details.
2. Did the writing achieve the writer's purpose?	**Add** explanations, descriptive details, arguments, or narrative details.
3. Are there enough details?	**Add** more details, facts, or examples to support your ideas.
4. Are there unrelated ideas or details that distract the reader?	**Cut** irrelevant or distracting information.
5. Are unfamiliar terms explained or defined?	**Add** definitions or other explanations. **Replace** unfamiliar terms with familiar ones.
Organization	
6. Are ideas and details arranged in the best possible order?	**Reorder** ideas and details to make the meaning clear.
7. Are the connections between ideas and sentences logical and clear?	**Add** transition words to link ideas: *therefore, for example, because,* and so on.
Style	
8. Is the meaning clear?	**Replace** vague or unclear words with words and phrases that are easy to understand.

Here is an example of a draft that has been revised, following the guidelines on the previous page.

President Woodrow Wilson had a ~~good~~ *creative* answer to the   **replace**

question, "How can we cut expenses at the White House?" He

replaced many members of the large gardening and lawn crew

with a herd of sheep. The sheep happily grazed on the White

House lawn. *In the process of eating, they also kept the lawn neatly trimmed.* During World War I, the sheep also made a patriotic   **add**

donation. When the Red Cross needed to raise funds for

supplies, ~~Woodrow~~ Wilson's sheep were sheared. The wool was   **cut**

sold at auction for $100,000, and the money was donated to

the Red Cross. ~~The Red Cross won the Nobel Peace Prize in 1917.~~   **cut**

Their coats ~~brought a lot~~ *produced ninety-eight pounds* of wool.   **replace**   **reorder**

EXERCISE 8   Revising a Paragraph

On your own paper, write a revision of the paragraph on Clemson Smith Muñiz that you evaluated for Exercise 7. Use your evaluation and the guidelines in this lesson to help you.

"must you correct everything i said say?"

Cartoon by George Dole.

PROOFREADING AND PUBLISHING

PROOFREADING

You're ready for one last look at the writing you've revised. This final look is called *proofreading.* When you proofread, you catch and correct any mistakes in spelling, grammar, usage, punctuation, and capitalization. Finding these mistakes is easier if you have put your paper aside for awhile. These guidelines will help you to put the final polish on your writing.

Guidelines for Proofreading
• Is every sentence a complete sentence?
• Does every sentence begin with a capital letter and end with an appropriate punctuation mark?
• Are all proper nouns and proper adjectives capitalized correctly?
• Are subject and object forms of personal pronouns used correctly?
• Does every verb agree in number with its subject?
• Are verb forms and tenses used correctly?
• Are pronouns used correctly?
• Are all the words spelled correctly?

Symbols for Revising and Proofreading	
Oklahoma <u>c</u>ity	Capitalize a letter.
up up the hill	Delete a word, letter, or punctuation mark.
the people Mexico	Insert a word, letter, or punctuation mark.
a singer talented	Change the order of words or letters.
The next morning	Begin a new paragraph.
a Citizen of France	Change to a lowercase letter.
Let's go	Add a period.

EXERCISE 9   **Proofreading a Paragraph**

The following paragraph contains twenty errors. Use proofreading marks to correct the errors. Some sentences may be correct.

[1] For more then two thousand years, the Bedouins lived have in the desserts of of North africa. [2] In fact, the name *Bedouin* means "desert dweller." [3] Many bedouins raise herds of shepe and goats [4] They continuously moves throughought the Desert, serching for water and new pasture. [5] Therefore, they live in tnets. [6] Each tent two rooms. [7] the front room is used to to greet visiters. [8] The back is room a combination kichen and bedroom

---

PUBLISHING

The final step of writing is *publishing*; it's your opportunity to share what you've written with other people. Here are a few suggestions for sharing your writing.

- Submit your writing for publication in the school newspaper or magazine. Or send it to your local newspaper. Most newspapers publish letters to the editors, and many accept feature stories.
- Submit your story or poem to a writing contest. There are many contests each year, and some are specifically for high school students. Ask your teacher, counselor, or librarian for information. You might win a prize!
- Compile an anthology of each classmate's favorite piece of her or his own writing. Make a copy of the collection for each contributor. Donate a copy to the school library.
- Send or give your article or story to someone who shares your interest in the topic or who may have shared the experience that you chose to write about.

EXERCISE 10   **Collaborating to Identify Publishing Opportunities**

Working with a partner or group, read the following descriptions of types of writing. Brainstorm as many ways as possible to publish each one. Have one member of the group record everyone's ideas on a separate piece of paper.

1. an article about a watercolor exhibit you enjoyed at a local museum
2. a story about your uncle Remo teaching you to ride a bike many years ago
3. a piece of persuasive writing about the importance of recycling
4. a poem about your grandmother's beautiful and gentle hands

USES OF PARAGRAPHS

DEVELOPMENT OF A MAIN IDEA

Most paragraphs have one *main idea.* The main idea, which tells what the paragraph is about, is usually expressed in a single sentence called the *topic sentence.* The topic sentence is a specific, limiting statement about the subject of the paragraph.

You'll often find the topic sentence as the first or second sentence of a paragraph. However, you can find a topic sentence anywhere in a paragraph. In the following paragraph, the topic sentence comes at the beginning.

> The potato is one of the world's best nutritional values. A single potato supplies half the vitamin C an adult needs daily. The quality of protein in a potato is better than that in the soybean, and a potato is 99.9 percent fat free. Potatoes are also an excellent source of fiber and potassium.

OTHER USES OF PARAGRAPHS

In many kinds of writing, such as popular magazines, newspapers, ads, and "how-to" manuals, you often find short (even one-sentence) paragraphs that don't really develop a main idea. They may be used (1) to show a transition from one idea to another, (2) to indicate a change in speakers, or (3) to make a point stand out.

> At 18,000 feet in the Andes, I would learn firsthand what people mean when they say that a breath of air contains half the oxygen a breath contains at sea level. [new speaker]
>
> "Above that level even fit climbers risk [fluid collecting in the brain] and possible death when they go up too fast to adapt," according to Dr. Charles S. Houston. [new speaker]
>
> On my climb, I would have to take many extra days to adjust to the lack of oxygen. I didn't want to hallucinate and stumble on the narrow trails.
>
> But altitude sickness was not the only danger I would face. [transition]
>
> What about landslides and mudslides? I knew that in 1985, twenty thousand Colombians drowned in a gigantic mudslide off Nevado del Ruiz in the Andes. [visual appeal]
>
> I did not want to become another casualty of those impressive mountains. [make a point stand out]

EXERCISE 1   Working Cooperatively to Study the Uses of Paragraphs

With two or three classmates, make a survey of the way paragraphs are used in popular magazines, newspaper articles, ads, "how-to" manuals, and movie, book, and restaurant reviews. On the lines provided, make notes on the different uses of paragraphs. Then name the sources where you found them. Include titles, dates, and page numbers in your notes. Find at least one example of each of these uses: developing a main idea, showing a transition from one idea to another, indicating a change in speakers, and creating visual appeal.

Popular magazines: _____

_____

_____

Newspaper articles: _____

_____

_____

Ads: _____

_____

_____

"How-to" manuals: _____

_____

_____

Movie, book, and restaurant reviews: _____

_____

_____

UNITY

A paragraph has *unity* when all the sentences work together to express or support one main idea. Sentences can work as a unit in one of three ways.

(1) All sentences relate to the main idea stated in the topic sentence. In the following paragraph, the topic sentence tells the main idea. Each of the supporting sentences provides details related to that idea.

> The Antarctic Treaty of 1959 is a highly successful agreement among twelve nations. These nations, in the interest of science, have forsworn territorial claims and banned military activity in Antarctica. Under the treaty, all member nations can conduct scientific inquiries in Antarctica, but they are obliged to share what they learn. The treaty has had such positive results that six more countries have signed it, and sixteen more have agreed to its terms.

(2) All sentences relate to an implied main idea. The following paragraph doesn't have a topic sentence. Each sentence, however, helps to support an implied main idea.

> Skiing probably started around 3000 B.C. in Norway. The oldest skis ever found date back to 2500 B.C. At that time, skiing was not just an outdoor sport. It was a way to travel through deep snowdrifts. In those days, the wooden runners, or skis, were connected to the skier only by thin straps on the toes. The equipment remained unchanged until the middle of the nineteeth century. In 1860 a man from Telemark, Norway, invented a binding that attached the skier's boots to his skis. These bindings laid the foundation for modern ski equipment.

(3) All sentences relate to a sequence of events. The following paragraph does not have a clearly stated main idea. However, each detail is part of the sequence of steps in making bark paper.

> The Otomi people in Mexico make bark paper mostly from jonote colorado trees. The papermaker separates the inner bark from the outer. This inner bark is boiled for hours in water that contains lime. Next, the papermaker rinses the strips of bark and arranges them in a grid pattern on a smooth board. Then he or she beats the bark with a stone until the fibers mesh. The sheet of paper is left on the board to dry in the sun.

EXERCISE 2   Identifying Sentences That Destroy Unity

In each paragraph below, draw a line through the sentence that doesn't support the main idea of the paragraph.

1. S. Josephine Baker became a doctor in 1898. Practicing medicine in New York City, she found terribly high infant mortality rates—up to 1,500 deaths a week in the summer. People didn't want to use the services of a woman doctor. Within ten years she had significantly decreased the mortality rate by educating mothers and other caregivers on the importance of proper ventilation and sanitation. She later organized vaccination programs to combat contagious diseases and to distribute uncontaminated milk.

2. Inuit tools and weapons are necessary in the Arctic, where life can depend on the perfection of the hunting weapon. A strong, straight, and well-balanced tool will be accurate and efficient. Harsh conditions in the Arctic mean that efficiency is a matter of life and death! A seal or fish missed because of an imperfectly made harpoon can escape entirely. It might be days before another is seen. The more perfect the tool or weapon, the more food there is to eat. Tools also served in the Inuit spiritual life.

3. Do you ever wonder why one word or phrase can have two opposite meanings? Think about the expressions "in apple-pie order" and "an apple-pie bed," for example. The first means neat and tidy, with everything just right. The second means a bed that's made wrong, so that you can't get into it. You may have heard the expression "upset the apple cart." Is the apple-pie phrase someone's joke, like slang that uses *bad* for *good*? Puzzling about these and other mysteries of the English language could be a lifetime occupation.

4. Well-planned cities are a bore compared with an old New England town. In a grid-plan city, all the streets are at right angles, so one always knows in what direction one is traveling. New England streets change direction, and frequently change their names! Street names are often quite unusual. In a grid-plan city, house numbers on every block start with a multiple of one hundred, so it is simple to know exactly how many blocks lie between any two street addresses. Each house faces the street squarely. A walk around the block, therefore, can be timed precisely and is always possible. New England houses, however, can face any angle.

COHERENCE: ORDER OF IDEAS

A paragraph in which all the ideas are sensibly arranged and clearly connected has *coherence.* You can create coherent paragraphs by paying attention to two things: (1) the order in which you arrange your ideas, and (2) the connections you make between ideas.

Arrange, or order, your ideas in the paragraph in a way that will make sense to readers. Often the subject you're writing about will suggest the most sensible order of ideas. Writers most often use one of the following four types of order.

Chronological Order. When you write about a series of actions or events, it makes sense to arrange the actions or events according to the times at which they happen, or in *chronological* (time) *order.* Notice how the following paragraph organizes information in the order of time.

> Whenever we try to go on a balloon ride, something goes wrong. The first date we made had to be changed because Tim was called out of town unexpectedly. The next time, a thunderstorm made us cancel the ascent. The last time, a heavy breeze blew up just as we were about to board. We're beginning to think we'll never get off the ground!

Spatial Order. When using descriptive details, writers sometimes use *spatial order* to arrange ideas. The details are arranged according to space—nearest to farthest, left to right, or any other reasonable arrangement. In the paragraph below, notice how the writer has arranged the details from top to bottom.

> *Opabinia* is a weird-looking animal discovered among the fossils of the Burgess Shale in British Columbia. Its head, which has five mushroom-shaped eyes, also has a flexible nozzle with pincers at the end of it. The nozzle probably enabled the creature to eat. The body has fifteen segments, most of which have gills attached. The tail has three sets of thin blades that point up and out.

Order of Importance. When trying to inform or persuade, you'll often arrange ideas in *order of importance.* Sometimes one idea or detail is more important than another. If so, you might arrange ideas with the most important idea first and the least important last. In another piece of writing, you may want to reverse the order and start with the least important idea. In the following paragraph, the writer begins with the least important detail and moves to the most important.

> My friend Bob is a lobster catcher, but he's thinking about changing jobs for the winter. Often the weather is wet and the seas are rough. His hands get cold and stiff in the frigid water, and it's hard to peg the lobsters or untangle the ropes with numb fingers. However, the worst days are the very cold ones, when the deck freezes. Then Bob, who works alone, worries about sliding out the open back of his boat, into the deadly cold of the ocean.

Logical Order. When you use the strategies of classification, including definition and comparison/contrast, you will usually group ideas in **logical order.** It may make sense to group ideas together to show how they are related. Logical order uses classification techniques to arrange ideas in a sensible way. In the example below, the details are arranged in two logical groups—those related to the past and those related to the present.

> Mauritius, an island nation in the Indian Ocean, developed rapidly in the 1980s. Before that, the country had a rapidly growing population and more than 20 percent unemployment. Sugar was the primary crop raised for export. Today, unemployment is about 3 percent, and income per person has doubled. The many new factories produce textiles that are now Mauritius's biggest export.

EXERCISE 3   Choosing an Order of Ideas

Rearrange the ideas in the paragraphs below in a sensible order that would work for each paragraph. On your own paper, list the numbers of the sentences in an appropriate order, and label the type of order you've used.

1. [1] One day Mr. Parenti asked me in to see how they had changed the house. [2] When I was seventeen (and six feet tall), I met the Parentis, who owned the house I used to live in. [3] First, I noticed how tiny the overstuffed furniture made the living room look. [4] Finally, the railing at the top, now minus my tooth marks, just barely cleared the top of my knee. [5] It had changed, all right. [6] Next, the stairs to the second floor, which had breathlessly stretched into dizzy heights, had been reduced to a dozen easy steps.

2. [1] Inside, every aisle had its dangers. [2] Trash barrels, lawn mowers, and bags of peat moss had wandered out the front door and were hanging out. [3] Finally, the case of tools and scissors along the back wall had to be locked, to protect browsers from the threatening inhabitants. [4] In one dark passage, brooms, rakes, and shovels stuck out their insensitive limbs to trip people. [5] The hardware store on the corner was unlike any other store I'd ever seen. [6] In another aisle, garden hoses and buckets created an obstacle course for people on their way to the paint department.

COHERENCE: CONNECTIONS BETWEEN IDEAS

Direct references and *transitional words* can help to make your paragraph coherent. These words and phrases act as connectors between and among ideas so that your paragraph is clear to readers.

Direct References. Referring to a noun or pronoun that you've used earlier in the paragraph is a *direct reference*. You can make direct references by (1) using a noun or pronoun that refers to a noun or pronoun used earlier, (2) repeating a word used earlier, or (3) using a word or phrase that means the same thing as one used earlier. In the following paragraph, the superscript numbers indicate the type of direct reference the writer is using.

> If you have friends or family members who[1] enjoy making puns, you[2] already know that the proper response to a pun[2] is a groan. Although some people make fun of this form of humor[3], great writers have used it[1] in their[1] works. One such writer[3], Lewis Carroll[3], the author[3] of *Through the Looking Glass* , was quite fond of the pun[2]. For example, he[1] uses plays on words in a series of somewhat familiar insects: the "Rocking-horse-fly[1]," the "Snap-dragon-fly[1]," and the "Bread-and-butter-fly[1]."

Transitional Expressions. Words and phrases that make a transition, or shift, from one idea to another are called *transitional expressions.* These words and phrases include prepositions that indicate chronological or spatial order, and conjunctions, which connect ideas and show relationships.

Comparing Ideas	also, and, another, besides, moreover, similarly, too
Contrasting Ideas	although, but, however, in spite of, instead, nevertheless, on the other hand, still, yet
Showing Cause and Effect	as a result, because, by, consequently, for, since, so, so that, therefore
Showing Time	after, at last, at once, before, eventually, finally, first, meanwhile, next, often, then, thereafter, when
Showing Place	above, along, around, before, behind, down, here, in, inside, into, next to, on, over, there, under, up
Showing Importance	first, last, mainly, more importantly, then, to begin with

In the following paragraph, the transitional expressions are underlined.

When I baby-sit, I read books to the children. I often find a moral message in the story. The message is usually obvious, such as "Smile, and the world smiles with you." Although the preschoolers don't seem to notice this preachiness, I find it irritating. However, I started to think: Aren't the books that I read also full of messages?

EXERCISE 4   Identifying Direct References and Transitions

On your own paper, make two lists of the connections in the paragraph below: one list of direct references and one list of transitions.

[1] The Lake Michigan beach was deserted when the party arrived early Sunday morning. [2] The lake hadn't frozen, but no boats were visible anywhere on the choppy blue waves. [3] The wind was brisk, so the seven people were all bundled up and had blankets with them, as well as several heavy baskets. [4] First, the two leaders, Rammel and Lily, spread the blankets on the cold, white sand. [5] Then Kenesha and Chet set up two hibachis and filled them with charcoal. [6] After a struggle with the wind, the cooks got the charcoal started. [7] When they got out the griddles and oil, paper plates and napkins escaped from the picnic basket, giving the rest of the party an excuse to keep warm by chasing after the paper. [8] Mainly, everyone stood around, laughing, talking, and warming their hands on mugs of coffee. [9] Eventually a few strangers jogged by, wondering at the unexpected festivity. [10] At last, when the pans were hot, the pancakes sizzled until they were brown, and everyone sat on the blankets to eat breakfast. People clutched their flimsy plates and enjoyed the end-of-the-year class picnic.

USING DESCRIPTION

When you need to focus on a subject, to tell what it's like, you have to examine its specific features. By using *description* as your strategy of development, you can arrange sensory details (sight, hearing, taste, touch, and smell) to support your main idea. You'll often use spatial order to organize a description, as in the following paragraph.

> The woman stood at a table that took up most of the room. Her hair was pulled back behind her ears; her glasses had slipped down to the front of her nose. On the table in front of her was an ironing board and a lavender chiffon dress. She was smoothing a strip of a stiff, white fabric over the dress. In the middle of the table lay a heap of gold wire hangers, some trimmings, and a large pair of black-handled, stainless shears. Across the table from her was another woman, a little younger, ironing an identical dress. All around the table other women bent over the same job—the same ironing board, dress, and shears. It was a typical scene at the dress shop.

EXERCISE 5   **Using Description as a Strategy**

Choose one of the subjects below. On your own paper, brainstorm to list the features that will help describe the subject you have chosen. Try to focus on sensory details (sight, hearing, taste, touch, and smell). After you have thought of as many ideas as you can, arrange them in spatial order.

1. a movie theater after a show

2. a favorite sports car

3. a basketball game

4. your favorite singer during a performance

5. an area of a shopping mall

USING EVALUATION

Evaluation means judging the value of something. You often evaluate a subject in order to inform readers or to persuade them to think or act differently.

An evaluation, or statement of opinion, should be supported with *reasons* showing *why* you made the judgment about the subject. One way to organize your reasons is by order of importance. Notice the reasons the writer of the paragraph below gives to support his opening statement.

EVALUATION	If you're worried about finding a job after high school,
REASON	volunteering can be a good tactic. Organizations that need volunteer help are often willing to train people to do certain jobs. Because they're likely to be less critical about the quality of work you do, you get a chance to practice
REASON	and improve your skills. Perhaps most importantly, volunteering can be a good way to meet people who can
REASON	share leads with you about job opportunities or recommend you to an employer.

EXERCISE 6   Using Evaluation as a Strategy

Choose two of the three subjects below, and evaluate them. On your own paper, write at least one sentence stating your opinion of each subject. Then list two or three reasons to support each judgment.

EX.   Broad Topic: Seat Belt Laws
           Evaluation: Drivers and passengers should be required by law to
                        wear seat belts.
             Reason 1: This law would encourage people to protect their
                        passengers.
             Reason 2: The number of accidental injuries would decrease.

1. a movie you have seen recently (Would you recommend it to someone else? Why, or why not?)

2. professionals participating in the Olympic Games (Would it make competition among countries fairer?)

3. laws restricting hunting, logging, and other activities in order to protect endangered species (Are they worth it?)

USING NARRATION

What happened on your first trip away from home? How do you make a loaf of bread? Why did we have an earthquake?

Answering these questions requires the strategy of *narration,* of looking at changes over a period of time. You may use narration to tell a story or incident (what happened on your trip), to explain a process (how to make bread), or to explain causes and effects (what causes an earthquake). You usually use chronological order to present ideas and information in paragraphs of narration.

TELLING A STORY

Writers use the strategy of narration to tell stories, either true or fictional, about events that take place over a period of time. In the following paragraph, the writer tells a story about an important event in Charlie's life.

> Charlie was a stray dog, so we never knew how old he was or who had owned him before us. However, one day, as we walked down a crowded sidewalk, Charlie heard the squeak of a rubber duck held by a toddler. He came to a sudden stop and stared at the toy. Because he seemed so interested in the toy, we bought him a plastic hamburger with a squeaker in it. Charlie got his new toy on Christmas Eve and played with it for three hours without a break. He tossed it in the air and caught it. He rolled it across the floor and pounced on it. He even occasionally let us toss it the length of the room so he could madly scramble after it. On Christmas Day he was so tired that he slept the whole day.

EXPLAINING A PROCESS

When you explain a process, you tell how something works or how to do something. In the following paragraph the writer explains how to sprout seeds.

> Sprouting herb seeds is easy if you follow these few steps. Fill small peat pots with sterile potting soil. Wet the soil, and spread the seeds very thinly. Next, cover the seeds with soil—a thin layer for small seeds, a heavier layer for large seeds. Water the covered seeds lightly. Then cover the pots with glass and newspaper, and set them in a warm place. As soon as shoots appear, remove the newspaper. Move the pots into a lighted, cooler place.

EXPLAINING CAUSE AND EFFECT

You also look at the way things change over time when you explain causes and effects. To make the cause-and-effect connections clear, events are given in the order in which they happened. In the following paragraph, the writer explains the causes for the Anasazi's leaving Chaco Canyon.

> The Chaco Canyon is no longer populated by the Anasazi, an ancient group of Native Americans, although it was once home to thousands. Some historians believe that it was a fifty-year drought that brought profound changes to the canyon. Because of the drought, the small amount of farmland couldn't produce enough to feed the large population. Social organizations started to break down, and most people moved to more productive areas. Eventually, dozens of large Chaco settlements fell into ruins.

EXERCISE 7   Using Narration as a Strategy

Follow the instructions for using narration, and develop prewriting for each of the items below. Write your lists on your own paper.

1. Select one of the subjects below, and list at least three actions that took place.

    a. a situation I want to forget (Make up the actions, if you like.)

    b. how people traveled on the Oregon Trail (Check in an encyclopedia or a history book.)

2. Select one of the subjects below, and list at least four steps in the process.

    a. how to make spaghetti sauce (If you don't know how, look in a recipe book.)

    b. how to recycle in your community (If you don't know what to recycle, ask someone at a recycling center.)

3. Select one of the subjects below, and list at least one cause and three effects.

    a. forgetting to set the clock ahead for daylight saving time

    b. a state legislature raising the driving age to eighteen

USING CLASSIFICATION

The word *perestroika* became popular during the late 1980s. What does it mean? When you answer this question, you're using the strategy of **classification.** You classify a subject by dividing it into its parts (the parts of a car), defining it (the word *perestroika*), or comparing and contrasting it with something else (dinosaurs and present-day lizards).

DIVIDING

Classifying by *dividing* means looking at the parts of a subject in order to understand the subject as a whole. For example, to explain the structure of a car, you may want to divide it into its systems—exhaust system, fuel system, and so on. The following paragraph uses the strategy of dividing to explain how to choose houseplants.

> When you select a houseplant, the most important consideration is how much light the plant needs. The light required falls into three main categories: bright, medium, and dim. If you have a sunny window, you can raise cacti or geraniums. Philodendrons do well in medium light filtered through a thin curtain. African violets and many ferns do well in the dim light from a window facing north.

DEFINING

To *define,* you first identify a subject as a part of a larger group or class. Then you discuss some features that make the subject different from other members of the class. In the following paragraph, the writer starts to define poetry.

> Poetry is an imaginative form of writing. It can be far removed from ordinary speech and familiar conversational patterns. Most often, however, poetry follows established rhymes and rhythms and uses ordinary words in unpredictable, lively ways. Some features often found in poetic writing include old-fashioned words or grammar, invented words, and unusual word order.

COMPARING AND CONTRASTING

You also use the strategy of classification when *comparing* subjects (telling how they're alike), *contrasting* them (telling how they're different), or when both comparing and contrasting. The following paragraph contrasts teahouses and coffeehouses.

> Tea and coffee are popular international beverages. However, the places that serve them can be curiously different. The traditional teahouse in Japan is decorated simply and is suitable for meditation. Coffeehouses in London, though, are busy public places of political debate and of business dealings. The locations of these houses also differ. Japanese teahouses are isolated in stylized gardens that represent nature in a purified form. The London coffeehouses are in some of the most crowded parts of the city. Finally, in Japan, the tea ceremony requires the study of Zen. The atmosphere of a London coffeehouse encourages discussions on many topics.

EXERCISE 8   Using Classification as a Strategy

Develop each main idea below by following the directions given in its classification strategy. Work in a group with two other classmates. Choose one member of your group to record on paper the group's ideas. Work together to list ideas, and then discuss strategies. Which was the most difficult to use? the easiest? How did the strategies help you stay focused on your subject?

Main Idea	Classification Strategy
1. Whatever your ability, there is a musical instrument that will suit you.	Look at the subject of musical instruments by dividing it into types. Then list details for each type to support this main idea.
2. Tae kwon do is an interesting sport.	Look at the subject of tae kwon do by defining it. Identify the larger group to which this sport belongs, and then list some features that make it different from other sports.
3. Because I like one novel, I would probably like another by the same author.	Compare and contrast two novels by listing their likenesses and differences.

THE THESIS STATEMENT

A *composition* is an essay or report that supports a single main idea. The main idea, or *thesis,* is expressed in a sentence called the *thesis statement.* This statement usually appears in the introduction. The rest of the composition supports the thesis statement by providing specific information or details.

A good thesis statement serves two functions: It introduces the topic of the composition, and it states a single, unifying idea about that topic. Consider the following thesis statement.

> Our country could save millions of gallons of water each year if ordinary citizens made simple changes in their everyday habits.

This thesis statement tells you that the topic of the composition is "saving water." It also tells you the main idea of the composition—that water can be saved by making simple changes in our everyday lives. The rest of the composition will have to support this statement by telling what simple changes people could make and how much water could be saved as a result.

Guidelines for Writing and Using a Thesis Statement

1. Use your prewriting notes. Before you begin to write, gather a lot of information about your topic. You might use reference books and personal interviews to collect facts and opinions. Then look over this information. Ask yourself which idea is most important. Look for a single main idea that ties together the details that you have gathered.

2. State both your topic and your main idea. Write a thesis statement that clearly presents your topic and the main idea that you want to communicate about that topic. Make sure that your main idea is narrow enough to be covered in a few paragraphs.

3. Change your thesis statement if you need to do so. Revise your thesis statement until it clearly says what you want it to say. As you gather information and write your composition, however, you may wish to further revise or to replace your original thesis statement. Feel free to do so.

> **4. Use your thesis statement to guide your writing.** Keep your thesis statement in mind as you write. The ideas and details that you include must support your thesis. Throw out any that don't relate to your thesis. By doing this, you can ensure that all of your composition will be focused on your main idea.

EXERCISE 1   Analyzing and Revising Thesis Statements

The following thesis statements need to be revised. The first one states the topic, but it doesn't present a main idea about that topic. The second one presents a main idea, but it doesn't clearly state the topic. On your own paper, rewrite each thesis statement so that it both states the topic and presents a main idea about the topic.

1.   This paper is about forming a rock-and-roll band.

2.   These terrible events can be avoided by taking common-sense precautions when picnicking, camping, or hiking in the woods.

EXERCISE 2   Cooperating to Write a Thesis Statement

Working with a partner, write a thesis statement to fit the topic and details given below. On your own paper, clearly express both the topic and the main idea in your thesis statement.

Topic: Life on Venus

Details:

- *literature*
    - —early science fiction stories picture Venus as having life
    - —Arthur C. Clarke's "History Lesson" is one such story
    - —Ray Bradbury's "All Summer in a Day" is another
- *atmosphere*
    - —weight of atmosphere on Venus is ninety times that of earth
    - —atmosphere of Venus contains very little oxygen, 96 percent carbon dioxide
    - —carbon dioxide in atmosphere of Venus traps heat
    - —temperature at surface of planet 900°F, hot enough to melt lead
    - —constant windstorms, with winds blowing 109 miles per hour just below cloud layer
- *investigation*
    - —American and Soviet space probes (*Mariner 2, Venera 13, Venera 14, Pioneer, Magellan*) have found no sign of life
    - —no response to radio communications

PLANNING A COMPOSITION

You probably wouldn't want to take a vacation without first making a plan. Planning what you are going to do ahead of time will help make any activity a success. When you write a long paper or composition, there are two kinds of plans that you can use—early plans and formal outlines.

EARLY PLANS

An *early plan*, also called a *rough,* or *informal outline,* is useful for organizing your ideas quickly. To make an early plan, sort your ideas or details into groups. Then arrange the groups in order.

GROUPING.   Once you have gathered ideas or details about your topic, group together those that have something in common. Write a heading for each group to show how its details are related. If some details do not fit into any group, put them in a separate list. These details may be useful later.

ORDERING.   After grouping your details, order the details within each group. Then order the groups themselves. There are several ways to order, or arrange, details.

Chronological (time) *order* presents events in the order that they happen.

Spatial order presents details according to where they are located.

Order of importance presents details from most important to least important, or vice versa.

Logical order presents your topic by dividing it into parts, by defining it, or by comparing and contrasting it with something else.

☞   **REFERENCE NOTE:** For more information on arranging details, see pages 17–18.

FORMAL OUTLINES

A *formal outline* is more structured than an early plan. A formal outline isn't necessary for every composition. However, referring to a formal outline can help make the structure of a composition clearer to both you and your reader.

To make a formal outline, arrange your details into main headings and subheadings, and label these headings with letters and numbers. You may create a *topic outline,* which uses phrases or single words. Or you may wish to create a *sentence outline,* which uses complete sentences. A sample topic outline appears at the top of the next page.

Title: Buying an Acoustic Guitar
Thesis statement: The following tips will help in finding a good deal when purchasing an acoustic guitar.

I. Sources of guitars

    A. Buying from music stores
        1. Sellers of new guitars
        2. Sellers of used guitars
    B. Buying from individuals
        1. Classified ads
        2. Bulletin board notices
        3. Guitar makers (luthiers)

II. Characteristics of guitars

    A. Price
    B. Age
    C. Type
    D. Manufacturer's design
    E. Quality
        1. Examining the construction
        2. Testing the sound
        3. Evaluating the ease of play

EXERCISE 3   Cooperating to Create an Early Plan

Below are some notes for a composition about computer games. On your own paper, write an early plan using these entries. Work with a partner to arrange the notes into two separate groups, one dealing with the history of computer games, and one dealing with types of computer games. Create headings for each group. Then order the entries within each group.

- Digital computers were manufactured in the 1950s.
- Race car simulation games are very popular.
- In simulation games, the computer creates for the user the illusion of a real-life experience, such as flying.
- In educational games, the user learns a skill, such as a foreign language, math, or grammar.
- Later games added high-quality graphics and sound.
- In interactive games, the user plays against the computer.
- Early computer games included chess and the Chinese game *Go*.
- Interactive games include chess, checkers, bridge, hangman, and tic-tac-toe.
- Flight-simulation games give the user the feeling of being in a cockpit, flying a plane.

EXERCISE 4   Creating a Formal Outline

Using the early plan you made for Exercise 3, create a formal outline on your own paper. Add a title and a thesis statement.

WRITING INTRODUCTIONS

The *introduction* to a composition serves three major purposes. It

- catches the audience's attention
- sets the tone, or shows the writer's attitude toward the subject (humorous, serious, critical, and so forth)
- presents the thesis statement, usually at the beginning or end of the introduction

NOTE The *body* of a composition is made up of paragraphs that support the main idea presented in the thesis statement. The body paragraphs should all work together to achieve *unity* and *coherence*. For information about unity and coherence, see pages 15–20.

TECHNIQUES FOR WRITING INTRODUCTIONS

Glance at a few magazine articles, and you will see that there are many different ways to write an introduction. Here are some common ones.

- **Begin by addressing the reader directly.** This technique is especially useful if you want to set an informal, friendly tone or if you want to involve the reader personally.

  "You are the WINNER of one of the following FABULOUS prizes." No doubt you have read such statements on pieces of mail delivered to your home. Don't believe them. While there are some legal, legitimate contests that operate by mail, many are frauds that can cost you time and money.

- **Begin with a simple statement of your thesis.** If your topic is interesting, you can catch your reader's attention by simply presenting your thesis statement.

  The most intelligent of all animals without backbones is the octopus. Like a human being, an octopus is capable of learning and of being trained.

- **Begin with a startling, unusual, or enlightening fact.** A new or unusual fact may cause your reader to want to read on to find out more.

  The wedding cake has not always been lovingly fed to the bride by her adoring husband. Originally, it was thrown at her by well-wishers! And the custom of throwing the bridal bouquet began with the bride tossing grains of wheat to hopeful, unmarried young women. Obviously, wedding traditions have changed over the years.

- **Begin with an example or anecdote.** One excellent way to involve a reader immediately is to give an example or to start with an **anecdote**, or little story.

> Once, many years ago, my mother was playing golf with some friends. Mom hit an amazing tee shot, but she and her friends could not find the ball. Finally, they looked into the hole. There was the ball. She had made a hole in one, something almost unheard of for an amateur golfer. One of her friends turned to her and said, "You're a regular Nancy Lopez." Obviously, the name "Nancy Lopez" has become synonymous with great golf shots. As Ms. Lopez's long string of success shows, she is the greatest female golfer in history.

- **Begin with an interesting or dramatic quote.** Often, writers use quotations from experts, authors, people mentioned in their compositions, or people whose personal experience relates directly to the composition's topic.

> "I'm tone deaf. The only time you'll catch me singing is in the shower." People often say something like this to describe their lack of musical ability. However, the truth is that with a little training, almost anyone can develop musical skills, including the ability to sing in tune.

- **Begin with a question or a challenge.** A question makes a reader want to read on to find its answer. A challenge makes the reader want to meet it.

> What would you do if you came face to face with a grizzly bear? An adult grizzly can run faster than any person and can knock down a tree. But your reaction to the creature could prevent a frightening experience from becoming a deadly experience.

- **Take a stand on an issue.** If you are writing a persuasive composition, you can start by stating your opinion forcefully. Your reader will then want to read on to find out how you support your opinion.

> School elections shouldn't be popularity contests. A student council represents the interests of students. I believe that before any student election, the candidates should hold debates to express their ideas and opinions about important issues facing the school.

- **Begin with an outrageous or comical statement.** If you are writing a humorous composition or a satire (to make fun of something), you might want to begin with a funny statement to set the tone.

> Instead of claiming "new and improved," my breakfast cereal should claim "less for your money." The box is smaller and contains less of the same old cereal. That's new, but its hardly an improvement. I don't know about you, but I'm tired of so-called upgrades by advertisers.

EXERCISE 5   Identifying Types of Introductions

On the line after each paragraph below, write the technique used in the attention-getting introduction.

1. Can a woman lead an American Indian nation, especially if it's the second largest group in the United States? The answer, of course, is "yes," as Wilma P. Mankiller has proved. Ms. Mankiller is the principal leader of the Oklahoma Cherokee, a nation with about 67,000 registered members.

   _____

2. At the beginning of the Civil War, President Lincoln thought he would need only 75,000 volunteers and that the war would be over in three months. However, the war lasted four years and was fought by four million armed soldiers. In terms of destruction of human life and property, this was by far the costliest war in American history.

   _____

3. "A picture is worth a thousand words," my mother used to say. If that's true, then Chinese words are worth a thousand ordinary words because Chinese words are written as picture-signs.

   _____

4. You can do it. You can get up off the couch and make yourself fit and healthy, without breaking your back with weights or developing shin splints from jogging. You can take an easy, safe road to physical fitness by walking every day.

   _____

EXERCISE 6   Cooperating to Write an Introduction

Work with a partner to write an introduction to a composition. Base your introduction on the formal outline that you created for Exercise 4. Use one of the techniques for writing introductions discussed in this lesson. Write the introduction on your own paper.

WRITING CONCLUSIONS

Imagine going to a movie and having the film break near the end. That would be disappointing. A movie, a book, or a composition needs a definite ending, or *conclusion.* There are many ways to write conclusions. Here are some of the methods often used by professional writers.

- **Refer to the introduction.** The following conclusion refers to the introduction about mail fraud on page 31.

    So, for these reasons, when I receive mail that says I've just won some grand prize, I stick it in an envelope and send it to the state attorney general's office, along with a note saying, "You might want to investigate this."

- **Offer a solution or make a recommendation.** This technique is particularly appropriate if your composition deals with a problem.

    How do we end all this pollution and congestion? How do we attract new business to the downtown area? Here's a radical proposal. Let's ban cars from the downtown area. Let's build parking garages outside the area, provide shuttle buses, and turn the downtown area into a mall. Imagine the downtown streets replaced by grass and trees. Imagine shoppers milling about, reading on park benches, and listening to open-air musicians. Sounds nice, doesn't it?

- **Restate your thesis.** Another way to end a composition is to restate your thesis in different words. The following conclusion restates the thesis presented in the sample introduction about Nancy Lopez on page 32.

    All the championships that she has won and all the money that she has made by playing in golf tournaments prove that Nancy Lopez is one of the finest women golfers in the history of the sport.

- **Pose a dramatic question or challenge.** By posing a question or a challenge, you can keep your reader thinking or move your reader to take some action.

    See for yourself. Try the walking program outlined above. In a month there will be a trimmer, stronger, healthier person walking around in your shoes.

- **Make a personal comment about your topic.** Ending on a personal note can touch your reader's emotions.

> Cherokees are justly proud of their history and their heritage. It's important to keep that heritage alive. My own great-great-grandmother was a Cherokee. Sadly, I know very little about her or about the life that she led. In two short generations, much of her history has been lost. We owe it to our ancestors not to let that happen.

- **Summarize your main points.** Yet another way to end a composition is to give a brief summary of the main points that you made in the body of the composition.

> It's clear, therefore, that playing in a rock-and-roll band isn't all play. There's a lot of hard work involved. You must find the right mix of musical talent. You must decide what material you plan to perform. You must find rehearsal space, gather equipment, and set up the equipment. And most of all, you must practice cooperatively. Doing all these things won't make your group another Bon Jovi or U2, but it's a start.

EXERCISE 7   Identifying Types of Conclusions

On the line after each of the following paragraphs, write the technique used in each conclusion.

1. As the previous facts and figures show, keeping exotic, wild pets such as rare birds, monkeys, and lions isn't a good idea. First, many such animals die when they are caught or are being transported. Second, wild animals can injure or even kill their owners by biting or scratching them. Third, these animals often carry diseases, such as polio, hepatitis, and rabies, that are harmful to humans.

   _____

2. My own experience with a grizzly in the wild is an example. Hiking in Alaska, I unexpectedly came upon a mother with her cubs. Because I was aware that a mother grizzly will attack if she believes that her cubs are in danger, I stood still. I didn't move. I looked at the bears. They looked at me. After a while, they moved on. Thankfully, my knowledge of grizzly bears had prepared me for this life-threatening situation.

   _____

3. These responsible actions on the part of the mayor have benefited many citizens in our community. Now, there's a simple way to show your gratitude: Vote in tomorrow's election to keep her in office.

---

4. So get out there and help make your world a healthier place. Start a recycling project at your school. Get your parents to recycle at work. Participate in town clean-up projects. Conserve gas, oil, and electricity whenever you can. It's your world to live in, clean or dirty.

EXERCISE 8   Writing a Conclusion

On your own paper, write the conclusion for a composition about computer games. Base your conclusion on the formal outline that you created for Exercise 4 (page 30). You may want to refer to the introduction you wrote for Exercise 6.

EXERCISE 9   Writing a Composition

Now you are ready to put together a complete composition. On your own paper, write a brief composition using the thesis statement, outline, introduction, and conclusion that you created for the topic "computer games." If you wish, you may choose another topic for your paper. Between your introduction and conclusion, you will need to create the body of your composition. To support your thesis statement, gather any additional facts and opinions that you might need. Reference books, magazines, newspapers, and personal interviews will help you gather information. Use the techniques you learned in Chapter 2 (pages 17–18) for ordering information. Be sure to give your composition a title when you are finished.

Shoe, by Jeff MacNelly, reprinted by permission: Tribune Media Services.

A STATEMENT OF PERSONAL GOALS

What's in your future? At this time in your life, that's a question you may be thinking about (or hearing from others) quite a bit. Your vision of what you want as an adult may be pretty clear or rather cloudy. Either way, trying to *state your personal goals* in writing helps define them. Writing to express yourself is a way to understand yourself—and perhaps to *become* yourself. A goal statement doesn't have to be a major formal document. It can be a personal journal entry, like this one.

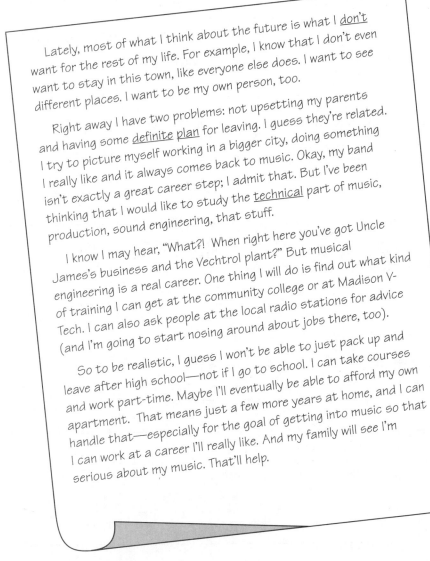

Lately, most of what I think about the future is what I <u>don't</u> want for the rest of my life. For example, I know that I don't even want to stay in this town, like everyone else does. I want to see different places. I want to be my own person, too.

Right away I have two problems: not upsetting my parents and having some <u>definite</u> <u>plan</u> for leaving. I guess they're related. I try to picture myself working in a bigger city, doing something I really like and it always comes back to music. Okay, my band isn't exactly a great career step; I admit that. But I've been thinking that I would like to study the <u>technical</u> part of music, production, sound engineering, that stuff.

I know I may hear, "What?! When right here you've got Uncle James's business and the Vechtrol plant?" But musical engineering is a real career. One thing I will do is find out what kind of training I can get at the community college or at Madison V-Tech. I can also ask people at the local radio stations for advice (and I'm going to start nosing around about jobs there, too).

So to be realistic, I guess I won't be able to just pack up and leave after high school—not if I go to school. I can take courses and work part-time. Maybe I'll eventually be able to afford my own apartment. That means just a few more years at home, and I can handle that—especially for the goal of getting into music so that I can work at a career I'll really like. And my family will see I'm serious about my music. That'll help.

Thinking About The Model

Reading this journal entry shows you that each statement of personal goals is unique. Yet the *process* of exploring ideals and obstacles is similar for all of us. To think more closely about this writer's expressive process, answer the following questions.

1. You might write about your goals in your journal to make them clear for yourself. The model entry starts with rather general goals about how and where the writer wants to live. What are the goals?

   _____

   _____

   The writer's journal entry also produces a career goal. What is it?

   _____

2. What practical steps toward this career does the writer mention?

   _____

   _____

   _____

3. Setting goals often means facing problems and obstacles. What obstacles does the model writer see?

   _____

   _____

   How does the writer suggest meeting the problems?

   _____

   _____

4. What personal values does this journal entry reveal? List briefly the things that you think matter to the writer.

   _____

   _____

ASSIGNMENT: WRITING A STATEMENT OF PERSONAL GOALS

Write a statement of personal goals for your journal. In your statement, you'll be looking to the future: what you want to be doing in five years, or perhaps at age twenty-five. You'll write to explore what's important to you and also how you can make it happen. A journal entry is personal and informal, but you may want others to read it: your teacher, a counselor, your family, or a friend.

Prewriting

Your personal goals are too important to be written without thought, so this journal entry requires some planning. The following steps will give you ideas for starting your thoughts, developing them, and ending up with a statement of real meaning.

Step 1:   Visualizing yourself in five years or at age twenty-five may be a good way to start. What picture pleases you most? Are you traveling? Are you working with children? Are you in the military? Are you at school studying art? Are you working outdoors? If a clear picture springs to mind, go directly to the lines below, and complete the sentence. If you can't form a clear picture, begin by focusing on areas like the following ones.

- **Location and surroundings:** How important is place to you? Do you love hot weather? Do you hate big cities? Would you like to stay where you are? *Where*, ideally, would you live, and *why*?
- **Favorite kinds of activities:** Suppose you volunteered to help at your high school, at a local business, or with a community group. What would you choose to do? What would you actually *look forward* to?
- **Your work "style":** Do you like to work with your hands? Do you work better in a team or alone? Do you like to create plans or to carry them out? Under what conditions do you really get things done?
- **Hates and horrors:** If ideas aren't flowing, there's nothing wrong with starting with what you *don't* want in your future. But after you state your vision of horror, ask yourself: Why do I dread this? How can I prevent it? What would be *totally unlike* it?

Complete this sentence:

When I am _____ years old, I see myself _____

_____

_____

Step 2:   Now test your goal a bit. Don't hesitate to shoot high, but be realistic too. You're writing to discover a future that's both fulfilling *and* possible. Set down some practical steps to reach your goal. Like the writer of the model journal entry, you'll have to look at needs or requirements (such as education) and possible problems (such as money). For the picture you created in *Step 1*, write responses on the lines that follow.

Needs or requirements of the goal: _____

_____

_____

Problems I'll face: _____

_____

_____

Practical steps I can take: _____

_____

_____

If you decide your first goals now look too much like fantasies, write some new ones. Use your own paper to freewrite about a different future, and come up with practical steps for achieving your goals.

Writing

Write your statement of personal goals in your journal. Keep in mind that someone else may read this entry. While your statement won't be like anyone else's, these suggestions can guide your writing.

1. Use your prewriting notes, but let your writing flow naturally. Don't hesitate to add details about your life now, your likes and dislikes, if they're important to your goals. If you're uncertain about some things—or have a new idea while you're writing—that's fine. Write those thoughts too.

2. In your entry, you may want to "paint the picture" of you in the future. Descriptive details may make the goals more real and the statement more interesting.

3. Be sure you include some practical actions or steps.

4. Express what the goals mean to you, why they're important. The focus of this writing is you, not "great careers for the nineties." Let your personal point of view come through.

If you already have a notebook or some other journal, write your goal statement in it. Or write your statement on the lines below.

_____

_____

_____

_____

_____

_____

_____

_____

_____

_____

_____

Evaluating and Revising

Usually, you write a journal just for yourself. You don't have to judge each entry or try to make it better. However, a goal statement is something you might share with another person. If so, you may want to evaluate it. You'll want to be sure it really communicates your goals and feelings—so make changes if necessary. Focus on whether you have **stated your goals clearly, included practical steps, and expressed what the goals mean to you.** If you like, write a revised entry on a separate sheet of paper.

Proofreading and Publishing

Consider showing your statement of personal goals to a good friend, a teacher, or your family. Be sure you keep a copy of it for yourself, though. You may want to check on your progress, revise the goals, or reject them entirely. A personal expression like this is very much open to change—just as you are.

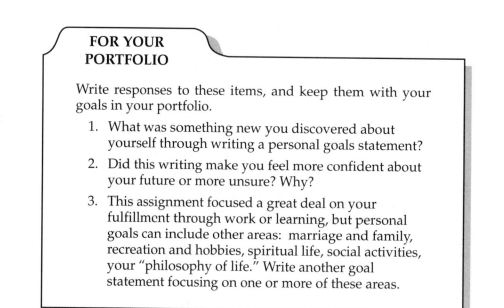

FOR YOUR PORTFOLIO

Write responses to these items, and keep them with your goals in your portfolio.

1. What was something new you discovered about yourself through writing a personal goals statement?

2. Did this writing make you feel more confident about your future or more unsure? Why?

3. This assignment focused a great deal on your fulfillment through work or learning, but personal goals can include other areas: marriage and family, recreation and hobbies, spiritual life, social activities, your "philosophy of life." Write another goal statement focusing on one or more of these areas.

A SHORT STORY

You are full of stories, whether you know it or not. You've been hearing, reading, watching, dreaming, and *living* them all your life. And you can write one, too. Still not so sure? Just give this chapter a chance to unleash your ideas and put them into *short story* form. You can start with something very real—like teenagers who want perfect looks. You can go off in a strange direction—as writers do in science fiction. Or you can do both—as the writer in the following story has done.

T-formity

Marlette Larkin

Sy stood in front of the mirror for about the twentieth time. He meant to look *good*. He'd been waiting seventeen years for this night, and even now he couldn't believe he'd made it. He pulled his certification card out of his beltpack (also for about the twentieth time): "Syzer.dos, Transformer Level I, valid June 16, 2395." He didn't like his laser image on the card, though. His ears looked like cabbage leaves.

Well, he could fix that now! He was a T-former at last! Sy could understand why the Earth Council didn't give people transforming power from the time they were born. Imagine if little kids could change their shape, size, and color whenever they wanted to. Disaster City. T-form Training started when you were thirteen. You got one brain chip installed at a time and had to pass some *mean* tests for the first card. So what if he was only a Level I—a greenie? He was allowed two transformations per day, and his only skin color choice was green, but it was a start.

Sy, though, had a secret. He gazed at his perfect ears in the mirror (his first change for the day). Maybe he should be seven feet tall tonight (that would be change number two). Red dreadlocks might be cool (that would be three). His secret? He could do all three if he wanted to! Every trainer said Sy was the best T-form student they'd ever seen. They didn't know how good. Even without a Level II chip, Sy had created his own brain program to do five changes per day—including orange. But Level II wasn't legal for him, and he was going to play it straight.

That meant he would do just one more T-form change for tonight. He decided to leave his head alone. With the ear change, his head was OK: deep brown skin, gray eyes, wide mouth, skyscraper-high white hair. He decided to go for super-broad shoulders. He'd noticed that Tara.mac, a really excellent Level II girl, was always hanging with *wide* guys. Poppp! Sy's shoulders moved out three inches on each side, stretching his crimson jumpsuit tight. All *right*!

When Sy got to the T-Time Club, Tara was already there. She was standing by the food belt with a whole lot of older T-formers who were acting like kings. He saw a few other greenies he knew, looking as scared and excited as he was. None of them had ever been inside the club before, because this was the first party since they'd graduated. It was packed and unbelievably cool. All the high-power T-formers looked great. They were tall or tiny, neon purple or midnight blue, slim or solid. The greenies just stared at them on the dance floor.

Sy took a deep breath and headed for Tara, who was wearing her black hair down to the floor. She'd always been friendly in the neighborhood, and he was relieved to see her smile.

"Hey, Sy," she said, "how do you like it? You really should try some of this great food." She pointed at the plate a guy was holding for her. The guy gave Sy a dirty look.

"You a greenie?" he asked. "You can always tell a greenie 'cause they only have two T-forms and need a hundred to look decent." He thought this was hilarious and laughed with his mouth full.

Sy tried to ignore Tara's friend, Gopher, but Gopher kept cutting him down. And Sy didn't think Gopher was so great. He was big, yes, but he looked mushy. Suddenly Sy couldn't stand it. He'd show this clown how to T-form, even if it was number three for the day. Muscles, that's what Sy wanted. Poppp! Out came gorgeous weight-lifter biceps. But also out shot his arm—right toward the plate Gopher held. Gopher got it in the chest: oozy gobs of seaweed dip.

"Yikes," said Tara, trying not to laugh.

"I'll get a towel," said Sy, scramming fast. He headed for the crowded dance floor, trying to disappear, but Gopher was following. "Man," he thought, "I am about to get colored black and blue." He could think of only one way to escape: T-form number 4. Sy didn't have time to plan. He just had to look really different really fast. And preferably really big. Sploosh! He was five feet tall and about 500 pounds.

"Crazy," admired a Level-IIIer he bounced into. "You think that's something? I can do better." Ripppp! He shot up to nine flaming-red feet. And the T-form contest was on. Splat! Plop! Whiz! Bodies were changing at warp speed. Arms and legs stretched out and tangled. Heads knocked. The macho guys got bigger and bigger. Girls popped out extra muscles to protect themselves. The greenies hugged the walls in terror. Sy managed to waddle to the edge of the dance floor, but he had to do something or he'd be crushed.

He had one T-form left—and he'd have to stay that way. He saw Gopher and three of his monster buddies looking like they'd pop. "Here goes," said Sy.

He T-formed and dived for cover.

The next thing Sy knew, blinding white lights were flashing, and somebody was gripping his arm like iron. Then he opened his eyes. He was under a table. The lights were real, not in his head, and the hand gripping him was Tara's. But Tara had hair about an inch long. She saw his surprise.

"It's me," she said. "Would you want to be in a riot with five feet of hair for people to grab? I notice you're not the new, improved Sy any more, either."

Whew, he'd done it. He touched his ears: cabbage. Too bad, he'd gone back 100 percent. Oh, well. At least Tara hadn't seen him at 500 pounds.

"Look," said Tara, "let's go. The lights mean all T-form chips are deactivated. Boy, that doesn't happen often! You probably feel lost, being a greenie. But don't worry. You'll get more experience."

That was exactly what Sy meant to do—at Level I.

Thinking About the Model

The model short story may have given you writing ideas already. It also showed you the basic *elements,* or parts, of a story. Answer the following questions to see how the writer used the elements to turn her idea into a story.

1. Stories have believable *characters,* even if the characters have made-up powers or are animals or machines. Who is the main character of "T-formity" ? What does he look like when the story begins?

   _____

   _____

   _____

   Who are other important characters? List one descriptive detail for each character.

   _____

   _____

2. The *setting* is the time and place of the story. "T-formity" is set on earth, far in the future. What is the year?

   _____

Setting also includes individual places where events take place. The model story's first setting is Sy's home. What is the second setting? List two details that help you picture this second setting.

_____

_____

What kind of *atmosphere,* or *mood,* do the above details and the futuristic time period create? Circle two words that could apply.

gloomy   fantastic   pitiful   lively

3. The *plot* is the sequence of events in a story. Plot is created and kept going by a *conflict,* or problem. The main character (or characters) may be lost on a mountain or may be facing a difficult personal choice. In the model, what conflict is the main character facing when the story starts? (Hint: What is his "secret"?)

_____

_____

Now, briefly list the main events of the plot.

_____

_____

_____

_____

4. In most stories, the plot builds in tension to a *climax.* A climax is a moment of keen interest or suspense (also called the *high point* or *turning point*) when the conflict will be settled. What is the climax of "T-formity"?

_____

_____

5. The *resolution,* or *outcome,* shows how the conflict is resolved. It also ties up any of the story's loose ends by giving final details about how things work out. What is the outcome of "T-formity"?

_____

_____

ASSIGNMENT: WRITING A SHORT STORY

Write a short story, using the basic storytelling elements of character, setting, conflict, and plot. Remember that the elements are meant to help your creativity: Let your imagination go, and entertain your readers. Write a story that *you* would like to read.

Prewriting

Step 1:   An idea: That's where your story starts. If those two little words seem like a BIG problem, relax. You can start developing story ideas from lots of things in your life:

- **dreams, nightmares, and fantasies:** Would you like to see a volcano in Hawaii? Did you dream you were skating through the mall? Did a nightmare have you running from a huge animal with a sharp beak?

- **people—family or strangers:** Does your family like to tell the story about your little cousin's "cinnamon" cookies—made with red-hot cayenne pepper? Did you see a girl at the bus stop wearing motorcycle boots and a lace dress?

- **newspapers, TV, and magazines:** Did you watch a news story about a flood at a laundromat? Did you read an article about teenagers camping out to get concert tickets?

Brainstorm some story starters here (take off from the examples above, if you like):

_____

_____

_____

Step 2:   Your final story idea has to have both a main character and a central conflict. *Someone* (or some *thing*—robot, pig, or whatever) has to have a *problem:* face danger, have a secret desire, get in a serious fix one way or another. You can use "What if?" questions to generate both elements. For example:

What if two best friends [the main characters] are the last people in line for one remaining concert ticket [the conflict]?

Check the story ideas you've written on the lines above. If they don't have both a main character and a conflict, brainstorm for these elements on a separate piece of paper, using "What if?" questions. Then write the story idea you like best on the lines on the following page.

Main character(s): _____

Conflict: _____

Step 3:   Describe your characters so that they're solid and real to readers. Can you see Sy in your mind's eye from reading the model story? (Probably you see several Sys!) That's because the writer described his "skyscraper-high white hair," "crimson jumpsuit," and more. Not all details are visual, of course. Imagine characteristics like these for your characters:

- age and appearance
- family and home
- voice and way of talking
- likes and dislikes
- favorite clothes
- strongest personality traits

You may not use all the details, but you'll *know* your characters.

Now use a separate sheet of paper to list details or to freewrite a paragraph about your main character(s).

Step 4:   What is your story's setting? Below, specify the time period and place(s) of the action. Then list some important or vivid details: weather? buildings? objects in a room? smells?

_____

_____

_____

Step 5:   Now decide the plot, the main events in the story. In the plot, you want to introduce the main character and get to the conflict quickly. You'll create a climax, or high point, of suspense, and then show the character trying to resolve the problem.

Plot Example

Conflict: The two best friends Joey and Shayne fight over the last ticket to the coming SirDogg concert.

Events: Joey buys the ticket, and Shayne angrily says, "You'll be sorry." At school, Shayne refuses to talk to Joey.

Climax: On concert night, Shayne is waiting outside Joey's house.

Resolution: Shayne apologizes for being childish and tells Joey to have a good time. Joey offers Shayne his ticket, but Shayne says no. Joey decides to surprise him with a concert T-shirt.

Plan your story by filling out the story map on the following page. Use your notes from Steps 2–4, and list details about setting, main character, and plot.

STORY MAP

SETTING

Time:_____

Place:_____

Details That Describe

Setting:_____

_____

_____

_____

MAIN CHARACTER

Name:_____

Details That Describe

Character:_____

_____

_____

_____

PLOT

Conflict:_____

_____

Events:_____

_____

_____

_____

_____

Climax:_____

_____

Resolution:_____

_____

Step 6:   **Dialogue**—what the characters say—is also important in stories. Dialogue moves the plot along and makes characters seem more real. How would an android woman speak? A furious, strict father? In dialogue, you should match the words to the character. Use informal English and slang if they're right for the speaker. In the model story, for instance, Gopher asks, "You a greenie?" This sentence fragment is fine because it sounds realistic. Here's another example of dialogue from "T-formity":

> "Crazy," admired a Level-IIIer he bounced into. "You think that's something? I can do better."

Choose an event from your story map, and write some possible dialogue for the characters involved. Always identify the speaker, and start a new paragraph when the speaker changes.

_____

_____

_____

_____

_____

_____

_____

_____

_____

_____

_____

_____

Writing

The story map on page 49 is your plan and guide. Now you'll write a rough draft, fleshing out the map's ideas and details in full sentences. The following suggestions will help you create a strong beginning, middle, and ending.

Beginning	• Introduce the main character(s). • Give any needed background information to set up the plot. • Grab the reader's interest early. Hint at or present the conflict, and use vivid details.

Middle	• Establish or deepen the conflict. • Use sharp details to make your characters, their actions, and the story's setting believable. • Use realistic dialogue to show emotions and attitudes. • Build action to a high point of interest or suspense.

Ending	• Resolve the central conflict. Show the reader how everything turns out.

 Evaluating and Revising

Now turn yourself into your audience. Decide how well your story interests readers and keeps them asking, "What next?" **Evaluate** which elements are strong and which seem weak. Then **revise** problem areas. You can use the **Questions for Evaluation** on the following page to review both your own story and a classmate's story.

Questions for Evaluation

1. Is the reader's interest captured from the beginning? If not, what descriptions, actions, or hint of conflict could be added?

2. Is the conflict established quickly? If not, what sentences could be changed, added, or moved?

3. Are the main characters vivid and believable? If not, what details could be added or changed? What dialogue could be improved or added?

4. Is the setting clear? Do details help readers picture it? If not, what details of time and of place—sight, sound, and smell—could be added?

5. Does the plot build in interest to a climax? If not, what actions or events could be added or cut to keep attention high?

6. Is the central problem resolved in a satisfying way? Does the ending answer final questions about what happens? If not, what could be added or changed to make the ending stronger?

Peer Evaluation

Exchange rough drafts with a classmate. Then follow these directions.

Step 1:   Read your classmate's rough draft. Read for the *story*—what it means and how entertaining it is—not for grammar and mechanics.

Step 2:   On your own paper, answer the **Questions for Evaluation** above. Remember not to let personal tastes influence your evaluation. Don't say things like, "Monster stories are boring." Decide whether the writer's elements *work well* for a monster story. For example, is the monster scary?

Self-Evaluation

Step 1:   Let some time pass before you reread your rough draft. Then pretend you're turning to a magazine short story for the first time. Ask yourself, "Does this opening pull me in? Does each paragraph pull me farther along?" Make quick notes if you want to.

Step 2:   Read your classmate's evaluation of your story.

Step 3:   On the following lines, which continue on the next page, answer the **Questions for Evaluation**. Compare the peer evaluation with your own evaluation, and mark the suggestions you'll use.

_____

_____

_____

_____

_____

_____

_____

_____

_____

Revise your story. You'll probably make bigger improvements if you take one element at a time. For example, you could make the plot tighter first, then work on character description, then add or rewrite dialogue, and so on.

 ## Proofreading and Publishing

After you've finished revising, you may think your story is perfect. It may seem that way—but you should take one last look to correct any remaining errors.

Step 1:   Reread your revised story for errors in grammar, usage, punctuation, capitalization, and spelling. Use a dictionary to check spellings you don't know. Carefully review the quotation marks and other punctuation in dialogue; see pages 301–306 for rules.

Step 2:   Make a clean copy of your revised and proofread story.

Step 3:   Almost everybody likes stories, so don't hide your tale from an audience. Here are some publishing ideas.

   A.   Does your school have computers that can sketch pictures? Or does it offer art classes? Ask your teacher about the possibility of arranging a collaborative project with computer or art classes to illustrate your class's stories. Then set up a library display.

   B.   Ask your teacher or library for the names of magazines and newspapers that publish high school students' creative writing, and submit your story.

   C.   Listen to some recordings of short stories, and then make an audiotape of your story. Play it in your car on family trips, or mail it to a friend or relative out of town.

FOR YOUR PORTFOLIO

Respond to these items, and keep the results with your story in your portfolio.

1. Draw either a scene from your story or the portrait of a character. If you're not an artist, then describe how you would film or videotape one of your scenes. Exactly what would you put on the screen?

2. Complete this sentence: *When I was writing this story, I got most involved or excited when . . .* If you never felt involved or enjoyed the writing, honestly explain why.

3. Find out about the author of a favorite story, and write a paragraph about him or her.

Calvin & Hobbes copyright 1986 Watterson. Reprinted with permission of Universal Press Syndicate. All rights reserved.

A CONSUMER REPORT

With so many products available in today's market, how do you choose which product is best for you? Is Brand X a better running shoe than Brand Y? What about the new, trendy Brand Z? To make an intelligent choice, you need information that compares and evaluates products and services. You need a *consumer report*. In the following consumer report, a member of the track team compares three types of running shoes for his high school newspaper.

On Track

Tyler Pope

An afternoon spent trying on different brands of running shoes is sure to result in a headache—maybe on top of a footache. As you stand bewildered before an enormous wall of shoes, the possibilities appear endless. For the serious runner, however, three brands of shoes quickly pull ahead to the first, second, and third positions—Cloud Nine Cumulus, HyFlyte, and Trophy II. Serious runners look at a shoe's fit, arch support, traction, and durability. They also look for a price tag smaller than a week's wages.

On the basis of my own hard training and having competed in several statewide meets this year, I can testify that Cloud Nine's newest running shoe, Cumulus, is a breakthrough for arch support. It truly delivers firmness without uncomfortable stiffness. Fit, traction, and durability also get above-average marks. And, at $69 a pair, Cumulus is an affordable high-quality shoe.

My previous brand, Icarus, has been on the market for three years. I wore the Icarus HyFlyte for the first two. During that time, the brand's fit and durability improved greatly. I would give equal marks on those features to HyFlyte and Cumulus. On the traditional cinder track, HyFlyte's traction ratings were good. They were much lower, though, for other surfaces, such as grass or cement. The shoe sells for $89.

Racer has been a popular brand for serious runners for five years. It's the choice of pros and many of my teammates. The newest model, Trophy II, just tinkers with the design of Trophy I. That best-seller was exceptional in fit, arch support, and durability. Trophy II, though, claims a revolutionary tread design. I don't see it. I examined the sole tread pattern of Trophy II and got a big surprise: The design is a close cousin to my Cumulus. The "new" traction isn't worth the price tag of $119 a pair.

Of these three good running shoes, I recommend Cloud Nine Cumulus first. Its fit, traction, and durability are all above average. HyFlyte and Trophy II are still winners, but in second and third place. Cumulus' dynamic arch support and low price speed it several steps ahead in the running-shoe race.

Thinking About the Model

In the model consumer report you've just read, the writer-runner does two things for his readers. He provides information, and he offers a recommendation. Think about how his recommendation is based on the kinds of information he presents. Answer the following questions on the lines provided.

1. A consumer report is informative, so the writer's opening paragraph makes clear his topic (running shoes) and his purpose (to help buyers choose). But *informing* readers doesn't mean *boring* readers. Name one entertaining detail or phrase in the first paragraph.

   _____

   _____

   _____

2. To give readers useful information, a consumer report must focus on *features* of the service or product. What features of running shoes does the writer discuss? (Hint: This writer chose to name all the features in his first paragraph.)

   _____

   _____

   _____

3. The writer *compares* the features for different shoes. What does he say about the feature of traction for each shoe?

Cumulus: _____

_____

HyFlyte: _____

_____

Trophy II: _____

_____

4. The writer has worn Cumulus and HyFlyte shoes, but not the Trophy II. How does he get information about Trophy shoes for readers?

_____

_____

5. The writer uses a different paragraph to explain each brand of shoe. In what order does he present the paragraphs (from best to worst, or vice versa)?

_____

_____

6. A consumer report usually ends with a recommendation for buyers and a summary of reasons for the recommendation. In the model report's last paragraph, what is the writer's advice to running-shoe buyers?

_____

_____

7. What reasons does he give for his first choice of shoe?

_____

_____

ASSIGNMENT: WRITING A CONSUMER REPORT

Write a consumer report for your school newspaper's "Wise Buys" column. Choose a product or a service, and compare the features of two or more companies, brands, or models. As you write, think about your audience, teenage consumers. What products do they want to know about? What features are important?

 ### Prewriting

Step 1:   To choose a product or a service, consider what interests you and other students—but also what's realistic! You may dream about European sports cars (who doesn't?), but are your readers really concerned over which one to buy? Think of

- products you have or may buy: CD player, bicycle, guitar, backpack, shampoo, lipstick, orange juice
- businesses or services you use: clothing stores, video rentals, restaurants, bike repair shops, hair stylists, campgrounds, city swimming pools

Brainstorm some topics on the lines below. One approach is to walk through, in your mind, a typical day or weekend. What do you use? What do you do?

Products: _____

_____

_____

_____

_____

_____

_____

_____

_____

_____

_____

_____

_____

Services or Businesses: _____

_____

_____

_____

_____

_____

_____

_____

_____

_____

_____

_____

_____

_____

Step 2:   Now choose one product or service to evaluate. Use these questions to review your ideas and settle on a topic.

A. **Can I identify at least two companies, brands, or models of the product or service?** Remember that you're giving readers a comparison. What choices do they face when buying the product or using the service?

B. **Can I easily get specific information about the product or service?** This doesn't necessarily mean paying for it or owning it. You may be able to make personal observations in other ways.

- Examine products in stores or at friends' homes.
- Read brochures and manuals.
- Ask questions.
- Explore a business's selection, prices, atmosphere, service.

In the chart below, list the product or service you'll write about, along with two or three companies, brands, or models you'll compare. An example for pizza is shown.

Example	Your Report
Product/Service: pizza	Product/Service: _____
Companies/Brands/Models	Companies/Brands/Models
1. Pizza Pizzazz	1. _____
2. Rudy's Pizza	2. _____
3. Pizza Now	3. _____

Step 3:   Next decide on the features you'll focus on. For example, some features for comparing pizza are crust, sauce, toppings, price, and the restaurant's service or delivery. Ask yourself, *What are the basic features I expect from this product or service? What matters to me?* Brainstorm features for your topic on the lines below. Then ask classmates if they have other suggestions.

_____

_____

_____

_____

_____

_____

_____

_____

_____

_____

_____

_____

Step 4:   For each company, brand, or model, gather information about the features through personal experience and observation. Look back at *Step 2, Question B,* for ways to observe. If you're comparing styling gels, you can easily do a personal test. If you're comparing music stores, you can inspect selection and prices and ask the clerks questions.

Use the chart on page 62 to record your observations. (If you need more room for notes or features, make your own chart on a separate sheet of paper.) Notice that your evaluation may turn up special features for some brands.

Step 5:   Study your evaluation results, and decide how you'll advise consumers. Ask yourself: *Based on what I've found out, what brand, model, or company do I prefer?* You may tell readers that only Rudy's pizza is worth eating. You may say that Rudy's and Pizza Now are equally good, but Pizza Pizzazz is not recommended. On the chart below, write the recommendation in a sentence. Then try to summarize your reasons. Just freewrite a summary now; you'll revise it later.

Evaluation of Features			
	Brand 1	Brand 2	Brand 3
Features	_____	_____	_____
1. _____	_____	_____	_____
	_____	_____	_____
2. _____	_____	_____	_____
	_____	_____	_____
3. _____	_____	_____	_____
	_____	_____	_____
4. _____	_____	_____	_____
	_____	_____	_____
Special features:	_____	_____	_____
	_____	_____	_____
Recommendation:	_____		
	_____		
	_____		

Summary of
reasons:
_____

_____

_____

_____

_____

_____

Writing

Use the notes on your chart to write a rough draft of your consumer report.
Rereading the model paper on pages 55–56 may help you too. Here is a plan to
follow as you write.

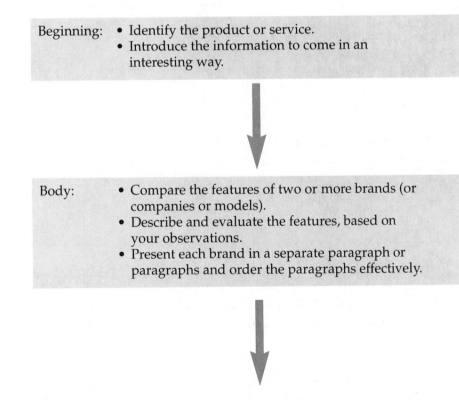

Beginning: • Identify the product or service.
            • Introduce the information to come in an
              interesting way.

Body: • Compare the features of two or more brands (or
              companies or models).
            • Describe and evaluate the features, based on
              your observations.
            • Present each brand in a separate paragraph or
              paragraphs and order the paragraphs effectively.

| Ending: | • Make a final recommendation to readers. |
| | • Summarize or restate reasons for the recommendation. |

 ## Evaluating and Revising

You've just evaluated a product or a service. Now you'll evaluate your report. What is good about it? What is not? What can you do to improve it—to revise it? You can use the following questions to evaluate your own consumer report and a classmate's report.

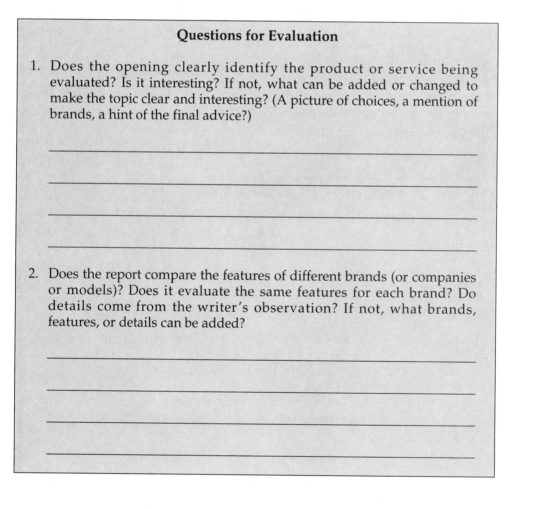

Questions for Evaluation

1. Does the opening clearly identify the product or service being evaluated? Is it interesting? If not, what can be added or changed to make the topic clear and interesting? (A picture of choices, a mention of brands, a hint of the final advice?)

_____

_____

_____

_____

2. Does the report compare the features of different brands (or companies or models)? Does it evaluate the same features for each brand? Do details come from the writer's observation? If not, what brands, features, or details can be added?

_____

_____

_____

_____

Questions for Evaluation, cont.

3. Is each brand presented in a separate paragraph or paragraphs? If not, how can the information be rearranged?

_____

_____

_____

_____

4. Is the order of brands effective? For example, are they ordered from best to worst, or vice versa? If not, how can the paragraphs be reordered?

_____

_____

_____

_____

5. Does the conclusion plainly state a recommendation? Does it summarize or restate the writer's reasons? If not, what recommendation do the evaluations of features lead to? What can be added about important reasons?

_____

_____

_____

_____

Peer Evaluation

Exchange rough drafts with a classmate, and follow these steps.

Step 1:   Read the consumer report carefully. But don't spend time checking grammar and mechanics: Give your attention to content.

Step 2:   Answer the **Questions for Evaluation** on your own paper. In your suggestions for the *If not . . . ?* questions, be as specific as possible.

Self-Evaluation

Next evaluate your draft, using these steps.

Step 1:   Read the peer evaluation of your paper. Ask your reviewer questions if it will help in revising. Note any answers or written comments you want to remember on the lines below.

_____

_____

_____

_____

_____

Step 2:   Reread your consumer report quickly. Then reread it more slowly, writing answers to the **Questions for Evaluation**.

Use both evaluations to guide the revision of your draft. Remember that you're writing to **inform** readers. If the evaluations show that your report lacks details about the products, go back to prewriting: brainstorm more features, or observe features more closely. When you revise, you can work directly on the draft or make a new copy incorporating the changes.

Proofreading and Publishing

Step 1:   Read your final revision for errors in spelling, grammar, usage, and mechanics. Read word by word for spelling and capitalization mistakes. Read sentence by sentence for other errors.

Step 2:   Correct errors by referring to the proofreading checklist on page 11. For help with capitalization, see pages 269–77.

Step 3:   Make a clean copy of your corrected report. Give it a title as if it will appear in the "Wise Buys" column of the school paper.

Step 4:   Publish your consumer report. After all, it's practical advice other students might want. Here are three ideas.

A. Consider publishing your consumer report electronically. Find the computer pros—teachers or students—at your school. They may know about electronic bulletin boards related to your topic. Other bicyclists, for example, might like to read a firsthand report on the new hybrid bikes.

B. Ask the school newspaper editor to start a "Wise Buys" column if the paper doesn't have one. Some local city papers have a "teen page" (or could start one) where you could publish your consumer report.

C. Ask the school media center to start a "Consumer Corner" so that other students can browse through, read, and even add to your class's consumer reports.

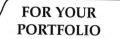

FOR YOUR PORTFOLIO

Write a brief response to each of the following questions and include them with your consumer report in your portfolio.

1. What effect has writing a consumer report had on your purchasing decisions? What's one consumer tip you learned for yourself?

2. What was the most difficult part of writing a consumer report? The easiest? Why?

3. What are the differences between writing to inform and other kinds of writing, such as writing to persuade?

A LETTER OF COMPLAINT

Does every product you buy work perfectly and live up to its claims? Is the service you receive always expert and courteous? If so, you're a rare (and lucky) person. Almost every consumer has a legitimate complaint sometime. How do you complain—and to whom? More important, how do you persuade that person to take action to solve your problem? One good way to voice your complaint and get results is to write a *letter of complaint*. The following letter was written to the manager of a local music store.

6789 Lincoln Avenue
Chicago, IL 60621
October 11, 1993

Cindy Hamadi, Store Manager
Sounds Galore
1000 State Street
Chicago, IL 60606

Dear Ms. Hamadi:

On October 1, I purchased the CD <u>Music, Music</u> by More Hot Music. When I played the CD for the first time, it skipped tracks 2 and 3. I have tried twice, unsuccessfully, to exchange the defective CD. I am now asking your help to resolve the problem.

On October 2, I called your store to report the skipping tracks. The clerk told me to return the CD within ten days for a full refund or an exchange. The next day I brought the defective CD and my receipt to your store for an exchange. Another clerk, Niki Jules, informed me that Sounds Galore was now sold out of <u>Music, Music</u> but that the CD would be restocked within a week. Yesterday I returned to get a new CD and was informed by yet another clerk, Franklin Crane, that unwrapped merchandise could not be returned or exchanged. This information completely contradicts the return/exchange policy the two other clerks had told me. Unfortunately, Franklin Crane was the only clerk in the store.

Today is the last day within the supposed ten-day return or exchange period. I have obviously tried to meet this deadline. Now, because two clerks gave me different information, I am left with a CD that doesn't work. I believe it is Sounds Galore's responsibility to state a clear return/exchange policy and make sure all employees know it. I would still like a new copy of <u>Music, Music</u>, but if it has not come in, I would like a full refund. Please respond, and I will bring the CD and my receipt to the store.

Sincerely,

Jason Smith

Thinking About the Model

The model letter of complaint on the previous page explains the problem and proposes a reasonable solution. Now that you've read the model, think about the information the writer uses to persuade the manager to solve the problem. Answer the following questions about the model letter of complaint.

1. The letter writer summarizes his complaint in the first paragraph. What is the complaint?

    _____

2. A letter of complaint must explain clearly what is wrong. Sometimes, as in the model letter, this explanation involves a series of events. Notice how the writer carefully details important events in *chronological order*. Fill in the missing *time phrase* or *event* in this list:

WHEN (time phrase)	WHAT (event)
"On October 1"	bought CD, found it defective
"On October 2"	called; clerk says refund/exchange within 10 days
"next day"	_____
_____	_____

3. All details that help define the problem or offer *evidence* are important. For example, in the model, what evidence (proof) of the purchase does the letter writer mention?

    _____

4. An effective letter of complaint closes with a *call for action*: the specific correction the writer wants. What two actions does the letter writer suggest to the store manager?

    _____

    _____

5. A letter of complaint should follow the form and tone of a business letter. Even though this writer is frustrated by his problem, he does not make threats or use rude or negative language. What *tone*, or feeling, does he use in his letter, and why?

    _____

    _____

ASSIGNMENT: WRITING A LETTER OF COMPLAINT

Write a letter of complaint about a problem you have had with a purchase or with a service. Address your letter to the manager of the store or to the customer service department of the company. In your letter, clearly state the complaint, and support it with full details. As you write, think about your tone and suggestion for action. What do you want the person or company to do about your complaint?

Prewriting

Writing complaint letters is definitely a skill you'll use in daily life. For this assignment, write a letter that you can actually mail. If you can't mail your letter (perhaps the store where you had a problem has closed), at least write about a real incident. The following steps will help you select an experience and plan your letter.

Step 1:   Think about problems you've had with a product or service. The problems can be *defects, confused orders, false advertising, mistakes in bills,* and *poor or rude service*. Here are just some examples:

- You order a T-shirt from a magazine ad and receive the wrong size and color.
- You make all payments on a layaway purchase, but the store's records say you still owe $10.
- A local radio station broadcasts the wrong date for the fund-raiser for your school trip.
- A warranty promises to replace a product within thirty days of purchase if the product doesn't work correctly. Neither the store nor the manufacturer will take responsibility for the warranty.

Brainstorm possible topics on the lines below. Name the product and service, and note the problem in a few words.

Products/Problems: _____

_____

_____

Service/Problems: _____

_____

_____

From these ideas, choose a problem

- **that you can detail** (you can list events or give any necessary product information)
- **that the company can correct** (you have a reasonable request that will "make things right")

On the lines below, summarize the complaint you will write about in one or two sentences.

Your letter's complaint: _____

_____

_____

Step 2: Decide where and to whom the letter should be sent. Who can take action on your complaint? Usually, for local complaints you will write to a store manager. If possible, telephone the store to get the manager's name. Writing to a specific person isn't necessary, but it's always a good idea. If you don't have an individual's name, you'll address the letter, "Dear Sir or Madam."

For complaints to out-of-town companies, you usually write to the customer service department—using "Dear Sir or Madam." Check the company's order forms, catalogs, or packing slips for complaint directions and an address.

On the lines below, write where you will send your complaint. Fill in the proper person (or department) and address.

Name, "Store Manager," or
"Customer Service Department": _____

Business/company name: _____

Street or P.O. Box: _____

City, state, ZIP Code: _____

Step 3: Now describe and discuss the specifics of what is wrong. Remember that to **persuade** someone to correct a problem, you have to give **evidence** that a problem exists. Here is what you want to make clear.

- the product or service you ordered, bought, or expected (an identifying description)
- why you aren't satisfied (the specific defect, error, poor service, etc.)
- any important dates, time periods, or people involved

- how the problem affected you (wasted money, lost time, inconvenience)

NOTE: Especially with complaints about mail orders—or products that need factory repairs—the company may give you directions about returning items, including your receipt, or stating the order number. Follow the directions whenever possible. And mention anything you send in your letter: "I am enclosing the cracked helmet and a copy of my receipt."

Write the specific details of your complaint below. Make rough notes first if you like. Then you can check information, add dates, or put events in chronological order.

_____

_____

_____

_____

_____

_____

_____

_____

_____

Step 4: Next, state exactly what you want the company to do about your complaint. You may suggest options, as the writer of the model letter did. He asked for a full refund OR a new *Music, Music* CD. On the lines below, write a solution that corrects your problem fairly.

_____

_____

_____

_____

_____

 Writing

Use your prewriting notes to draft your letter of complaint. Write the draft on the blank letter form on the next page. The chart that follows explains how to use proper business form and what to put on each line.

Parts of a Business Letter	
Heading	Divide the letter in half by drawing an imaginary line vertically down the middle. Begin the heading to the right of the line. Write these parts of the heading on separate lines. • your street address • city, state, and ZIP Code (A comma follows the name of the city.) • date of letter (A comma separates the day of the month from the year.)
Inside Address	Leave a margin at the left of the letter. Begin the inside address at the margin. Include these parts on separate lines. • the name of the person you are writing to or the title (*Store Manager*) or the department (*Customer Service*) • the name of the store or company • street address of the store or company • city, state, and ZIP Code of the store or company
Salutation	Begin the salutation, or greeting, at the left margin. Begin the first word and all nouns with a capital letter (*Dear Sir or Madam* or *Dear Ms. Smith*). A colon follows the salutation.
Body	Explain your complaint, and request a solution. Indent the first line of each paragraph.
Closing and Signature	Line up the closing under the heading. You might write *Sincerely* or *Yours truly*. Only the first word should be capitalized. A comma follows the closing. Skip four lines, and type or print your name. Sign your name in the space just below your closing.

[heading]

[inside address]

: —[salutation]   ⌐[body]

[closing]

[signature]

[typed or printed name]

 Evaluating and Revising

Now that you've drafted your letter of complaint, you have a chance to improve it. Getting satisfaction for your complaint depends on the strength of your letter. Uncover any weaknesses, and revise them. You will use the following **Questions for Evaluation** for your letter and for a classmate's letter.

Questions for Evaluation

1. Does the opening paragraph of the letter clearly state the complaint or problem? If not, what could be added or changed?

2. Does the letter provide full information about what is wrong or unsatisfactory? If not, what details could be added?

3. Are events (if any) organized in chronological order? If not, which events should be rearranged?

4. Does the letter of complaint close with a clear and reasonable statement of what the writer wants? If not, what specific solution to the problem could be added?

5. Is the letter's tone reasonable and calm? If not, what words or phrases could be cut or changed?

Peer Evaluation

Exchange rough drafts with a classmate, and follow these steps.

Step 1:   Read your classmate's letter as if you had to respond to the complaint. Focus on the letter's information, not on grammar and mechanics at this point.

Step 2:   Answer each question in the **Questions for Evaluation,** either in writing or in a conference with the writer.

Self-Evaluation

Evaluate your own draft by following these steps.

Step 1:   Again, put yourself in the store manager's (or the company's) shoes. This isn't as easy to do for your own letter as for someone else's, but it will yield results. Read your draft closely. Would you be persuaded?

Step 2: Answer in writing the **Questions for Evaluation**. Then listen to, or read, your classmate's answers to the questions. What suggestions are similar to yours? What suggestions are different? Decide on the suggested corrections you'll use.

Now revise your letter, using both evaluations. Whenever you or your peer reviewer answered "no" or "sort of" to an evaluation question, keep revising until you can say "yes." You can make corrections directly on your draft; you can rewrite your draft; or you can start all over again with prewriting.

Proofreading and Publishing

Now is the time to worry about your letter's mechanics and appearance. A manager who reads a letter filled with errors may question the writer's carefulness and may dismiss the complaint. Could the writer also have a careless memory? a loose way with details?

Step 1: Check each word carefully for correct spelling. Check in a dictionary if you are uncertain how a word is spelled.

Step 2: Proofread the letter of complaint for errors in capitalization, grammar, usage, and mechanics. Refer to the proofreading checklist on page 11.

Step 3: Be sure you've followed proper business form. Recheck the chart and letter form on pages 74 and 75. Then make a clean copy of your revised letter of complaint.

Step 4: Use one of the following suggestions to publish your letter.

- Mail your letter.
- If you are not mailing your letter to a store or company, send it to the Better Business Bureau or the Chamber of Commerce. The class could send several letters. In a cover letter to the president, explain your assignment, and ask for a practical evaluation of the letters. You might also ask a representative to talk to the class about complaint letters from the business person's perspective.
- Use your letter as you role-play a conversation between a consumer and the store manager.

FOR YOUR PORTFOLIO

Write down your answers to these questions to accompany your letter of complaint in your portfolio.

1. Role-play a manager and write a reply to a letter of complaint. Exchange letters of complaint with someone in your class. Write an answer to the letter. After you and your partner have exchanged replies, make copies so that you can put both replies —yours and your partner's— in your portfolio.

2. Have you ever lost you cool when making a complaint? Or when something new broke? In other words: What problem made you really *angry*? Freewrite what happened, or write it as a scene with dialogue. Then complete this thought: *The difference between writing to show anger and writing a complaint letter is . . .*

COORDINATING IDEAS

8a   Equally important ideas in a sentence are called *coordinate ideas*.

To show that ideas are coordinate, join them with a coordinating conjunction (*and, but, or, for, nor, so, yet*) or another connective.

(1) When you use a coordinating conjunction, a semicolon, or a semicolon and a conjunctive adverb to combine two independent clauses, the result is a *compound sentence*.

EXAMPLES   Karla drew a map of Ethiopia, **and** I created the map key. [coordinating conjunction]
Karla drew the map**;** I created the key. [semicolon]
The map was extremely detailed**; therefore,** we worked on it for several hours. [semicolon and conjunctive adverb]

(2) In addition to linking coordinate independent clauses, you can also link coordinate words and phrases in a sentence.

EXAMPLES   **A weathered sign and an iron lamppost** stood at the corner of the lane. [compound subject]
The pitcher **wound up and hurled a fast ball**. [compound predicate]
Should we go to the concert with **Dr. Ramírez or Ms. Podenko**? [compound object of a preposition]
Straining at the reins and snorting loudly, the horse charged ahead. [coordinate verbal phrases]

NOTE   When you join two independent clauses with a coordinating conjunction, you usually put a comma before the conjunction. However, a comma isn't necessary if the clauses are short and easy to understand.

COMMA NECESSARY   They asked Hillary Rodham Clinton to speak**, and** she accepted their invitation.
COMMA UNNECESSARY   Geraldo read and I listened.

8b   Ideas joined by a coordinating conjunction must be of equal importance. Otherwise, the sentence will contain *faulty coordination*.

When unequal ideas are presented as equals, the true relationship between them becomes unclear. Avoid faulty coordination by putting less-important ideas into phrases or subordinate clauses.

FAULTY   We stopped to buy a picnic lunch, and we missed the train.
REVISED   **Because we stopped to buy a picnic lunch,** we missed the train.
or
By stopping to buy a picnic lunch, we missed the train.

EXERCISE 1   Writing Sentences with Coordinating Ideas

On your own paper, combine and rewrite the sentences below. Follow the directions in parentheses for coordinating sentences or sentence parts.

EX.   1.   After lunch we will go swimming. After lunch we will read. (Use a coordinating conjunction.)

    1.   After lunch we will either go swimming or read.

1. Wellington is the capital of New Zealand. Wellington is one of New Zealand's largest cities. (Use a coordinating conjunction.)

2. Genevieve was bored with the movie reviews in the newspaper. She tried to get her reviews published. (Use a semicolon and a conjunctive adverb.)

3. I am allergic to strawberries. I love their flavor. (Use a coordinating conjunction.)

4. "I'm sure we'll see Kristi Yamaguchi in the Olympics," Chris said. She said, "She's our country's best skater." (Use a semicolon.)

5. Bill Peet is a writer. He is a cartoonist also. (Use a coordinating conjunction.)

6. We enjoyed reading the play. It is better to see it on stage. Use a semicolon and a conjunctive adverb.)

7. Patwin only had time to look for gophers. He only had time to make dinner. (Use a coordinating conjunction.)

8. Lian had gone to her first class. She hoped it would last all morning. (Use a semicolon.)

9. Gladi always won her races against Kanoa. Gladi didn't win this time. (Use a semicolon and a conjunctive adverb.)

10. Should we give Yat Chou a ride? Should we give Chin a ride? (Use a coordinating conjunction.)

EXERCISE 2   Revising Sentences to Correct Faulty Coordination

On your own paper, revise the italicized part of each sentence below to correct faulty coordination. Use the hint given in parentheses to help you.

EX.   1.   *She grew potatoes in her garden,* and we ate a lot of potato soup. (Use *because.*)

    1.   Because she grew potatoes in her garden, we ate a lot of potato soup.

1. *It rarely rains in the desert,* and very few plants grow there. (Use *because.*)

2. I bought a volume of poems, and *Edna St. Vincent Millay wrote the poems.* (Use *by.*)

3. *Mariana prepared her notes on index cards,* and it was easy for her to organize them. (Use *because.*)

4. We let Alnaba have the horseshoe set. *We had not used it for years.* (Use *since.*)

5. Mom took the car to work. *Her train was delayed.* (Use *after.*)

SUBORDINATING IDEAS

To make the main ideas stand out in your writing, you need to downplay, or *subordinate*, the less important ideas.

8c   You can subordinate an idea in a sentence by putting the idea in a subordinate clause.

The subordinate clause explains or expands the thought expressed in the independent clause.

(1) A subordinate *adverb clause* modifies a verb, an adjective, or an adverb in a sentence. Adverb clauses usually express the relationship of *cause or reason, time or place, purpose or result*, or *condition*.

You introduce an adverb clause with a subordinating conjunction (*after, although, because, if, since, when, whenever, where, while*). The subordinating conjunction you use shows your reader the relationship between the ideas in the adverb clause and those in the independent clause.

EXAMPLES   One rain forest plant is called the cannonball tree **because its fruit is large, round, and heavy**. [*Because* shows cause or reason.]

After the storm, we picked up the fallen branches. [*After* shows time.]

I turned on the porch light **so that Marcus could find his way in the dark**. [*So that* shows purpose or result.]

I will meet you at the game **if I finish my homework in time**. [*If* shows under what condition.]

(2) A subordinate *adjective clause* modifies a noun or pronoun in a sentence.

An adjective clause usually begins with *who, whom, whose, which, that*, or *where*. Before you use an adjective clause in a sentence, decide which idea you want to emphasize and which you want to subordinate.

TWO IDEAS   The kapok tree is an enormous plant. It thrives in the rain forest.

COMBINED   The kapok tree, **which is an enormous plant**, thrives in the rain forest.

or

The kapok tree is an enormous plant **that thrives in the rain forest**.

> **(3) A subordinate *noun clause* can serve as a subject, a direct object, a predicate nominative, or an object of a preposition.**
>
> You can introduce a noun clause with *that, how, what, whatever, who,* or *whoever.*
>
> TWO IDEAS   Julio won the election. Pearl told me.
>
> COMBINED   Pearl told me **that Julio won the election.** [noun clause as direct object]

EXERCISE 3   Subordinating Ideas by Using Adverb, Adjective, and Noun Clauses

For each item below, make the sentence in italics a subordinate clause, and combine it with the other sentence. The hints in parentheses will tell you what words to use at the beginnings of the clauses. You may need to delete or change some words from the italicized sentence. Write your revised sentences on your own paper.

EX.   1. *The parade began.* Snow started falling. (Use *before.*)

    1. Before the parade began, snow started falling.

1. Desert locusts are grasshoppers. *They often fly together in swarms.* (Use *that.*)
2. Gloria Estefan is a performer. *I respect and admire her.* (Use *whom.*)
3. Oil and natural gas are two natural resources. *They are found in desert regions.* (Use *that.*)
4. I need to buy a new notebook. *This one is falling apart.* (Use *because.*)
5. *Shan will be a famous actor someday.* I am convinced. (Use *that.*)
6. *The game ended.* The coach congratulated the quarterback. (Use *after.*)
7. *An early French king was nicknamed Louis the Sluggard.* I read. (Use *that.*)
8. I have a cousin named Maria. *She lives in the Dominican Republic.* (Use *who.*)
9. *This stew contains leeks and turnips.* The chef told me. (Use *that.*)
10. *I go to Houston.* I try to see a game at the Astrodome. (Use *whenever.*)
11. *The osprey is a bird that fishes.* The osprey nests in tall trees at the water's edge. (Use *which.*)
12. Lorraine's father liked the movie *Hamlet. This movie starred Mel Gibson.* (Use *which.*)
13. *I will be late for dinner again.* I will not be able to watch television for a week. (Use *if.*)
14. *Jamil does something with his table tennis bat.* It is certainly effective. (Use *whatever.*)
15. Mauricio is going on a trip to New Orleans. *He is competing in a debate tournament.* (Use *because.*)

USING PARALLEL STRUCTURE

You can make your writing smoother and clearer by checking your sentences for *parallel structure*.

8d You create *parallel structure* in a sentence by using the same grammatical form to express equal, or parallel, ideas.

For example, you pair a noun with a noun, a phrase with a phrase, a clause with a clause, and an infinitive with an infinitive.

(1) Use parallel structure when you link coordinate ideas.

NOT PARALLEL   I like movies and to listen to popular music. [noun paired with an infinitive]

PARALLEL   I like **movies** and popular **music.** [noun paired with a noun]

(2) Use parallel structure when you compare or contrast ideas.

NOT PARALLEL   For an athlete, playing fairly should be as important as to win. [gerund paired with an infinitive]

PARALLEL   For an athlete, **playing** fairly should be as important as **winning**. [gerund paired with a gerund]

(3) Use parallel structure when you link ideas with the correlative conjunctions *both . . . and, either . . . or, neither . . . nor,* or *not only . . . but also.*

NOT PARALLEL   I want either to win the contest or getting at least an honorable mention. [infinitive paired with a gerund]

PARALLEL   I want either **to win** the contest or **to get** at least an honorable mention. [infinitive paired with an infinitive]

EXERCISE 4 Revising Sentences by Using Parallel Structure

On your own paper, revise the following sentences by using parallel structure. If a sentence is correct, write *C*. [Note: There may be more than one way to revise each sentence.]

EX.   1. Dorothy Parker became famous for writing poetry and as a short story writer.

     1. Dorothy Parker became famous for writing poetry and short stories.

1. To practice hard is just as important as having natural musical talent.

2. Juan likes baking bread and to make his own chili sauce.

3. On my vacation, I look forward to taking long walks and ~~to~~ reading mystery stories.

4. The doctor told me that I was healthy *but should be* and ~~to~~ eat more fresh fruits and vegetables.

5. Both canoeing and ~~to~~ water-ski are great aquatic sports.

6. Ben Vereen is both a dancer and ~~he is~~ a talented actor.

7. Gina prefers drawing in pencil rather than ~~painted pictures~~ *my pictures*.

8. Neither skating nor ~~to go for a~~ swim is allowed at the river.

9. Henri is not only a straight-A student but ~~also~~ he ~~is~~ a member of the track team.

10. I think that we will either watch a video or ~~to~~ play basketball tonight.

11. Yoshi not only went to band practice but ~~also to~~ the fair.

12. Not only the Missouri River but also the Ohio River empties into the Mississippi River.

13. I have never found writing poetry as difficult as ~~it is to~~ writ*ing* a research paper.

14. When you are playing defense, is it more important that you be in position than ~~to know~~ *knowing* where the ball is?

15. Ms. Gelfand said we could either write a dance ~~for our~~ *as a* final or perform one.

16. I have never been to Yosemite nor ~~gone~~ to Yellowstone.

17. Both in diving and ~~when doing~~ gymnastics, the athlete's toes should be pointed.

18. Our guide taught us not only how ~~to~~ avoid ticks but also preventing chigger attacks.

19. I either wanted a whole-wheat bagel ~~or raisin~~ *raisin* bread with my milk and the Sunday paper.

20. Because the drama society has four performances this weekend, I shall have time for neither playing with my nephew nor ~~to go~~ on a picnic.

21. I like looking at the apple blossoms and ~~to~~ eat the crisp apples.

22. Bob enjoys both reading old books and ~~to~~ collect them.

23. Our school has not only an auditorium but ~~also there is~~ a small rehearsal stage.

24. I did not enjoy the movie, ~~but the~~ acting was enjoyable.

25. Neither Peter wears plaids, ~~nor~~ does anyone else in his family.

SENTENCE FRAGMENTS AND RUN-ONS

A sentence should express a complete thought. Each complete thought in your writing should come to a full stop.

8e If you punctuate a part of a sentence as if it were a complete sentence, you create a *sentence fragment*.

(1) One type of sentence fragment is a phrase fragment. A *phrase* is a group of related words that does not contain a subject and a verb.

FRAGMENT   The elf owl made its nest. **In a saguaro cactus.** [prepositional phrase]

SENTENCE   The elf owl made its nest in a saguaro cactus.

(2) Another type of fragment is a subordinate clause fragment. A *subordinate clause* has a subject and a verb, but it does not express a complete thought.

FRAGMENT   A tropical rain forest is a hot, moist region. **Where more than four hundred types of trees may grow**.

SENTENCE   A tropical rain forest is a hot, moist region where more than four hundred types of trees may grow.

8f If you run together two sentences as if they were a single thought, you create an error called a *run-on sentence*.

There are two kinds of run-on sentences. A *fused sentence* has no punctuation at all between the two complete thoughts. A *comma splice* has only a comma separating them.

FUSED   Archie Griffin played football at Ohio State University he won the Heisman Trophy in 1974 and 1975.

COMMA SPLICE   Each year, sportswriters and sportscasters elect the winner of the Heisman Trophy, it is awarded to the nation's outstanding college football player.

You can fix a run-on sentence in several ways.

(1) Make two sentences.

EXAMPLE   Archie Griffin played football at Ohio State University. **He** won the Heisman Trophy in 1974 and 1975.

(2) Use a comma and a coordinating conjunction.

EXAMPLE   Archie Griffin played football at Ohio State University**, and** he won the Heisman Trophy in 1974 and 1975.

(3) Change one of the independent clauses to a subordinate clause.

EXAMPLE   Archie Griffin, **who** won the Heisman Trophy in 1974 and 1975, played football at Ohio State University.

(4) Use a semicolon.

EXAMPLE   Archie Griffin played football at Ohio State University; he won the Heisman Trophy in 1974 and 1975.

(5) Use a semicolon and a conjunctive adverb or transitional expression.

EXAMPLE   Archie Griffin played football at Ohio State University; **in fact,** he won the Heisman Trophy in 1974 and 1975.

EXERCISE 5   Revising Fragments and Run-ons

On your own paper, revise each sentence fragment or run-on sentence below. If a sentence is correct, write *C.*

EX.   1. The Chicago Bulls picked Croatian player Toni Kukoc in the 1990 NBA draft, however he didn't join the team until 1993.

    1. The Chicago Bulls picked Croatian player Toni Kukoc in the 1990 NBA draft; however, he didn't join the team until 1993.

1. The Bulls offered Kukoc a seven-year contract. For $17.6 million.

2. Kukoc played basketball in the European League, on an Italian team called Bennetton Treviso. Before he came to Chicago.

3. Throughout Europe, Kukoc was hailed as a great player in fact he was named European Player of the Year three times.

4. Kukoc looked forward to playing with the Chicago Bulls. Especially because he wanted to play with Michael Jordan.

5. He had played against Michael Jordan. When Jordan played for the American team at the 1992 Olympics.

6. Kukoc was disappointed when he learned that Jordan retired from basketball in 1993.

7. However, Kukoc and his wife and son moved to Chicago, he was ready to begin his career in the NBA.

8. Kukoc averaged nineteen points a game. During his last year on the Italian team.

9. Because he was almost seven feet tall, he could play two positions. Point guard and forward.

10. The Bulls needed new talent when Michael Jordan retired therefore they were fortunate to get Toni Kukoc.

REVIEW EXERCISE

A. Revising a Paragraph for Clarity

On your own paper, revise each faulty sentence below to make it read clearly and smoothly.

EX. [1] Women have ruled many nations, and they have ruled nations throughout history.

[1] *Throughout history, women have ruled many nations.*

[1] Several queens ruled in ancient Egypt, and they were named Cleopatra. [2] The most famous Cleopatra ruled from 51 B.C. to 30 B.C., and she was both intelligent and ambitious. [3] Queen Victoria ruled for sixty-three years, and she was the queen of Great Britain. [4] She ruled with wisdom, strength, and to be fair. [5] Another woman has ruled Britain for many years, and she is the queen and named Elizabeth II. [6] For more than ten years of Elizabeth's reign, another woman also led Britain, not as queen but she was prime minister. [7] Margaret Thatcher became prime minister in 1979, and she was Britain's first female prime minister. [8] She was reelected in 1983, and the people voted her back into office in 1987. [9] Golda Meir served in Israel as foreign minister, member of parliament, and then she was prime minister from 1969 to 1974. [10] Benazir Bhutto was elected prime minister of Pakistan in 1988, and she was the first woman to lead a modern Muslim state.

B. Revising Paragraphs to Eliminate Fragments and Run-ons

On your own paper, revise the following paragraphs to eliminate the sentence fragments and run-on sentences.

EX. 1. The Dallas Museum of Art has expanded and grown. Because of a huge new wing that was donated by Nancy Hamon.

1. *The Dallas Museum of Art has expanded and grown because of a huge new wing that was donated by Nancy Hamon.*

1   Museum Director Richard Brettell has used the new space. To change
2 the way the museum exhibits its collections. The collections have been
3 reorganized into five sections, and each section is a "museum" by itself
4 and each section represents a continent. For example, the museum's

5   collection of European art is in a section. Now called the Museum of

6   Europe. Soon the collection of African art will become its own "museum,"

7   additionally the collection of Asian art will, too. The Museum of the

8   Americas contains art from South America, Central America, and North

9   America in fact the collection contains everything from ancient Native

10   American jewelry and pottery, to Inuit carvings, to modern paintings by

11   Andrew Wyeth.

12   The Dallas Museum of Art has always had an impressive collection. Of

13   pre-Columbian art from Mexico and South America. Dallas seems just the

14   right place for a museum. That unites North and South America. The city

15   has a rich Hispanic heritage. Because it has a large Hispanic population

16   and because Texas was once part of Mexico. One gallery within the new

17   Museum of the Americas contains ancient fabrics and pottery, they came

18   from the Moche and Nasca cultures. Another gallery displays art of

19   ancient Mexico. Particularly from the cultures of the Olmec and the Maya.

C.   Working Cooperatively to Write a Story Beginning

Below are some sentence fragments you and a partner can use to write a story beginning. Add words and punctuation to make a coherent paragraph with complete sentences. Write your paragraph on your own paper.

pride of lions in Africa

most of them sleeping

a herd of wildebeests

to drink water from the lake

mid-afternoon sun shining

not having eaten anything all day

running as a herd

especially slow because of an injured hoof

long, sharp horns and strong leg and neck muscles

no match for a half-dozen lions

COMBINING BY INSERTING WORDS

You can add details to your sentences and variety to your writing style by combining short, choppy sentences that contain related ideas.

8g You can combine short sentences by taking a key word from one sentence and inserting it into another sentence.

Sometimes you can use the word from one sentence as a modifier in another sentence. Other times you will need to change the word into an adjective or adverb before you can insert it.

Using the Same Form	
ORIGINAL	Winona picked up the puppy. She picked it up gently.
COMBINED	Winona picked up the puppy **gently**.
ORIGINAL	Ricardo is a painter. He is talented.
COMBINED	Ricardo is a **talented** painter.
Changing the Form	
ORIGINAL	The truck rolled up the hill. Its speed was slow.
COMBINED	The truck rolled **slowly** up the hill. [changed to adverb]
ORIGINAL	I accepted the award. It filled me with excitement.
COMBINED	**Excited**, I accepted the award. [changed to adjective]

EXERCISE 6   Combining by Inserting Single-Word Modifiers

On the lines provided, combine each pair of sentences by inserting an adjective or adverb from the second sentence into the first sentence. The hints in parentheses will help you to know what kind of modifier to insert.

EX. 1. Charlie finally found the trail to the bottom of the mountain. What relief he felt! (Add –*ed*.)
        Relieved, Charlie finally found the trail to the bottom of the mountain.

1. Ramona danced the role of the white swan. Her steps were graceful. (Add –*ly*.) _____

    _____

2. The science students worked on their lab reports. The reports were difficult. _____

    _____

3. Do you like the taste of lemonade? Do you like its tartness? (Drop *–ness.*)

   _____

4. "I need more parsley for the stew," the cook said. "It must be fresh parsley."_____

   _____

5. I opened the letter from Diana Ross. What a thrill I felt! (Add *–ed.*)_____

   _____

6. Molière was a French playwright. He was gifted. _____

   _____

7. Let me put your jacket in the dryer for a few minutes. It's wet. _____

   _____

8. I wasn't prepared for the ending to the play. It was a surprise. (Add *–ing.*)

   _____

9. The children were startled when the balloon popped. It happened all of a sudden. (Add *–ly.*) _____

   _____

10. Ms. Myoki has donated a gift to the hospital. She is generous. (Add *–ly.*)

    _____

11. My brother only likes to eat vegetables that are cooked. He is finicky. _____

    _____

12. The volleyball team won a game yesterday. The game was close. _____

    _____

13. I listened to crickets outside my bedroom window last night. I listened closely. _____

    _____

14. Lee can't come over for dinner tonight. It's unfortunate. (Add *–ly.*) _____

    _____

15. Our school band is among the best in the state. The band is very talented.

    _____

COMBINING BY INSERTING PHRASES

A *prepositional phrase* is a group of words consisting of a preposition, a noun or pronoun that serves as the object of the preposition, and any modifiers of that object.

8h **You can usually combine two related sentences without any change in form by taking a prepositional phrase from one sentence and inserting it in the other. You can also combine sentences by changing part of a sentence into a prepositional phrase.**

ORIGINAL   We sat and talked. We were under the oak tree.
COMBINED   We sat **under the oak tree** and talked.

ORIGINAL   My grandfather came to the United States. The year was 1939.
COMBINED   My grandfather came to the United States **in 1939.**

A *participial phrase* contains a participle and words related to it. The whole phrase acts as an adjective.

8i **Sometimes you can lift a participial phrase directly from one sentence and insert it into another sentence. Other times you will need to change a verb into a participle before you can insert the idea into another sentence.**

ORIGINAL   My favorite poem is "The Gift Outright." It was written by Robert Frost.
COMBINED   My favorite poem is "The Gift Outright," **written by Robert Frost.**

ORIGINAL   I raised my hand. I knew the answer.
COMBINED   **Knowing the answer,** I raised my hand.

An *appositive phrase* is made up of an appositive and its modifiers. The phrase identifies or explains a noun or a pronoun.

8j **You can sometimes combine sentences by placing one of the ideas in an appositive phrase. The appositive phrase should be set off by a comma (or two commas if you place the phrase in the middle of the sentence).**

ORIGINAL   William Butler Yeats helped establish the Abbey Theatre in Dublin. He was a leading Irish poet and dramatist.
COMBINED   William Butler Yeats**, a leading Irish poet and dramatist,** helped establish the Abbey Theatre in Dublin.
or
A leading Irish poet and dramatist, William Butler Yeats helped establish the Abbey Theatre in Dublin.

EXERCISE 7   Combining by Inserting Phrases

Combine each pair of sentences below by making a phrase out of one sentence and inserting it into the other sentence. Write your answers on your own paper.

EX. 1. Fung called the meeting to order. He hit the table with a gavel.

 1. Hitting the table with a gavel, Fung called the meeting to order.

1. I found a five-dollar bill. It was lying on the sidewalk.
2. In French class, we are reading *Père Goriot*. It is a novel by Balzac.
3. Julia spoke to the children. Her voice was soft.
4. Giorgio sprinted toward the finish line. He wanted to break a record.
5. The Navajo people settled in the American Southwest around A.D. 1000. They migrated from northern regions.
6. I found your black socks. They were under the sofa.
7. In the museum, we saw a statue of a woman. It was carved out of marble.
8. The star of the movie *Jaws* was a mechanical shark. It was nicknamed "Bruce" by crew members on the movie set.
9. Uncle Lars is a philatelist. That is someone who collects stamps.
10. Lima is located on the Pacific Ocean. It is the capital of Peru.
11. "Jabberwocky" is a poem by Lewis Carroll. It uses a lot of invented words.
12. The moose crashed through the bushes. It disappeared in seconds.
13. All my sweaters are in a bag. The bag contains mothballs.
14. The fish in that aquarium are guppies. That aquarium is coated with algae.
15. The hedge was a row of barberry bushes. It badly needed pruning.
16. Tap water is not fit to drink. I mean the water in this town.
17. Traditional Turkish coffee is brewed in an *ibrik*. It is brewed over a flame.
18. Anne opened the front door. She put down her packages first.
19. The national instrument of Japan is the *shaku hachi*. The Japanese make it from bamboo.
20. That broom is made of cinnamon roots. It scents my whole house.
21. We went for a long walk. We walked under large willow trees.
22. Sheila watered the plant. She admired the plant's beauty.
23. My mother runs a homeless shelter. She cares about people in the community.
24. My favorite teacher and I stood and talked for a long time. We were in the hallway.
25. My brother moved many of his belongings to college. The date was September 10.

COMBINING BY COORDINATION AND SUBORDINATION

8k **You can combine sentences that contain *coordinate*, or equally important, ideas by using either a coordinating conjunction (*and, but, or, nor, so, for, yet*) or a correlative conjunction (*both . . . and, either . . . or, neither . . . nor*).**

ORIGINAL   Sonya will take you home. Les will take you home.
COMBINED   **Either Sonya or Les** will take you home. [compound subject]

ORIGINAL   I might watch the game. I might listen to a tape.
COMBINED   I might **either** watch the game **or** listen to a tape. [compound predicate]

ORIGINAL   We looked everywhere for the cat. We couldn't find her.
COMBINED   We looked everywhere for the cat, **but** we couldn't find her. [compound sentence]

You can also form a compound sentence by linking independent clauses with a semicolon and a conjunctive adverb (*however, likewise, therefore*) or just a semicolon.

EXAMPLE   Maria, Kim, and Max went to the mall**; however,** we wanted to go to the skating rink.

8l **If two sentences are unequal in importance, you can combine them by placing the less-important idea in a subordinate clause.**

ORIGINAL   Gregory Hines starred in the musical *Jelly's Last Jam*. Hines is a talented dancer and actor.
COMBINED   Gregory Hines, **who is a talented dancer and actor,** starred in the musical *Jelly's Last Jam*. [adjective clause]

ORIGINAL   Hines was superb in the role. He won the Tony Award in 1992 for Best Actor in a Musical.
COMBINED   **Because Hines was superb in the role,** he won the Tony Award in 1992 for Best Actor in a Musical. [adverb clause]

ORIGINAL   *Jelly's Last Jam* was a terrific show. Many critics agree on that.
COMBINED   Many critics agree **that *Jelly's Last Jam* was a terrific show.** [noun clause]

☞   **REFERENCE NOTE:** For more about subordinate clauses, see pages 165–171.

EXERCISE 8   Combining by Coordinating Ideas

On your own paper, combine each pair of related sentences below by forming a compound subject, compound verb, or compound sentence.

EX.   1. Sonja may answer the question. Jill may answer the question.
   1. Either Sonja or Jill may answer the question.

1. John Tyler grew up in Virginia. He became governor in 1825.
2. The Statue of Liberty was designed by Frédéric Bartholdi. Its pedestal was designed by Richard M. Hunt.
3. Moose roam through Isle Royale National Park in Michigan. Wolves roam through Isle Royale National Park in Michigan.
4. I am a fan of the Boston Red Sox. The team didn't do well this year.
5. Was Edmund Spenser named poet laureate of England? Was Ted Hughes named poet laureate of England?
6. I heard the alarm clock buzz. I woke up at five o'clock.
7. The squirrel begged for food. It stole seeds from the feeder.
8. Sutki showed us some kachina dolls. Una did also.
9. Li Hua wanted to take the left turn. Sandra said we should turn right.
10. The July Fourth party was not well attended this year. Not many people went to the Labor Day picnic.

EXERCISE 9   Combining by Subordinating Ideas

On your own paper, combine each pair of sentences by turning one sentence into a subordinate clause.

EX.   1. August Wilson is a playwright. He wrote *The Piano Lesson*.
   1. August Wilson is the playwright who wrote The Piano Lesson.

1. In *Close Encounters of the Third Kind*, a ship lands in Wyoming. The ship came from outer space.
2. Archibald Leach began a career as an actor. He changed his name to Cary Grant.
3. Actor and comedian Danny Kaye wanted to help children. He became an ambassador for UNICEF.
4. Harrison Ford may make another "Indiana Jones" movie. My sister told me that.
5. Robert Redford gained fame as an actor. Then he became a spokesperson for conservation and solar energy.

VARYING SENTENCE BEGINNINGS

Not all sentences have to begin with a subject. Make your writing more interesting by varying the beginnings of your sentences.

8m You can improve the overall style of your writing by beginning some sentences with introductory words, phrases, or clauses.

When you vary sentence beginnings, you must sometimes reword the sentences for clarity. Be sure to place phrase modifiers close to the words they modify.

SUBJECT FIRST We were surprised, so we jumped to our feet.

REVISED **Surprised,** we jumped to our feet. [introductory single-word modifier]

SUBJECT FIRST My mother used a circular saw to cut the boards.

REVISED **Using a circular saw,** my mother cut the boards. [introductory verbal phrase]

SUBJECT FIRST Sly knew that he would have to beat Ossie in order to win the race.

REVISED **In order to win the race,** Sly knew that he would have to beat Ossie. [introductory prepositional phrase]

SUBJECT FIRST I read the novel *To Kill a Mockingbird* before I saw the movie version.

REVISED **Before I saw the movie version of *To Kill a Mockingbird*,** I read the novel. [introductory clause]

EXERCISE 10   **Varying Sentence Beginnings**

On the lines provided, revise the following sentences by varying their beginnings. The hint in parentheses tells you which type of beginning to use.

EX. 1. Francine raced down the court and caught the pass from Ella May. (*phrase*)

Racing down the court, Francine caught the pass from Ella May.

1. Franco called me because he needed directions to the meeting. (*clause*) _____

_____

2. I suddenly understood the problem. (*single-word modifier*) _____

_____

3. We collected several specimens of quartz during our hike. (*phrase*) _____

    _____

4. I'll need to make more biscuits to feed all those hungry children. (*phrase*) __

    _____

5. It was clear by the time the first half ended that the Steelers had improved.

    (*clause*) _____

    _____

6. My father sends me a postcard whenever he takes a business trip. (*clause*) __

    _____

7. It was lucky that the rain stopped before the game started. (*single-word*

    modifier) _____

    _____

8. Marta walked into the kitchen and asked, "What's for dinner?" (*phrase*) ___

    _____

9. Jerald needed information, so he went to the library. (*phrase*) _____

    _____

10. This land was a meadow before the housing development was built.

    (*clause*) _____

    _____

11. Thi gave me a big hug as he departed. (*clause*) _____

    _____

12. We ordered fish and chips from the place at the corner. (*phrase*) _____

    _____

13. Do not forget to bring the blanket and jug also. (*word*) _____

    _____

14. Her shirts were neatly pressed and folded because she was neat. (*clause*)

    _____

15. We played kickball in the yard after watching the baseball game. (*phrase*) __

    _____

VARYING SENTENCE STRUCTURE

You can improve your writing style by varying the structure of your sentences.

8n **When writing a paragraph, use a variety of sentence structures rather than a string of simple sentences. Whenever possible, use a mix of simple, compound, complex, and compound-complex sentences.**

Paragraph with Simple Sentences
The city of Bayeux is in Normandy. Normandy is in northern France. A famous tapestry hangs in a museum in Bayeux. It is called the Bayeux Tapestry. The tapestry was made more than nine hundred years ago. The tapestry is made of linen. It has pictures. The pictures are stitched in wool. It tells the story of the Norman Duke William. It is a true story. In A.D. 1066, William sailed to England with an army of Norman soldiers. He waged war on King Harold of England. William won the war at the Battle of Hastings. He became king of England. He also earned his historical nickname. It is "William the Conqueror."

Revised Paragraph with Varied Sentence Structure
The city of Bayeux is in Normandy, which is in northern France. In a museum in Bayeux hangs the famous Bayeux Tapestry. It was made more than nine hundred years ago. The tapestry is made of linen, and its pictures, which are stitched in wool, tell the true story of the Norman duke William. In 1066, William sailed to England with an army of French soldiers, and he waged war on King Harold of England. After William won the war at the Battle of Hastings, he became king of England. He also earned his historical nickname, "William the Conqueror."

☞ **REFERENCE NOTE:** For information about the four types of sentence structure, see page 173.

EXERCISE 11 **Revising a Paragraph to Vary Sentence Structures**

On your own paper, revise the paragraph below. Use sentence-combining techniques to vary the sentence structures.

EX.   1   The Bayeux Tapestry contains about fifty different pictures.
         2 The pictures tell the history of William's victory.

         1   The Bayeux Tapestry contains about fifty different pictures that
         2 tell the history of William's victory.

1   The Bayeux Tapestry has been called "the world's oldest cartoon strip."

2   Its many pictures stretch out over a length of 230 feet. Its height is only

3   about twenty inches. According to the tapestry, in A.D. 1051, King Edward

4   of England made a promise to Duke William of Normandy. King Edward

5   was the cousin of William's father. Edward had no children of his own.

6   William would be king of England when Edward died. Edward wanted to

7   seal that promise. Edward sent his brother-in-law, Harold Godwinson, to

8   France to see William. He told Harold to confirm the promise to William.

9   Harold went to France. He delivered the message. He promised his

10   support to William as the next king of England. But then King Edward

11   died. Harold double-crossed William. He claimed the throne for himself.

12   William was forced to declare war. At the Battle of Hastings, Harold died.

13   William won the war. He became king of England.

EXERCISE 12 **Writing a Nomination**

It's time to choose the person to receive the Athlete of the Year Award, and your school newspaper is publishing students' nominations for the award. Write at least five sentences to nominate your favorite athlete. If you want your reader to be convinced that your choice is the best one, you'll need to make your sentences lively and clear. Capture your readers' attention by using a variety of interesting sentence structures.

EX.   1. As an athlete who shows determination and courage, Nikki Farris deserves
          the Athlete of the Year Award.

REDUCING WORDINESS

8o **To avoid wordiness in your writing, use only as many words as you need to make your point.**

Choose simple, clear words rather than unusually complicated ones. Don't repeat words or ideas unless it's absolutely necessary. Use these steps to revise wordy sentences.

(1) Take out a whole group of unnecessary words.

WORDY   Before going to the supermarket, we made a list of the groceries we needed in order to make the food that we intended to eat for dinner.

BETTER   Before going to the supermarket, we made a list of the groceries **we needed for dinner.**

(2) Replace complicated words and expressions with simple, clear ones.

WORDY   The immature dog put his forward extremity on my lap and emitted a jubilant utterance.

BETTER   The **puppy** put his **front paw** on my lap and **barked happily**.

(3) Reduce a clause to a phrase.

WORDY   Ahab, who was the captain of the ship, wanted to find Moby-Dick.

BETTER   Ahab, **the captain of the ship,** wanted to find Moby-Dick.

(4) Reduce a clause or a phrase to one word.

WORDY   I put the glass that was broken into the bin for recycling.

BETTER   I put the **broken** glass into the **recycling** bin.

Wordy	Better
at this point in time	now
at which time	when
in spite of the fact that	although
in the event that	if

EXERCISE 13   Reducing Wordiness in Sentences

On the lines provided, revise each of the sentences below to make them less wordy. If a sentence doesn't need improving, write C on the line.

EX.   1.   Can you tell me at which time practice for cheerleaders commences?

    Can you tell me when cheerleaders' practice begins?

1.   In the event that precipitation occurs, the field for football will be wet. ____

2.   The words of the speaker could not be heard due to the fact that he expressed himself in subdued tones. _____

3.   I brushed the dirt and grime off my shirt and got back in the saddle on top of the horse. _____

4.   That program on television was on television at 7:00 P.M. last night. _____

5.   Elena, who is my little sister, appears to have gained a few inches in height. _____

6.   Resources that are natural in the state of Texas include oil and gas. _____

7.   The fact is that Peter infrequently enjoys partaking of sandwiches that are filled with tuna fish. _____

8.   The balloon, in a sudden way, deflated itself due to a puncture. _____

9.   Dr. Hsu, who was born in Canton, is an expert on the art of China. _____

10.   In the event that you do not succeed in finding a notebook to buy at that store, try to locate a notebook at the downtown branch. _____

CHAPTER REVIEW

A. Revising Sentences for Clarity

On your own paper, revise the sentences below to eliminate faulty coordination or faulty parallelism. [Note: There may be more than one way to revise each sentence.]

EX. 1. Hillary likes broccoli better than eating peas.

    1. Hillary likes broccoli better than peas.

1. Jumping rope is as constructive an exercise as to jog.
2. I tipped the glass, and the milk spilled.
3. Esther works in a convenience store, and it is located on Wyoming Avenue.
4. The cast needs more rehearsals and to get new costumes.
5. Janine is talented not only as a singer but she also dances.
6. We need paint and to have new curtains.
7. The back door opens, and the dog ran outside.
8. Sybil is not only skilled as a math student, but also in science.
9. I want more books and to have time for reading.
10. Teresa likes hockey better than playing baseball.

B. Revising Sentences to Eliminate Fragments and Run-ons

On your own paper, revise each item below to eliminate sentence fragments and run-on sentences. If a sentence is correct, write C.

EX. 1. Bonsai is the art of pruning small trees. So that they appear to be large trees in miniature.

    1. Bonsai is the art of pruning small trees so that they appear to be large trees in miniature.

1. The art of bonsai began in ancient China, the name *bonsai* means "to plant in a tray."
2. The practice was adopted by the Japanese. During the eleventh or twelfth century.
3. The form of the bonsai tree follows certain standards, basic to its form is the three-branch triangle, it represents heaven, a human, and earth.
4. What is important is not how old a bonsai is. But how old it appears to be.
5. A bonsai tree needs care, never let it dry out, water it daily with a fine mist.

C.   Combining Sentences

On your own paper, combine each pair of sentences below. Change an idea in one sentence into a phrase or clause, and insert it into the other sentence.

EX.   1.   Joe ran to catch up with me. He waved the tickets and yelled, "I got them!"

   1.   Running to catch up with me, Joe waved the tickets and yelled, "I got them!"

1.   The sidewalk outside Veterans Stadium was filled. Many eager people were standing in line.
2.   Joe works at a store. It is just around the corner from the stadium.
3.   His boss is also a Phillies' fan. He gave Joe the day off to stand in line.
4.   "Buy me a ticket, too," Joe's boss said. "That's all I ask."
5.   Joe waited all morning in the pouring rain. Joe was able to buy three tickets to game four of the World Series.

D.   Revising Sentences for Variety

On your own paper, revise each of the sentences or pairs of sentences below to vary the style. The hint in parentheses will tell you how to revise.

EX.   1.   The sun rose. We saw many colorful sailboats out on the bay. (*Change to a complex sentence.*)

   1.   When the sun rose, we saw many colorful sailboats out on the bay.

1.   We took our seats. The performance began. (*Change to a complex sentence.*)
2.   I moved as quickly as possible as I crossed the street. (*Begin with a phrase.*)
3.   Joni lost her way on the hike. I found her. (*Change to a compound sentence.*)
4.   I went backstage after the performance to meet the band. (*Begin with a phrase.*)
5.   Gil will give you a ride home after the show is over. (*Begin with a clause.*)
6.   My friend Gina arrived home early in the afternoon. She began her homework. (*Change to a complex sentence.*)
7.   I gave the volunteer coordinator my phone number as we walked to our cars. (*Begin with a clause.*)
8.   My rabbits were hungry. I fed them. (*Change to a compound sentence.*)
9.   I bought a map of the area before our drive because I didn't want to get lost. (*Begin with a clause.*)
10.   I ate carrot sticks as I studied for my test. (*Begin with a clause.*)

VARIETIES OF AMERICAN ENGLISH

In the United States, there are many language variations called *dialects*. There are *regional dialects*. For example, people living in eastern New England generally speak differently than people living in the South. There are also *ethnic dialects*. People of different nationalities and cultural heritages often bring to American English new words and expressions. That is how American English grows.

The most widely used variety of the English language is called *standard English*. It is not limited to a particular region or ethnic group. It is used all over the country, and all over the world, by people of all backgrounds. It is the variety of English that is used in formal writing and in formal speech. In everyday conversation, people freely use dialect and nonstandard English. However, it is important to learn how to write and speak in standard English in order to make your meaning clear to a general audience.

EXERCISE 1   Identifying Dialect Differences

Each of the word groups below is a definition of a familiar item. On the line following each one, write at least one popular or regional word or phrase used to name each item. [Note: There will be more than one way to answer each item.]

EX.   1.   a metal pushcart that can contain groceries

   cart; basket; buggy

1.   a yellow or white bread made from cornmeal

_____

2.   a long sandwich filled with meat, cheese, tomato, and lettuce

_____

3.   a large, shallow pan used for cooking on top of the stove

_____

4.   a large truck with a cab and a trailer, used for hauling freight

_____

5.   a folded paper item used to carry groceries

_____

6.   a large store where food and household supplies are sold

_____

7. a thin band of stretchy material used to hold things together, such as a pile of note cards

_____

8. a container used for throwing away unwanted materials in a home or office

_____

9. a menu item that consists of meat or cheese or vegetables wrapped inside a thin circular layer of cooked dough

_____

10. waterproof footwear

_____

11. a playground structure used by two people facing each other, seated at either end of a board, the ends of which go up and down

_____

12. a hot beverage made from milk and chocolate

_____

13. a soft, usually brimless hat

_____

14. a large kitchen appliance used for cooking, baking, and broiling

_____

15. a garden tool used for digging

_____

16. a piece of upholstered furniture that seats two or more people

_____

17. a room in some homes used for informal events and the watching of television

_____

18. a car and driver that a person can hire to ride to another location, such as across a city or to an airport or train station

_____

19. a fixture that provides drinking water in a public place

_____

20. a piece of hand luggage, usually carried by women, to hold money, papers, pens, and so on

_____

FORMAL ENGLISH

The kinds of languages you use in different situations are called *levels of usage*. In English, the two standard levels of usage are *formal English* and *informal English*.

FORMAL ENGLISH   My younger brother is not a capable driver.
INFORMAL ENGLISH   My kid brother ain't a good driver.

When you write, you should use formal English for essays and research reports. Use informal English when you write personal letters, journal entries, short stories, and plays. When you speak, use formal English at such formal occasions as banquets and job or college interviews. Use informal English in everyday conversations.

FEATURES OF FORMAL AND INFORMAL ENGLISH			
Words in formal English are often . . .	**Example**	**Words in informal English are often . . .**	**Example**
longer	repair	shorter	fix
precise	polite	vague	nice
serious	celebrity	offhand	big shot
restrained	amusing	exaggerated	hysterical
Spelling of formal English is often . . .	**Example**	**Spelling of informal English is often . . .**	**Example**
in full	does not	in contractions	doesn't
conventional	through	unconventional	thru
Grammar in formal English is often . . .	**Example**	**Grammar in informal English is often . . .**	**Example**
complex	The man who came to my aid gave me directions.	compound	The guy came over and told me how to get there.
complete	I will see you later.	fragmentary	Check you later.

EXERCISE 2   Classifying Language as Formal or Informal

Analyze each sentence below. If the language is formal English, write *FE* on the line before the sentence. If the sentence uses informal English, write *IE* on the line before the sentence, and rewrite the sentence in formal English on your own paper.

EX.   __IE__   1.   I am really into Mexican food.

I enjoy Mexican food.

_____   1.   That truck is going pretty fast.

_____   2.   The model in the vacation ad is absolutely a geek.

_____   3.   The aroma of baking bread captured my attention.

_____   4.   I can't stand action flicks.

_____   5.   May I offer my congratulations, Ian?

_____   6.   Your room appears disorganized.

_____   7.   I was so out of it that I couldn't remember what my gig was about.

_____   8.   The guy on the phone was from the electric company place, and he left a message for you.

_____   9.   At some point in the future, I will no longer require additional assistance in mathematics.

_____   10.   The tenant shall remit payment in full on the first of the month.

Calvin and Hobbes   by Bill Watterson

Calvin & Hobbes copyright 1987 Watterson. Reprinted with permission of Universal Press Syndicate. All rights reserved.

COLLOQUIALISMS AND SLANG

Two types of expressions in informal English are *colloquialisms* and *slang*.

Colloquialisms are words and phrases of conversational language. People use them every day. Many colloquialisms are *idioms*, words and phrases that mean something different from the literal meanings of the words. Colloquialisms can add a lively, realistic tone to dialogues in plays and short stories. However, use them with care in your writing. If your reader is unfamiliar with the word or phrase, your meaning will be unclear.

EXAMPLES Your answer is **right on target**. ["correct"]
What's up? ["What is happening?" or "What is new in your life?"]

Slang is highly informal language that consists of either made-up words or conventional words used in new ways. Slang words and phrases go in and out of fashion. Popular slang from last year may have already been replaced by new words. Use care when you use slang in your writing. Like colloquialisms, slang can add a realistic tone to dialogue. Its meaning, however, may be unclear to your readers.

EXAMPLE The music is **rad**. ["good, enjoyable"]
The concert was **awesome**. ["exciting, terrific, great"]

EXERCISE 3 Identifying and Revising Colloquialisms and Slang

Underline each colloquialism or slang expression in the following sentences. Then, on the line provided, revise the sentence so that its meaning is clear to all readers. [Note: There may be more than one way to revise each sentence.]

EX. 1. At the bottom of the application, write your John Hancock on the line.

   At the bottom of the application, write your signature on the line.

1. You can stow your gear in the bedroom closet.

   _____

2. His parents pushed him to become an award-winning athlete.

   _____

3. Chita Rivera was pleased to get rave reviews for her performance.

   _____

4. I was in over my head on the project, so I asked for volunteers to help me.

_____

5. Because she thinks dinosaurs are radical, she really enjoyed the movie _Jurassic Park_.

_____

6. Gino was pro-recycling, so he worked hard on the curb-collection campaign.

_____

7. After listening to my grandmother's old records, I've really gotten into jazz.

_____

8. Did you fall for his story about seeing aliens in the meadow last night?

_____

9. Because he is so tight with his money, he rarely gives donations to charitable organizations.

_____

10. I refuse to wear this gorilla get-up to the costume party.

_____

EXERCISE 4   Writing an Informal Dialogue

On your own paper, write ten sentences of an informal dialogue between yourself and a friend. In the dialogue, discuss a musical group, a concert, a television program, or a short story. One of the people in your dialogue should have a positive reaction to the subject, and the other person should have a negative reaction. Use informal, everyday, conversational language. In parentheses, give "translations" for any slang or colloquial words or phrases that readers may not understand.

EX.   Denise: I guess I'm just not into that kind of music. (don't enjoy)
      Jonah: Well, I think it's rad. (good)

EUPHEMISMS AND GOBBLEDYGOOK

Euphemisms are indirect, agreeable words and phrases that are sometimes used in place of direct but unpleasant or offensive ones. Euphemisms are appropriate when they are used as a courtesy. However, too many euphemisms can weaken your writing and make your exact meaning and true feelings unclear. Use direct, clear language whenever possible.

EUPHEMISMS   I'm sorry that your grandfather **passed away**. ["died"]
My uncle is a **sanitation engineer**. ["garbage collector"]

Gobbledygook is wordy, puffed-up language. Writers sometimes make the error of using gobbledygook to attain a formal, impressive tone. However, formal English does not have to include long, confusing sentences and difficult words. Use clear, straightforward language so that your readers will understand your meaning.

GOBBLEDYGOOK   A plethora of precipitation may have a deleterious effect on our luncheon on the lawn.
CLEAR ENGLISH   Too much rain may spoil our picnic.

EXERCISE 5 **Revising to Eliminate Euphemisms and Gobbledygook**

On the lines provided, rewrite each sentence below in clear, direct, straightforward English, eliminating any euphemisms or gobbledygook. You may need to look up some of the words in a dictionary. [Note: There may be more than one way to revise each sentence.]

EX.   1. The thieves are currently serving their sentences at a correctional institution.

      The thieves are now serving their sentences at a prison.

1. In our state, all motorists must don restraining devices while operating their vehicles.

2. At eventide, a luminous celestial satellite appeared overhead.

3. Because his low motivation interfered with his work, Mr. Johnson was relieved of his duties by the company.

4. Operators of vehicular transportation should avoid confrontations with pedestrians.

_____

5. I'm afraid that the candidate misrepresented himself.

_____

6. Our governor is disinclined to increase our revenues on consumer spending.

_____

7. The juvenile male person removed currency from his savings account held in trust by his financial institution.

_____

8. That building is an educational institution for youthful offenders.

_____

9. At a quarter after the midday hour, personnel of both genders in our company will congregate.

_____

10. Someone has misappropriated the accessory that contains my currency.

_____

11. While I am absent from the community, you can disseminate information to me by epistle.

_____

12. Shera inhabits her domicile with two fraternal siblings and a pet feline.

_____

13. Joel achieved a vertical ascent to the pinnacle of Mount Everest.

_____

14. The automotive merchant proclaimed that the venerable vehicle had been operated previously.

_____

15. Individuals who are the victims of a widely familiar upper-respiratory affliction may have a requirement of forcefully projecting air and mucus from their nasal cavities.

_____

CHAPTER REVIEW

A. Working Cooperatively to Rewrite a Passage

The following dialogue takes place between two people on a street corner. However, the dialogue seems unrealistic, because the people are using extremely formal English. In fact, they often use gobbledygook. Working with a partner, rewrite the passage on your own paper to make it more realistic. Replace formal expressions with informal English. [Note: There will be many different ways to revise the dialogue.]

EX.   [1] Harvey: At what hour will the athletic competition commence?
      1. Harvey: When does the game start?

[1] May: I remain unaware of the scheduling for this evening's event.

[2] Harvey: Is it your understanding that the team representing our community will achieve a victory?

[3] May: That is my heart-felt desire, my trusty companion. Nevertheless, the team that will be conducting themselves in opposition to our team contains a multitude of highly capable participants.

[4] Harvey: Exactly what is your meaning? If it pleases you, inform me of your position on this matter. Is it your theory that our team may be foiled in its endeavor to achieve victory?

[5] May: It is my consideration on this matter, having expended several moments in weighing each side of the situation with the greatest of care, that our team members may not live up to your expectations. I believe they will be confronted by great difficulty.

[6] Harvey: Upon what factual basis have you constructed this opinion?

[7] May: You have become such an enamored follower of our team that you have become unable to observe it from the point of view of an objective observer! Some of the participants encounter enormous perils and tragedy during their experiences involving the projectile hurled by the pitcher. In actuality, I feel it would be sufficiently accurate to state that our team is somewhat horrific when it participates in the batting portion of the event!

[8] Harvey: Nevertheless, there does not exist in the known areas of the planet a more capable handler of the bat than our premiere participant, Reggie Blackburn.

[9] May: However, consider my verbal expressions. A singular individual cannot compensate, even with the totality of his strengths and talents, for a large conglomeration of participants with inferior skills!

[10] Harvey: The situation may prove that your observations are well taken. However, I will continue to voice my support for our participants in a boisterous manner.

B.   Revising to Eliminate Colloquialisms, Euphemisms, and Gobbledygook

On the line following each sentence below, rewrite the sentence in standard English, using clear, straightforward words and phrases.

EX.   1.   The high-spirited child uttered a disagreeable expression.

The poorly behaved child made a rude remark.

1.   It's up to you—a movie or a concert this Saturday night?

2.   I'm afraid that these apples are past their prime.

3.   Leon said, "Get real!" when Jane dissed him.

4.   We were held up in traffic.

5.   Do not procrastinate in obtaining an inoculation against influenza.

6.   Workers engaged in the manufacture of clothing have benefited from legislation effectively precluding the profitable operation of sweatshops.

7.   My dog displays a variety of breeds in his heritage.

8.   The pearls in this necklace are faux.

9.   Refrain from unnecessary verbal communication in the library.

10.   This mature cheese delivers a scent to my olfactory region.

NOUNS

The Eight Parts of Speech			
noun	adjective	pronoun	conjunction
verb	adverb	preposition	interjection

10a   A *noun* is a word used to name a person, a place, a thing, or an idea.

PERSONS   skater, Haruki Murakami, grandfather, police
PLACES   valley, Connecticut, nation, gymnasium
THINGS   apple, Grammy Award, fever, life, cactus
IDEAS   friendship, trust, worry, value, liberty

10b   A *common noun* names any one of a group of persons, places, things, or ideas. A *proper noun* names a particular person, place, thing, or idea.

COMMON NOUNS   woman, nation, event, holiday, language, car, bridge, road
PROPER NOUNS   Chien-Shiung Wu, China, Academy Awards,
   Valentine's Day, Italian, Toyota, London Bridge, Route 66

10c   A *concrete noun* names an object that can be perceived by one or more of the senses (hearing, sight, smell, taste, or touch). An *abstract noun* names a quality, a characteristic, an emotion, or an idea.

CONCRETE NOUNS   guitar, cafeteria, Idaho, Bob Vila, lamp
ABSTRACT NOUNS   skill, bravery, love, charm, solitude, humor

10d   A *collective noun* names a group.

COLLECTIVE NOUNS   class, swarm, fleet, crew, group, team

10e   A *compound noun* consists of two or more words used together as a single noun. Some compound nouns are written as one word, some as separate words, and others as hyphenated words.

COMPOUND NOUNS   sidewalk, telephone pole, bull's-eye, Jonas Salk

EXERCISE 1   Classifying Nouns

Classify each of the nouns below by writing *comm.* for *common* or *prop.* for *proper.* Then, if the noun is *compound*, write *comp.*, and if it is *collective*, write *coll.* Separate your answers with a semicolon.

EX.   1. family ____*comm.; coll.*____

1. football   _____
2. dancer   _____

3. Robert Dole   _____
4. hotel   _____

5. Buick	_____	13. team		_____
6. Labor Day	_____	14. Ohio		_____
7. vegetable	_____	15. orange		_____
8. piano	_____	16. sunflower		_____
9. sister-in-law	_____	17. shower		_____
10. honesty	_____	18. totem pole		_____
11. Japan	_____	19. South America	_____
12. child	_____	20. herd		_____

EXERCISE 2   Classifying Concrete and Abstract Nouns

On the line before each of the sentences below, classify each italicized noun. Write *con.* for *concrete* or *abs.* for *abstract.* Separate your answers with a semicolon.

EX. _____*con.; abs.*_____   1. The *coach* thanked the players for their *dedication* to the team.

_____   1. That *play* was written by *Tennessee Williams.*

_____   2. Abraham Lincoln earned a *reputation* for *honesty.*

_____   3. The *United Nations* tries to ensure world *peace.*

_____   4. Early on, Pablo Picasso showed great *talent* as an *artist.*

_____   5. Examples of *pasta* include *spaghetti,* macaroni, and penne.

_____   6. Horticulturists are *people* who study the art and science of growing fruits, vegetables, and *flowers.*

_____   7. Civil rights *laws* provide equal *opportunities* to all people.

_____   8. *Connie Chung* is a newscaster on *television.*

_____   9. Use *caution* when handling chemicals in the *laboratory.*

_____   10. In what *year* did the *wedding* of George and Martha Washington occur?

_____   11. The *audience* applauded the speaker's *ideas.*

_____   12. *Grapes* spilled out of the *bowl* and onto the table.

_____   13. The *sunset* was the color of a ripe *peach.*

_____   14. The *popularity* of the author was well known in *China.*

_____   15. His *success* was due to his *humor.*

PRONOUNS

10f A *pronoun* is a word used in place of a noun or of more than one noun.

Personal Pronouns	I, me, my, mine, we, us, our, ours, you, your, yours, he, him, his, she, her, hers, it, its, they, them, their, theirs
Relative Pronouns	who, whom, whose, which, that
Interrogative Pronouns	who, whose, what, whom, which
Demonstrative Pronouns	this, that, these, those
Indefinite Pronouns	all, another, any, anybody, anyone, anything, both, each, either, everybody, everyone, everything, few, many, more, most, much, neither, no one, nobody, none, one, other, several, some, somebody, someone, such
Reflexive/ Intensive Pronouns	myself, oneself, ourselves, yourself, yourselves, himself, herself, itself, themselves

NOTE In this book, the words *my, your, his, her, ours,* and *their* are considered possessive pronouns rather than adjectives. Follow your teacher's instructions in referring to such words.

A word that a pronoun stands for is called its **antecedent.** A pronoun may appear in the same sentence as its antecedent or in a following sentence. The antecedent may be a noun or another pronoun.

EXAMPLE **They** went home. Kim followed **them.** [*They* is the antecedent of *them.*]

EXERCISE 3 Identifying Pronouns

Underline the pronouns in the following sentences.

EX. 1. Were <u>both</u> of Mia's parents born in Taiwan?

1. Those are the boots Jim bought yesterday.

2. Would you like more salad?

3. A few of Sally's friends have planned a surprise party.

4. W. H. Auden was the poet who wrote "The Composer."

5. Rafael built that computer table himself.

6. Everyone on the debating team is ready to begin.

7. Now extinct, the *Dunkleosteus* was a fish that was as big as a bus.

8. This is the phone number to call if the girls want to order some sandwiches.

9. Are the books on the dining room table mine?

10. The following morning, neither of the cars would start.

11. Anything we asked of Mr. and Mrs. Tong, they gave us gladly.

12. Since it was so late, the boys decided to sleep over, not trusting themselves to stay awake during the long drive home.

13. My parents say that much of the time young people watch television.

14. If you want it done right, I advise you to do it yourself.

15. Which of the computers has the software for teaching graphing?

EXERCISE 4   Identifying Pronouns and Their Antecedents

Underline the pronouns in the paragraph below. Circle the antecedent of each pronoun.

EX.   [1] Grandma Moses began painting when <u>she</u> was seventy-six years old.

[1] Grandma Moses' colorful pictures are valued today because they are filled with innocence and have a fresh, primitive style. [2] Many of the paintings hang in art museums. [3] Each of the scenes has a rural setting. [4] Grandma Moses based the paintings on memories she had of her childhood. [5] They were fond memories of a peaceful life on farms in Virginia and northern New York. [6] Several of the paintings show busy people, working and having fun. [7] Some are working in the fields or picking apples or hanging quilts out on a clothesline. [8] Grandma Moses taught herself to paint. [9] She never took art lessons; she apparently never needed them. [10] Grandma Moses lived 101 years, and in her last year, she painted twenty-five pictures.

ADJECTIVES

10g An *adjective* is a word used to modify a noun or pronoun.

To *modify* means "to describe or to make more definite" the meaning of a word. Adjectives modify nouns or pronouns by telling *what kind, which one,* or *how many/how much.*

What kind?	**old** book, **blue** sky, **warm** water
Which one?	**that** game, **those** lights, **his** stereo
How many?	**six** days, **nine** judges, **many** friends

The most frequently used adjectives are *a, an,* and *the.* These words are called *articles.*

A and *an* are **indefinite articles.** They indicate that a noun refers to one of a general group. *A* is used before words beginning with a consonant sound; *an* is used before words beginning with a vowel sound. *An* is also used before words beginning with the consonant *h* when the *h* is not pronounced.

EXAMPLES   **A** lion crouched in the tall grass.
This is **an** excellent essay, Clarice!
An hour passed while we chose **a** hat for the scarecrow.

The is the **definite article.** It indicates that a noun refers to someone or something in particular.

EXAMPLE   **The** blackbird sat in **the** cedar tree, sheltered from **the** rain.

Sometimes nouns are used as adjectives.

EXAMPLES   Have you ever been to an **auto** race? [*Auto,* usually a noun, is used as an adjective modifying the noun *race.*]
Is that machine the new **carpet** cleaner? [*Carpet,* usually a noun, is used as an adjective modifying the noun *cleaner.*]

NOTE   Some pairs or groups of nouns are considered compound nouns. By checking a dictionary, you can avoid confusing a noun that is used as an adjective with a noun that is part of a compound noun.

EXAMPLES   country club, blood bank, road map, United States

EXERCISE 5   **Identifying Adjectives in Sentences**

Underline the adjectives in each of the sentences below, and circle the word each adjective modifies. Do not include *a, an,* or *the.*

EX.   1. Onesimus developed a <u>successful</u> (cure) for smallpox in 1721.

1. Smallpox is a serious disease that causes a high fever.

2. Also a contagious disease, it was causing many people to die at the time.

3. Onesimus based the new medicine on an old remedy he knew.

4. That remedy had been a popular and common medicine in Africa.

5. Onesimus was an African American slave.

6. The Puritan leader who owned Onesimus sent the medicine to a Dr. Boylston.

7. Dr. Boylston tried the remarkable medicine on three smallpox victims.

8. The sick people became well.

9. Onesimus did not receive immediate credit for his tremendous discovery.

10. The dishonest Dr. Boylston took all credit for himself.

EXERCISE 6   **Using Adjectives in Sentences**

In each sentence below, add interesting adjectives to modify the nouns and pronouns. Write your sentences on your own paper.

EX.   1. The workers took the truck to the building.
    1. The fatigued workers took the rusty, old-fashioned truck to the gigantic building.

1. Scott gave a book to his father.

2. Camara donated toys and tools for the sale.

3. Marian packed a lunch for the picnic.

4. The athlete ran across the field.

5. The warrior fought the animal and rescued the child.

6. Which book have you chosen for your report?

7. For days, the woman made her baskets.

8. During the day, we washed cars and raked the leaves.

9. The children gave gifts to their friends at the party.

10. Rosie painted a picture of the meadow for her relatives.

VERBS

10h **A *verb* is a word that expresses action or a state of being.**

(1) An *action verb* expresses physical or mental activity.

EXAMPLES   leap, sail, break, scoop, consider, forget, hope, believe

(2) A *transitive verb* is an action verb that takes an *object*—a word that tells who or what receives the action.

EXAMPLES   The cows **crossed** the pasture. [The action of the verb *crossed* is received by *pasture*.]
Tyrone **tuned** his car's engine. [The action of the verb *tuned* is received by *engine*.]

(3) An *intransitive verb* is an action verb that does not take an object.

EXAMPLES   The children **laughed.**
A letter **came** from your friend in Norway.

A verb can be transitive in one sentence and intransitive in another.

EXAMPLES   Shulka **wrote** a play. [transitive]
Shulka **wrote** carefully. [intransitive]

(4) A *linking verb*, or *state-of-being verb*, connects the subject with a word that identifies or describes it.

The most commonly used linking verbs are forms of the verb *be: am, is, are, was, were, being,* and *been.* Other common linking verbs include *appear, become, feel, grow, look, remain, seem, smell, sound, stay, taste,* and *turn.*

EXAMPLES   This tree **is** a sycamore.
That music **sounds** distorted.

Many linking verbs can be used as action verbs as well.

EXAMPLES   The chicken **tasted** good. [The verb links the subject, *chicken,* to a word that describes it, *good.*]
Did you **taste** the chicken? [The verb describes an action taken by the subject, *you.*]

(5) A *verb phrase* consists of a *main verb* and at least one *helping,* or *auxiliary, verb.* Common helping verbs are forms of *be,* forms of *have,* forms of *do,* and the auxiliaries *can, could, may, might, must, shall, should, will,* and *would.*

EXAMPLES   **did** speak, **must have been** sleeping, **is** working

EXERCISE 7   Identifying and Classifying Transitive and Intransitive Verbs

In the sentences below, underline each verb or verb phrase. Then identify the verb as transitive or intransitive. Write *trans.* for *transitive* or *intr.* for *intransitive* on the line before each sentence.

EX.   1.   _intr._   Marc grew tall.

_____   1.   The veterinarian treated my cat.

_____   2.   Georgia rented a movie last night.

_____   3.   You skate particularly well.

_____   4.   Nadine is calling the dentist for an appointment.

_____   5.   I have grown many herbs in pots on my windowsill.

_____   6.   The twins are racing down the hill.

_____   7.   When did the bus leave?

_____   8.   For a three-year-old, Harley speaks very clearly.

_____   9.   Uncle Pierre drove to Texas last summer in an old car.

_____   10.   I named my cat "Humphrey" in honor of Humphrey Bogart.

EXERCISE 8   Identifying Verb Phrases and Helping Verbs

In each sentence below, underline the verb phrase once and the helping verb or verbs twice.

EX.   1.   Everyone in the auditorium was cheering for Tia.

1.   Tomorrow we are starting a new literature selection.

2.   I have been studying German for two years now.

3.   Did Marilyn give you her new phone number?

4.   He must have been hoping for a raise in pay.

5.   The trees in the meadow have dropped their leaves.

6.   We might go to the park after the game.

7.   Does Andrew watch *Jeopardy* every night?

8.   Benji would like more broccoli.

9.   You should have seen the hot-air balloon in the field last night.

10.   I must have lost my library card.

ADVERBS

10i An *adverb* is a word used to modify a verb, an adjective, or another adverb.

Adverbs modify by telling *how, when, where,* or *to what extent.*

How?	The rescue team worked **frantically.** The drummer plays **well.**
When?	Will winter be here **soon?** I **occasionally** play basketball.
Where?	The shutters flew **open.** Do ospreys travel **far?**
To what extent?	Cleve **nearly** won the race! I've **never** seen an ocean.

EXAMPLES   The bank closes **promptly** each day. [*Promptly* modifies the verb *closes,* telling *when* the bank closes.]
I thought that the play was **rather** exciting. [*Rather* modifies the adjective *exciting,* telling *to what extent.*]
The police officer acted **quite** heroically. [*Quite* modifies the adverb *heroically,* telling *to what extent.*]

EXERCISE 9   Identifying Adverbs and the Words They Modify

Underline the adverbs in each of the following sentences. Draw brackets around the words they modify. Then identify the words modified by writing *v.* for *verb, adj.* for *adjective,* or *adv.* for *adverb* on the line before the sentence.

EX.   ___adj.___   1. Joseph Bruchac is a nationally [famous] storyteller.

_____   1. The trash barrel is nearly empty.

_____   2. My cousins from Nevada visit frequently.

_____   3. Suddenly, all the bright lights dimmed.

_____   4. We never found the lost necklace.

_____   5. They finished their meeting quite quickly.

_____   6. Geraldo and Demi were thoroughly happy with the results.

_____ 7. Did you play well in yesterday's game?

_____ 8. Turn the lever slowly so you don't break it.

_____ 9. Fish are rarely caught in this river.

_____ 10. These lines are slightly uneven.

_____ 11. Quite soon, we will have the election results.

_____ 12. The sheep grazed in a gently rolling meadow.

_____ 13. You can put the stack of boxes here.

_____ 14. Did you ever meet a famous person?

_____ 15. The food at that Chinese restaurant is really great.

EXERCISE 10   Using Adverbs in Sentences

Complete each sentence below by writing an appropriate adverb on the line provided. The word or phrase in parentheses tells you what information the adverb should give about the verb, adjective, or other adverb.

EX. 1. I have __almost__ finished my book. (*To what extent?*)

1. They will return the books _____ . (*When?*)

2. Barbara picked up the papers _____ . (*How?*)

3. Robert De Niro _____ plays tough characters. (*When?*)

4. Sit _____ . (*Where?*)

5. My friends _____ recognized me in my costume. (*To what extent?*)

6. This story was _____ exciting. (*To what extent?*)

7. The players on the opposing team played _____ . (*How?*)

8. The package should arrive _____ . (*When?*)

9. I'll put your sandwich _____ . (*Where?*)

10. Edna visits her older sister at college _____ . (*When?*)

11. Helen speaks _____ quickly. (*To what extent?*)

12. The flock of geese are nesting _____ . (*Where?*)

13. He has _____ visited Puerto Rico. (*When?*)

14. _____ gently, Jonah bandaged my arm. (*To what extent?*)

15. _____ , I agreed to be president of the club. (*How?*)

REVIEW EXERCISE 1

A. Identifying Nouns, Pronouns, and Adjectives

On your own paper, identify the italicized words in each of the sentences below by writing *n.* for *noun,* *pron.* for *pronoun,* or *adj.* for *adjective.*

EX. 1. *Those* are the *best* amplifiers on the market today.

    1. pron.; adj.

1. *We* went for a *long* hike around Lake Sunapee.

2. Fern still remembers the *friends* she made in *Iran.*

3. The *woods* were peaceful and *dark.*

4. Please fill out the application with your *full* name and *address.*

5. The *Liberty Bell* is near Independence Hall in *Philadelphia.*

6. *Everyone* on the bus was anxious to get to the *next* station on time.

7. I wish that *I* had continued my *piano* lessons.

8. Eleanor had bought the *latest* newspapers for her *mother* to read.

9. He couldn't find *either* of his *shoes.*

10. Is *it* a fact that elephants have *remarkable* memories?

B. Classifying Verbs

On the line before each of the following sentences, identify the italicized verb as an action verb or a linking verb. If it is an action verb, tell whether it is transitive or intransitive. Write *a.v.* for *action verb,* *l.v.* for *linking verb, trans.* for *transitive,* and *intr.* for *intransitive.*

EX. _a.v., intr._ 1. They *were calling* to the hikers on the rocky slopes.

_____ 1. People *are* often happy when they find unexpected treats.

_____ 2. The bread *seems* slightly stale, don't you think?

_____ 3. Where *did* you *buy* that silly hat?

_____ 4. The students *remained* in their seats after the performance.

_____ 5. The cat *sat* outside most of the day, enjoying the sunshine.

_____ 6. Who *has borrowed* my tennis racquet?

_____ 7. They *became* worried when the hikers did not return.

_____ 8. *Do* you *remember* all of your lines for the play?

_____ 9. Katya *worked* hard all afternoon, raking leaves.

_____ 10. It seems late; what time *is* it?

C. Identifying Adjectives and Adverbs

On the line before each sentence below, identify the italicized words by writing *adj.* for *adjective* or *adv.* for *adverb*. Then underline the word or words that each adjective modifies, and circle the word or words each adverb modifies.

EX. _adv. ; adj._ 1. Rather *quickly*, *black* clouds (appeared) in the sky.

_____ 1. *Humorous* advertisements *often* appear on television.

_____ 2. The game *certainly* ended in a *surprising* way.

_____ 3. Thank you for your *extremely thoughtful* letter.

_____ 4. *Yesterday* we saw a *young* bear close to our tent!

_____ 5. *Usually* you have to work hard to become a *great* athlete.

_____ 6. Tyrone finished the *history* project *easily*.

_____ 7. I had *hardly* begun to speak when an *older* gentleman interrupted me.

_____ 8. We were *very* happy to hear about the *Latin* award that you won!

_____ 9. *Unexpectedly*, a visitor arrived at the *information* booth just before closing time.

_____ 10. Ramón *unexpectedly* brought up *several* interesting questions at the meeting.

_____ 11. *Certainly*, water helps young plants to develop *strong* roots.

_____ 12. I did *not* know that Sandra Day O'Connor is the *first* woman to serve on the U. S. Supreme Court.

_____ 13. The *mushroom* soup was *truly* delicious.

_____ 14. Does popcorn *really* contain any *nutritional* value?

_____ 15. The *church* bus usually arrives at this corner *promptly* at 6:00 A.M.

_____ 16. How *often* do you watch the *evening* news on television?

_____ 17. The senators were *quite firm* in their support of the president.

_____ 18. Walking can *certainly* be an *excellent* form of exercise.

_____ 19. *Clearly*, I understand your *unusual* point of view.

_____ 20. *Yesterday* we visited the Smithsonian Institution in Washington, D. C., and stayed at a *nearby* hotel.

PREPOSITIONS

10j A *preposition* is a word that shows the relationship of a noun or pronoun to some other word in the sentence.

A preposition always introduces a *phrase.* The noun or pronoun that ends a prepositional phrase is the ***object of the preposition.*** In each of the following examples, the object of the preposition is *me.* Notice how the prepositions show six different relationships between *sang* and *me.*

EXAMPLES Sabrina sang **to** me. Sabrina sang **after** me.
Sabrina sang **with** me. Sabrina sang **before** me.
Sabrina sang **for** me. Sabrina sang **beside** me.

Commonly Used Prepositions				
aboard	before	by	like	through
about	behind	concerning	near	to
above	below	down	of	toward
across	beneath	during	off	under
after	beside	except	on	until
against	besides	for	onto	up
along	between	from	outside	upon
among	beyond	in	over	with
around	but (mean-	inside	past	within
at	ing *except*)	into	since	without

NOTE The same word may be either an adverb or a preposition, depending on its use in a sentence.

EXAMPLES A motorcycle zoomed **by.** [adverb]
A motorcycle zoomed **by** us. [preposition]

Prepositions can also be compound.

Compound Prepositions		
according to	in addition to	next to
because of	in front of	on account of
aside from	instead of	prior to

EXERCISE 11   Identifying Prepositions and Their Objects

Underline each preposition in the sentences below. Draw a bracket around its object.

EX.   1.   Tony Thornton competed <u>for</u> an important boxing [title].

1.   Tony Thornton is an African American mail carrier who works in New Jersey.

2.   He delivers mail to over four hundred homes.

3.   In addition to that job, Tony has another large interest and talent.

4.   He is a contender for the super-middleweight boxing championship.

5.   Tony, who is thirty-three years old, is a lifetime resident of New Jersey.

6.   In one boxing match in 1993, Tony faced James Toney, a much younger boxer.

7.   Tony boxed well, but he lost the match in a twelve-round decision.

8.   Tony's co-workers at the post office sometimes make some good-natured jokes.

9.   Because of his two interests, they call him "The Punching Postman."

10. However, his co-workers also share great respect for Tony.

11. They agree that he is a dedicated postal worker who never lets his job suffer because of his boxing talent.

12. Before a boxing match, Tony spends many hours training.

13. He sometimes misses work after a match, though.

14. Usually, instead of resting, Tony delivers the mail the very next morning!

15. His co-workers support Tony, whether he becomes the super-middleweight champion of the world or not.

EXERCISE 12   Describing an Amusement Park

You have been employed by a large entertainment company to plan a new amusement park. On your own paper, draw a diagram of the park. Show what rides, forms of entertainment, restaurants, and other attractions might be found there. Then, also on your own paper, write fifteen sentences describing the park. Use at least ten prepositions in your sentences, and include at least three compound prepositions. Underline the prepositions you use.

EX. 1.   <u>Inside</u> the park <u>next to</u> a Stone Age man, stands a giant statue <u>of</u> a prehistoric mammoth.

CONJUNCTIONS AND INTERJECTIONS

10k A *conjunction* is a word used to join words or groups of words.

(1) *Coordinating conjunctions* join words or groups of words used in the same way.

Coordinating Conjunctions						
and	but	for	nor	or	so	yet

EXAMPLES   The workshop has a bench saw **and** a sander in one corner.
Advance ticket sales were slow, **but** many people showed up
at the door.

(2) *Correlative conjunctions* are used in pairs to join words or groups of words used in the same way.

Correlative Conjunctions		
both . . . and	neither . . . nor	whether . . . or
either . . . or	not only . . . but (also)	

EXAMPLES   **Both** moose **and** caribou live in the north country.
The comedian's routine was **not only** funny **but also**
appropriate to the occasion.

(3) A *subordinating conjunction* begins a subordinate clause and connects it to an independent clause.

Commonly Used Subordinating Conjunctions			
after	because	since	when
although	before	so that	whenever
as	even though	than	where
as if	how	that	wherever
as much as	if	though	whether
as though	in order that	unless	while
as well as	provided	until	why

EXAMPLES   Did Otto decide **whether** he would take that class?
We should take a taxi **since** the bus is late.

> **10l   An *interjection* is a word that expresses emotion. It has no grammatical relation to other words in the sentence.**
>
> An interjection is set off from the rest of the sentence by an exclamation point or a comma.
>
> EXAMPLES   **Hey!** Watch out for that truck!
> **No,** there aren't many stars out tonight.

EXERCISE 13   Identifying and Classifying Conjunctions

Underline the conjunctions in the sentences below. In the space above each conjunction, write *coor.* for *coordinating conjunction, corr.* for *correlative conjunction,* or *sub.* for *subordinating conjunction.*

EX.   1. Lee Seong Chul was a great spiritual leader, *and* he inspired many people.

1.   Until Uncle Jeff bought the farm, he lived in the city.

2.   Some students will finish the story before the class is over.

3.   When Stephanie was born, the whole family sent flowers.

4.   Horses, donkeys, and ponies ran freely in the pasture.

5.   Mexico is a country of both ancient, abandoned cities and new, busy centers.

6.   The people of River Junction, where I grew up, always looked out for all the young people.

7.   Dad sang the song and made up the words.

8.   Not only giant pandas but also red pandas live in bamboo forests in the mountains of Asia.

9.   Gina said her essay was too long, yet we all agreed that it was wonderful.

10.   Legend has it that the emperor Nero played the fiddle while the city of Rome burned.

EXERCISE 14   Using Interjections

On your own paper, write a sentence using each of the interjections below.

EX.   1. hey
   1. Hey! Haven't I seen you on television?

1. ouch	3. well	5. oh	7. why	9. ah
2. help	4. yes	6. wow	8. whew	10. ugh

DETERMINING PARTS OF SPEECH

10m The part of speech of a word is determined by the way the word is used in a sentence.

EXAMPLES   Menino will win the election. You can **bank** on it. [*Bank* is used as a verb.]
Deposit your paycheck in the **bank**. [*Bank* is used as a noun.]

EXERCISE 15 Classifying the Parts of Speech

Above each italicized word in the paragraph below, write the word's part of speech. Write *n.* for *noun*, *pron.* for *pronoun*, *v.* for *verb*, *adj.* for *adjective*, *adv.* for *adverb*, *prep.* for *preposition*, *conj.* for *conjunction*, or *intj.* for *interjection*.

EX.   [1] Gina heard a *loud* crash.   *(adj.)*

[1] Gina *ran* to the *open* window. [2] *Outside*, the wind was howling *and* shaking the shutters of her old house. [3] At first, she couldn't see *what* had caused the *crash* that she had heard. [4] "I'd better go *outside* and have a *look*." [5] A large, *knotted* oak tree, planted by *her* grandfather many years ago, had fallen to the ground. [6] "*No!* It's just horrible, you beautiful old tree," *she* said. [7] *After* the storm, Gina helped her grandfather saw the *branches* and trunk of the tree into firewood. [8] As he worked, he said, "*That* was a great tree, almost like a dear friend, and I'll *surely* miss it." [9] For the *rest* of the fall and the cold winter months that followed, the yard *seemed* empty and sad without the oak tree. [10] Although *neither* of them spoke about it, the loss of their "old friend" *saddened* Gina and her grandfather. [11] Then, one *spring* morning, Gina saw a brand-new oak tree, which had sprouted from a *buried* acorn. [12] Gina rushed *into* the house and gave a *shout* to her grandfather. [13] *When* her grandfather saw the tiny seedling, he said, "Let's water it *well* and *put* a little fence around it to keep it safe." [14] *Both* of them knew that *oak* trees take years and years to grow into big trees. [15] But that didn't matter, *for* the seedling seemed *like* a gift from the old tree.

REVIEW EXERCISE 2

A. Identifying Parts of Speech

In the paragraph below, identify the part of speech of each italicized word. Write *n.* for *noun*, *pron.* for *pronoun*, *v.* for *verb*, *adj.* for *adjective*, *adv.* for *adverb*, *prep.* for *preposition*, *conj.* for *conjunction*, or *intj.* for *interjection*.

EX.   [1] If pets *crowd* your home, take a lesson *from* Sandee Chreiman.

[1] *This* Pennsylvania woman cares for forty-three animals in her *home.*
[2] She doesn't find *all* those animals a *bother.* In fact, she thinks of them as a big, happy family. [3] *Yes,* some of them *sometimes* get into mischief. [4] *Some,* like the twelve cats and the five *dogs,* may occasionally jump on the furniture. [5] Others, such as the twenty-four ferrets, steal little items found *around* the house and hide *them* under Sandee's dresser. [6] Her *pet* bird watches all this activity from a *perch* overhead, while her pet rat sits quietly, munching on raisins. [7] *All* of Sandee's pets are special to her, but perhaps the ferrets are the *most* special. [8] Sandee has rescued many *pet* ferrets from *animal* shelters. [9] *Too* many people buy ferrets as pets and then decide *that* they don't want the animals. [10] Although ferrets are timid animals, *when* they are frightened, they may bite. [11] *That* is usually when the pet owner *takes* the ferret to a shelter. [12] Sandee rarely gets bitten by her *friendly* ferrets, *for* she understands that they need gentle care. [13] At Sandee's house, *that* care involves big, airy cages in an *upstairs* bedroom. [14] Because the ferrets *enjoy* running and playing, Sandee often opens the cages and lets the ferrets run *through* the house. [15] The ferrets have many friends among the five dogs, who often *let* the ferrets ride *around* the house on their backs.

B. Describing Your Personal Flag

A nation's flag often has special symbols on it that tell about the nation and about the beliefs of its people. Design a flag for yourself that has four sections. The flag should tell about you. On your own paper, write a short paragraph of at least ten sentences describing your personal flag. Use and label each of the eight parts of speech at least once.

EX.   The top two sections of my personal flag represent my personality and my dreams. One part has a red rose in it; the other has a beautiful bird.

CHAPTER REVIEW

A. Identifying Nouns, Pronouns, and Adjectives in Sentences

Classify each italicized word in the sentences below by writing *n.* for *noun, pron.* for *pronoun,* or *adj.* for *adjective* above the word. For each adjective, circle the word it modifies.

               n.   *adj.*   *adj.*   *n.*

EX.   1. *Garrett Augustus Morgan* invented *many valuable* (tools).

1. *His* mother, Elizabeth Reed Morgan, was a *former* slave with African and Native American ancestry.

2. He sold his first invention, a tool to tighten *belts* on sewing machines, for *fifty* dollars.

3. Morgan invented a *fireproof* hood; attached to it was a small tank carrying *fresh* air.

4. *This* hood eventually became the gas mask, *which* Morgan patented in 1914.

5. Another invention that made Morgan famous was the automatic *traffic* light.

B. Determining the Parts of Speech of Words

In the following paragraph, identify the part of speech of each italicized word or expression. On the line before each sentence, write *n.* for *noun, adj.* for *adjective, pron.* for *pronoun, v.* for *verb, adv.* for *adverb, prep.* for *preposition, conj.* for *conjunction,* or *intj.* for *interjection.*

EX. [1] <u> prep. </u> Wherever I go, I buy a postcard *for* my album.

[1] _____ *Last* year, I went to Chicago to visit my cousin Sheila.

[2] _____ I bought a card that had a picture of the Art Institute on *it*.

[3] _____ *Outside* the museum's main entrance are two gigantic statues.

[4] _____ *Each* one is a lion. [5] _____ They *guard* the museum like silent, powerful friends. [6] _____ *According to* the card, the lions were created by an American sculptor named Edward Kemeys. [7] _____ *Since* that trip, I have collected other postcards with statues and monuments on

them. [8] _____ My *favorite* grandfather sent me a postcard from

Paris. [9] _____ *Because* he knew of my interest in monuments, his card

pictured the Arc de Triomphe. [10] _____ I've *never* before seen a

monument in such a busy place. [11] _____ *Wow!* The card says that

twelve major avenues meet in the circle surrounding the arch.

[12] _____ My grandfather's note said that all those roads can create a

traffic nightmare. [13] _____ The monument celebrates the *courage* of the

soldiers of Napoleon, a historic leader of France. [14] _____ Along the

monument's *outside* walls are a group of statues by the French sculptor

François Rude. [15] _____ A flame that will burn *forever* has been

installed beneath the arch to honor France's Unknown Soldier.

C.   Writing Sentences with Words Used as Specific Parts of Speech

On your own paper, write fifteen sentences according to the guidelines below.
Underline the part of speech that has been asked for in each sentence.

EX.   1. Use *down* as a preposition.
       1. The river flows <u>down</u> the hill.

1. Use *some* as an adjective.
2. Use *so* as an adverb.
3. Use *touch* as a noun.
4. Use *where* as an interrogative pronoun.
5. Use *where* as a subordinating conjunction.
6. Use *by* as a preposition.
7. Use *outside* as an adverb.
8. Use *because of* as a compound preposition.
9. Use *either . . . or* as a correlative conjunction.
10. Use *oh* as an interjection.
11. Use *taste* as a linking verb.
12. Use *might* as a helping verb.
13. Use *cover* as a verb.
14. Use *cover* as a noun.
15. Use *but* as a coordinating conjunction.

SUBJECTS AND PREDICATES

11a A sentence consists of two parts: a *subject* and a *predicate*. A *subject* tells *whom* or *what* the sentence is about. A *predicate* tells something about the subject.

                PRED.   S.   PRED.

EXAMPLES   When do | autumn leaves | fall from the branches of the trees?

In this example, the words labeled *subject* make up the **complete subject**. The words labeled *predicate* make up the **complete predicate**. Notice that parts of the complete predicate can come before and after the subject.

11b A *simple subject* is the main word or group of words in the complete subject that tells *whom* or *what* the sentence is about.

                                  S.

EXAMPLES   Who was the research <u>scientist</u> on this project?

                                      S.

                Decorating the float, the <u>students</u> kept warm with mittens and mugs of hot tea.

NOTE In this book, the term *subject* refers to the simple subject unless otherwise indicated.

11c A *simple predicate* is a verb or verb phrase in the complete predicate that tells something about the subject.

                        PRED.

EXAMPLES   Alfredo <u>wrote</u> clearly and eloquently.

                    PRED.   PRED.

                <u>Did</u> Julia ever <u>find</u> the concert tickets?

NOTE In this book, the term *verb* refers to the simple predicate (a one-word verb or a verb phrase) unless otherwise indicated.

EXERCISE 1 Identifying Complete Subjects and Simple Subjects in Sentences

In each of the following sentences, underline the complete subject once and the simple subject twice.

EX. 1. The old <u>sleigh</u> provided the only transportation during the blizzard.

1. The energetic kitten unraveled the ball of yarn.

2. My lab partner completed the science project on time.

3. Each member brought a list of suggestions to the meeting.

4. The orange chrysanthemums brightened Mr. Hwang's autumn garden.

5. Fresh dandelion greens are tasty in a salad.

6. Mrs. Wharton hoped for a better view of the purple martin.

7. At the track meet, Derek, along with Kate and Gloria, broke several records.

8. After ripping up the carpet, Donna refinished the wooden floors.

9. Piles of red and gold leaves covered the lawn, the driveway, and the front porch steps.

10. Dusty bookcases lined the walls of the abandoned house.

EXERCISE 2   Identifying Complete Predicates and Verbs in Sentences

In each sentence below, underline the complete predicate once and the verb twice. Be sure to include all parts of a verb phrase.

EX.   1. Today we will clean the entire apartment.

1. Yesterday we were walking by the new museum.

2. Angela bought large bags of birdseed at the supermarket.

3. On Saturday George took fresh bread to his neighbors.

4. We will make a quilt from those colorful scraps of fabric.

5. I am learning about everyday life in Israel.

6. Julian saw frogs and fish in the pond behind Robin's house.

7. Nell wanted answers immediately.

8. I have requested dozens of my favorite songs.

9. I gave Josephine fresh corn, tomatoes, and lettuce.

10. Jerry and I will baby-sit this weekend.

11. Into the compost pile Kim dumped the vegetable scraps.

12. Did Randy go outdoors to help his father?

13. Katy volunteered at the library.

14. All the seedlings grew into huge vines with plump pumpkins.

15. Each of the visitors remarked on the interesting new exhibit at the Museum of Modern Art.

COMPOUND SUBJECTS AND COMPOUND VERBS

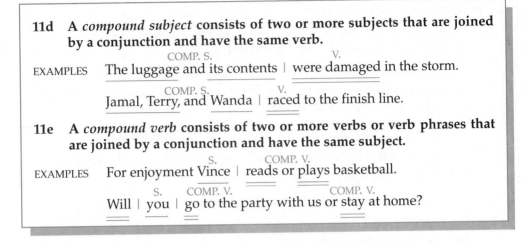

11d   A *compound subject* consists of two or more subjects that are joined by a conjunction and have the same verb.

EXAMPLES   The luggage and its contents | were damaged in the storm.

Jamal, Terry, and Wanda | raced to the finish line.

11e   A *compound verb* consists of two or more verbs or verb phrases that are joined by a conjunction and have the same subject.

EXAMPLES   For enjoyment Vince | reads or plays basketball.

Will | you | go to the party with us or stay at home?

EXERCISE 3   Identifying Compound Subjects and Compound Verbs

In each of the sentences below, underline the subject once and the verb twice. Include all parts of a compound subject or a compound verb and all words in a verb phrase.

EX.   1. Leon and Cesar butter and toast their bread for breakfast.

1. As early as 2600 B.C., the Egyptians baked and toasted bread.

2. Toasting or roasting can remove mold and moisture from the bread.

3. In the eighteenth century, people in Great Britain and people in North America called two connected forks a toaster.

4. The fork toaster sandwiched the bread and toasted it over a fire.

5. Tin and wire formed a cage-shaped toaster in the nineteenth century.

6. This toaster held four slices of bread and sat over a coal stove.

7. At the turn of the century, with the invention of electric toasters, toast could finally be made and enjoyed without lighting a stove.

8. Toasters quickly became popular and were installed in kitchens and even in bedrooms.

9. In 1919, a mechanic invented the pop-up toaster and filed for a patent.

10. Springs and a timer were built into the new, automatic toaster.

EXERCISE 4   **Using Compound Subjects and Compound Verbs to Combine Sentences**

Combine each of the following groups of two or three short sentences into one longer sentence by using compound subjects or compound verbs. Write each new sentence on the line provided.

EX. 1. In the evening, Emily called to remind me about band practice. Jason called to remind me about band practice, too.

In the evening, both Emily and Jason called to remind me about band practice.

1. The house painters scraped the wood-framed house. They also primed the house. Finally, they painted the house.

_____

2. This summer, Mr. Ruffolo traveled by train to Canada. Mrs. Ruffolo rode the train to Canada, too.

_____

3. After cleaning the garage, Lucas played basketball. Then he ate dinner. Finally, Lucas studied for his exam.

_____

4. Grilled swordfish is especially tasty. Grilled salmon is tasty, too.

_____

5. Mosi enjoys a game of chess. Eric and Julio enjoy playing chess, too.

_____

6. After school yesterday, Nina met Felicia at the health food store. Rosa was also at the health food store.

_____

7. Yesterday morning, Frank jogged two miles. Next, he ate breakfast. Then he showered and dressed for school.

_____

8. Amanda wrote her first short story. She showed it to her friend Betsy.

_____

9. After skiing, Pearl removed her hat and gloves. She took off her boots. Then she warmed her feet by the fireplace.

_____

10. After the art history lecture, Cora went to the library. Ben went to the library.

_____

FINDING THE SUBJECT OF A SENTENCE

11f   To find the subject of a sentence, ask *Who?* or *What?* before the verb.

EXAMPLES   The **team** of doctors **worked** hard to save the patient. [Who worked? *Team* worked.]

Across the finish line **jumped** the winning **frog.** [What jumped? The *frog* jumped.]

(1) The subject of a sentence expressing a command or a request is always understood to be *you*, although *you* may not appear in the sentence.

EXAMPLES   Eat a balanced meal for good health. [Who is being told to eat? *You* eat.]

Please read me the directions again, Kim. [Who is being asked to read? *You* read.]

(2) The subject of a sentence never appears in a prepositional phrase.

EXAMPLES   A **flock** of birds flew above the tall pine trees. [What flew? *A flock* flew. *Birds* is the object of the preposition *of*.]

A **group** of friends gathered near the doorway. [Who gathered? *Group* gathered. *Friends* is the object of the preposition *of*.]

(3) The subject of a sentence expressing a question usually follows the verb or a part of the verb phrase.

EXAMPLES   **Is** the **cat sleeping** on top of the desk? [What is sleeping on top of the desk? The *cat* is.]

When **was Carolyn elected** president of the student council? [Who was elected? *Carolyn* was elected.]

Were your **friends** early? [Who was early? *Friends* were.]

(4) The word *there* or *here* is never the subject of a sentence.

In the following examples, the words *there* and *here* are used as adverbs telling *where*.

EXAMPLES   There are the four suitcases we want to take. [What is there? The *suitcases* are there.]

Here is your new video game. [What is here? The *game* is here.]

In the following example, the word *there* is used as an *expletive*—a word that fills out the structure of a sentence but does not add to the meaning.

EXAMPLE   There are two reasons for the delay of the game. [What are? *Reasons* are.]

EXERCISE 5   Identifying Subjects and Verbs

In each of the sentences below, underline the subject once and the verb twice. Include all parts of a compound subject or a compound verb and all words in a verb phrase.

EX.   1. At an early age, <u>Pablo Picasso</u> <u>showed</u> unusual artistic talent.

1. The son of an art teacher, Picasso was born in Spain in 1881.

2. At the age of twenty, he traveled to Paris for the first time.

3. Picasso's early paintings show the influence of other painters and his mastery of traditional techniques.

4. Despite the early-twentieth century popularity of Fauvism, Picasso followed his own path and questioned standard art forms.

5. Picasso and Georges Braque rejected the formal use of shapes and tried to show three dimensions in their paintings.

6. Together, the two painters developed Analytical Cubism.

7. Throughout their experiments with form, both common and unusual colors appeared in their artwork.

8. Picasso often placed various objects in his paintings.

9. His collages sometimes included newspaper, string, or wire.

10. In 1917, Picasso's interest in Classicism and his later connection with the Surrealists led to more analytical works.

11. His series of paintings and drawings with unusual figures of dancers started emerging from his studio in 1923 and developed over the next ten years.

12. In the 1930s, bull-fighting subjects appeared in Picasso's paintings.

13. His most important work during that time is the large mural *Guernica*.

14. Painted in 1937, *Guernica* is nearly twenty-six feet long and expresses Picasso's personal response to the Spanish Civil War.

15. Frightening images remained part of Picasso's work through World War II.

DIRECT OBJECTS AND INDIRECT OBJECTS

11g   A *complement* is a word or a group of words that completes the
meaning of a verb.

INCOMPLETE   Jose Rodríguez threw

COMPLETE   Jose Rodríguez threw the **ball.**

Generally, a sentence includes at least one complement. However, some
sentences contain only a subject and a verb.

                            s.   v.   v.
EXAMPLES   Knute sang.   Run! [The subject *you* is understood.]

Direct objects and indirect objects are two kinds of complements.

11h   A *direct object* is a word or group of words that receives the action of
a verb or shows the result of the action. A direct object tells *whom* or
what after a transitive verb.

EXAMPLES   Angelina met **Susan** and **me** at the library. [Met whom? *Susan
and me.*]
Ms. Campbell recited the **poem** from memory. [Recited what? *Poem.*]

NOTE   For emphasis, a direct object may come before a subject and a verb.

EXAMPLE   What an excellent safety **record** the driver holds! [Holds
what? *Record.*]

11i   An *indirect object* is a word or group of words that comes between a
transitive verb and a direct object and tells *to whom* or *to what,* or
for whom or *for what,* the action of the verb is done.

EXAMPLES   Mr. Jacobs showed our **class** slides of Albert Pinkham Ryder's
paintings. [Showed to whom? *Class.*]
Pedro gave the **shelter** his extra wool sweaters and pants. [Gave
to what? *Shelter.*]

NOTE   Do not confuse an adverb for a complement. Also, do not mistake a
word in a prepositional phrase for a complement.

EXAMPLES   Janet plays **well.** [The adverb *well* tells *how* Janet plays.]
Janet plays **with the band.** [The noun *band* is the object of
the preposition *with.*]

EXERCISE 6   Identifying Direct and Indirect Objects

Underline the direct objects once and indirect objects twice in each of the sentences below. [Note: Not every sentence has an indirect object.]

EX.   1. Jared fed his baby brother a bottle of milk.

1. The department gave Constance a surprise retirement party.
2. Lorenzo collected aluminum cans and plastic bottles for recycling.
3. Mrs. Duffy fed her roses the new plant food.
4. The engineer showed David and Mateo the design for the water system.
5. What a dramatic role the actor played!
6. The judge gave her a lenient sentence.
7. Sam demonstrated the new machinery to the production staff.
8. Aunt Sarah brought my sister and me a gift from her trip.
9. Melvin showed Ruben and Sally his notes on the political debate.
10. Brandon served the guests fresh sea bass and a salad.
11. Ramon and Maya built a front porch for their mother's house.
12. The architect showed the principal the plans for the school's new gym.
13. Emily's brilliant news articles won the magazine many awards.
14. The stranger gave us directions to the nearest museum.
15. Mr. Chan showed the students a slide show about early computers.

EXERCISE 7   Writing Direct Objects and Indirect Objects

On your own paper, finish the sentences below according to the guidelines. In your sentences, underline the direct objects once and and indirect objects twice.

EX.   1. Vera told _____ . (*Add a direct and an indirect object.*)
         1. Vera told me a secret about the new recreation center.

1. Please give _____ . (*Add a direct and an indirect object.*)
2. Stan read _____ . (*Add a direct and an indirect object.*)
3. Do you know _____ ? (*Add a compound direct object.*)
4. Cassie suggested _____ . (*Add a direct object.*)
5. She promised _____ . (*Add a direct and an indirect object.*)
6. Tito wrote _____ . (*Add a direct and an indirect object.*)
7. I understand _____ . (*Add a direct object.*)
8. Ho handed _____ . (*Add a direct and an indirect object.*)
9. Joel interviewed _____ . (*Add a direct object.*)
10. We showed _____ . (*Add a direct and an indirect object.*)

OBJECTIVE COMPLEMENTS

> **11j** An *objective complement* is a word or group of words that helps complete the meaning of a transitive verb by identifying or modifying the direct object.
>
> An objective complement may be a noun or an adjective. The complement may also be compound.
>
> EXAMPLES Eli and Joy named their son **Kai.**
>
> Tony painted the fence **green** and **white.**
>
> Only a few verbs take an objective complement: *consider, make,* and verbs that can be replaced by *consider* or *make,* such as *appoint, call, choose, elect, name, cut, paint,* and *sweep.*

EXERCISE 8 Identifying Objective Complements

Underline the objective complement in each of the sentences below.

EX. 1. The contestants considered the questions <u>difficult</u>.

1. The judge found the jury's decision surprising.

2. The students elected Veronica treasurer.

3. They named the new restaurant Pasta Pasta.

4. Ben painted the kitchen walls blue.

5. Nina made the shower invitations pink and silver.

6. Herb swept the sidewalk clean.

7. The neighborhood appointed Kim chairperson of the block party.

8. Many student volunteers made the dance a success.

9. Lena named her two dogs Holly and Chester.

10. The salesperson called the hand cream miraculous.

11. Tomás cut the puzzle pieces smaller.

12. The summer rains made the islands green and lush.

13. Everyone thinks him reliable.

14. Jiro thought the exam simple.

15. Katherine dyed the wool purple.

REVIEW EXERCISE

A. Identifying Complete Subjects and Verbs

For each sentence below, put brackets around the complete subject. Then underline the simple subject once and the verb twice. Be sure to include all parts of a compound subject or a compound verb.

EX. 1. [Antonia and Maria] visited their friends over summer break.

1. My friends Sylvia, Anna, and Felicia live in California.

2. The bus ride lasted many hours and exhausted Antonia and Maria.

3. The bus driver and the passengers stopped for meals in small towns.

4. Antonia and Maria had seats near the driver.

5. Arriving in San Franciso, Antonia and Maria saw their

   friends' waving hands and smiling faces.

B. Identifying Direct Objects, Indirect Objects, and Objective Complements

Identify the italicized complement in each of the following sentences. On the line before each sentence, write *d.o.* for *direct object*, *i.o.* for *indirect object*, or *obj. c.* for *objective complement*.

EX. _d.o._ 1. Mesopotamians invented the *umbrella* 3,400 years ago.

_____ 1. Early umbrellas protected *Mesopotamians* from the desert sun.

_____ 2. Even today, ancient traditions decide the *use* of the umbrella.

_____ 3. In many African societies, umbrella bearers protect *chiefs* from the sun.

_____ 4. The ancient Egyptians considered the umbrella *religious* and *heavenly*.

_____ 5. As a high honor, a leader might offer *someone* the umbrella.

_____ 6. Whether made of palm leaves, feathers, or stretched papyrus, the Egyptian umbrella and its shade symbolized royal *protection*.

_____ 7. The Greeks and Romans borrowed the *idea* of the umbrella from the Egyptians.

_____ 8. Greek women considered the white parasol a *status symbol*.

_____ 9. In the first century A.D., a Roman emperor gave *women* the right to protect themselves from the rain with umbrellas.

_____ 10. Roman women gave their paper *umbrellas* a coating of oil.

SUBJECT COMPLEMENTS

A *subject complement* is a word or word group that completes the meaning of a linking verb and identifies or modifies the subject.

11k A *predicate nominative* is the word or group of words that follows a linking verb and refers to the same person or thing as the subject of the verb.

EXAMPLES   Mary Cassatt was a famous impressionist **painter.** [The noun *painter* refers to the subject *Mary Cassatt*.]

Mrs. Fitzgerald was **one** of the school board candidates. [The pronoun *one* refers to the subject *Mrs. Fitzgerald*.]

11l A *predicate adjective* is an adjective that follows a linking verb and modifies the subject of the verb.

EXAMPLES   The autumn sky is **blustery.** [The adjective *blustery* modifies the subject *sky*.]

All of the contestants looked **nervous** but **excited.** [The adjectives *nervous* and *excited* modify the subject *All*.]

NOTE   A predicate nominative or a predicate adjective may be compound.

EXAMPLES   The winners are **Adela** and **Pedro.** [compound predicate nominative]

Our weather was **cold, rainy,** and **windy.** [compound predicate adjective]

EXERCISE 9   Identifying Linking Verbs and Subject Complements

In each of the following sentences, underline the subject complement once and the linking verb twice. On the line before the sentence, identify the complement by writing *p.n.* for *predicate nominative* or *p.a.* for *predicate adjective*.

EX.   _p.a._ 1. Last night the honking geese <u>sounded</u> <u>lonely</u>.

_____ 1. Usually, autumn nights are quiet and calm.

_____ 2. From my bedroom window, the trees look bent and craggy.

_____ 3. In my backyard, the tree with the thick, black trunk is an oak.

_____ 4. Of all the trees in our yard, the oak is the oldest one.

_____ 5. Now all of the trees are bare.

_____ 6. What a wonderful season autumn is!

_____ 7. The days grow shorter.

_____ 8. Cool temperatures and brisk winds feel refreshing.

_____ 9. An autumn moon can be golden and bright.

_____ 10. Of the four seasons, autumn appears the most colorful time to me.

_____ 11. Neighbors are busy with preparations for the cold weather.

_____ 12. Mulching trees and bushes is a necessary chore before the arrival of winter.

_____ 13. The bush with the bronze, drooping blossom heads is a hydrangea.

_____ 14. The hydrangea flowers remain bronze all through the winter.

_____ 15. Those striking flowers with the yellow petals and black centers are black-eyed Susans.

_____ 16. Both black-eyed Susans and bee balm are good sources of seeds for birds in winter.

_____ 17. Bee balm smells spicy.

_____ 18. After a frost, bee balm leaves become gray and brown.

_____ 19. In autumn, almost all of the flowers look scraggly and worn.

_____ 20. The season of renewal is spring.

EXERCISE 10   Writing Subject Complements

Complete each of the sentences below with the type of subject complement requested in parentheses. Write your answers on the lines provided.

EX.   1. The runners in the park are (_predicate adjective_) _____energetic_____ .

1. My cousin Tita is (_predicate nominative_) _____ .

2. The trees are (_predicate adjective_) _____ .

3. The winners of the music scholarships are (_compound predicate nominative_) _____ .

4. All of the candidates look (_compound predicate adjective_) _____

_____ .

5. The owner of the new home on Sierra Street is (_predicate nominative_)

_____ .

CLASSIFICATION OF SENTENCES

Sentences may be classified according to purpose.

11m A *declarative sentence* makes a statement. It is followed by a period.

EXAMPLES George Washington was the first president of the United States**.**
The front tires on the car are flat, and I will have to fix them**.**

11n An *interrogative sentence* asks a question. It is followed by a question mark.

EXAMPLES Have you ever traveled to Colorado**?**
Do you like stir-fry made with vegetables and tofu**?**

11o An *imperative sentence* makes a request or gives a command. It is usually followed by a period. A very strong command, however, is followed by an exclamation point.

EXAMPLES Please give me the date of my dentist appointment**.**
Stop running**!**

11p An *exclamatory sentence* expresses strong feeling or shows excitement. It is followed by an exclamation point.

EXAMPLES What a motivating speech she gave**!**
Oh, you were hired for the job**!**

EXERCISE 11 Classifying the Four Kinds of Sentences

Classify each of the following sentences. On the line before each sentence, write *dec.* for *declarative*, *inter.* for *interrogative*, *imp.* for *imperative*, or *excl.* for *exclamatory*. Then add the appropriate end mark to each sentence.

EX. _imp._ 1. Please lend me your copy of *As You Like It*

_____ 1. Have you finished your writing assignment

_____ 2. Call the paramedics—now

_____ 3. Fruits and vegetables are good for you, and you should eat two to four servings of each daily

_____ 4. Is Boston the capital of Massachusetts

_____ 5. What is your favorite movie

_____ 6. What an inspired leader she is

_____ 7. I've heard that downhill skiing can be an exciting and exhilarating sport, but it looks dangerous to me

_____ 8. Which do you enjoy more, Chinese food or Italian food

_____ 9. Please call Phoebe after school

_____ 10. Mr. DeSoto told me that repairing plaster walls can be difficult and time-consuming work

_____ 11. Help me

_____ 12. Have you ever traveled to Spain

_____ 13. Kim and Alex are the best artists in our class, but Ernesto has the most original ideas

_____ 14. What an amazing performance that was

_____ 15. Write your answers on a separate piece of paper

_____ 16. Oh, no, you've ruined the experiment

_____ 17. When did you publish your first story

_____ 18. Dogs can be loyal companions; however, they do require a good deal of care and attention

_____ 19. What did you eat for breakfast

_____ 20. Poor thing, you look absolutely exhausted

_____ 21. My friends will be arriving soon

_____ 22. How long is that scarf

_____ 23. Stop the show

_____ 24. Please give Jeremy the message as soon as he gets home from work

_____ 25. Oh, I'm late

EXERCISE 12   Writing Sentences

On your own paper, write ten sentences using each of the four types of sentences at least once. After each sentence, write *dec.* for *declarative, inter.* for *interrogative, imp.* for *imperative,* or *excl.* for *exclamatory.* Be sure to add the appropriate end mark to each sentence.

EX.   1. Do you know the answer? (inter.)

CHAPTER REVIEW

A. Identifying Subjects, Verbs, and Complements

On the line before each sentence below, identify the underlined word or word group by writing *s.* for *subject*, *v.* for *verb*, or *c.* for *complement*. Classify each complement by writing *d.o.* for *direct object*, *i.o.* for *indirect object*, *obj. c.* for *objective complement*, *p.n.* for *predicate nominative*, or *p.a.* for *predicate adjective*.

EX. _____*c. (p.n.)*_____ 1. The Marx Brothers were popular <u>comedians</u> on the stage, the screen, and the radio.

_____ 1. Famous for their inventive humor, the <u>Marx Brothers</u> made film versions of their stage comedies in the late 1920s.

_____ 2. *Duck Soup, Animal Crackers,* and *A Night at the Opera* are their best-known <u>pictures</u>.

_____ 3. Groucho Marx was a <u>master</u> of the wisecrack.

_____ 4. In his unpredictable style, Groucho often <u>strode</u> with bent knees across the stage floor.

_____ 5. In contrast to Groucho's busy actions, Harpo Marx calmly played <u>music</u> on the harp.

_____ 6. A third brother, Chico Marx, played the <u>piano</u> and even smashed it on one occasion.

_____ 7. All five of the original Marx brothers were <u>successful</u>, but Gummo Marx left the act.

_____ 8. During World War II, Chico became a band leader, and Zeppo was a theatrical <u>agent</u>.

_____ 9. Groucho Marx brought his <u>fans</u> much entertainment as the television quizmaster on *You Bet Your Life*.

_____ 10. Many years have passed since Julius Henry Marx named his memorable character <u>Groucho</u>.

B. Classifying Sentences

Identify each of the following sentences. On the line before each sentence, write *dec.* for *declarative*, *inter.* for *interrogative*, *imp.* for *imperative*, or *excl.* for *exclamatory*. Then add the appropriate end mark to each sentence.

EX. ___*dec.*___ 1. The raspberry bushes produced many berries this year

_____ 1. Please open the door for me

_____ 2. Why wasn't Marlene in school today

_____ 3. Tamisha wants to be a photographer

_____ 4. What an important scientific breakthrough this is

_____ 5. We cleaned the house before leaving for the movie

_____ 6. Visit the seashore's fine seafood restaurants and miles of beaches

_____ 7. Are you registering for the photography workshop

_____ 8. What a wonderful birthday

_____ 9. Is there a job opening for a cashier on weekends

_____ 10. The extended forecast calls for a chance of snow flurries on Wednesday

C. Writing Sentences

On your own paper, write one sentence according to each of the guidelines below. In your sentences, underline the words that indicate the italicized sentence parts. Also, use a variety of subjects, verbs, and complements in your sentences.

EX.   1. an interrogatory sentence with a compound indirect object
    1. Did you bring <u>Harry</u> and <u>Cora</u> their new books?

1. a declarative sentence with a *compound subject*
2. an exclamatory sentence with a *direct object*
3. a declarative sentence with a *predicate nominative*
4. an interrogative sentence with a *compound predicate adjective*
5. an imperative sentence with an *indirect object*
6. an interrogative sentence with a *compound verb*
7. a declarative sentence with a *direct object*
8. an exclamatory sentence with an *indirect object*
9. an interrogative sentence with a *predicate nominative*
10. an imperative sentence with a *compound direct object*
11. an exclamatory sentence with a *predicate adjective*
12. a declarative sentence with an *indirect object and a direct object*
13. an imperative sentence with a *compound verb*
14. an interrogative sentence with a *compound direct object*
15. a declarative sentence with a *compound verb*

PREPOSITIONAL PHRASES

12a A *phrase* is a group of related words that is used as a single part of speech and does not contain both a verb and its subject.

12b A *prepositional phrase* is a group of words consisting of a preposition, a noun or pronoun that serves as the *object of the preposition*, and any modifiers of that object.

EXAMPLES   The brick house **with the green shutters** is Jaime's home. [The noun *shutters* is the object of the preposition *with*.]
Behind it are a vegetable garden and raspberry bushes. [The pronoun *it* is the object of the preposition *Behind*.]

An object of a preposition may be compound.

EXAMPLE   **Near the garden and raspberry bushes,** wasps are building a nest. [Both *garden* and *bushes* are objects of the preposition *Near*.]

☞ **REFERENCE NOTE:** For lists of prepositions, see page 125.

EXERCISE 1   Identifying Prepositional Phrases and Their Objects

Find the prepositional phrase in each of the following sentences. Underline the preposition once and the object of the preposition twice.

EX.   [1]   We drove <u>through</u> the <u>park</u> to see the ice skaters.

[1] Ice skaters swirled across the frozen pond. [2] Above them shone a bright moon and starry sky. [3] Spectators watched from the park benches. [4] Everyone was bundled in bulky, woolen layers. [5] Occasionally, a spectator went into the warming house. [6] Only the skaters, with their glowing faces, seemed oblivious of the cold. [7] Inside the warming house, a young park employee named Salvadore tended a crackling fire and served hot cider. [8] Pairs of skates were lined up by the hearth. [9] Salvadore stoked the fire and from the window longingly watched the skaters. [10] He was eager to join the other skaters and glide across the ice in his new skates. [11] Under his breath, he muttered something. [12] A few

more spectators came through the door of the warming house. [13] One of the spectators stood beside Salvadore. [14] He was a tall, elderly gentleman wearing a bright red scarf around his neck. [15] "Young man, why aren't you on the ice?" he asked Salvadore. [16] Salvadore explained that he was working but pointed to his skates underneath a bench. [17] After much discussion, Salvadore loaned the man his skates. [18] On the man's feet, the skates gleamed. [19] Thanking Salvadore, the man bowed and skated swiftly across the pond. [20] Salvadore smiled as his new friend twirled in front of the spectators, the tail of his bright red scarf waving behind him.

EXERCISE 2   Writing a Design Report

Write a description of your dream house for an architect. Remember to include bathrooms and closets. On your own paper, write ten sentences about your house. Include at least ten prepositional phrases. Underline each prepositional phrase that you use.

EX.   1.   A large closet <u>for coats</u> is <u>to the right.</u>

THE QUIGMANS   by Buddy Hickerson

"We the people, of the people, for the people, by the people, above the people, under the people, beside the people, behind the people..."

Overly thorough, lesser known Founding Father Clive Fishburne delivers his Preposition Proclamation.

ADJECTIVE PHRASES AND ADVERB PHRASES

12c An *adjective phrase* is a prepositional phrase that modifies a noun or a pronoun.

An adjective phrase tells *what kind* or *which one*. An adjective phrase always follows the word it modifies.

EXAMPLES   A glass **of iced tea** is refreshing. [The phrase modifies the noun *glass*, telling *what kind*.]

Her eyes looked like those **of her mother.** [The phrase modifies the pronoun *those*, telling *which ones*.]

The treasure **at the edge of the old graveyard** was never found. [The phrase *at the edge* modifies the noun *treasure*. *Edge* is the object of the preposition *at*. The phrase *of the old graveyard* modifies *edge*.]

12d An *adverb phrase* is a prepositional phrase that modifies a verb, an adjective, or an adverb.

An adverb phrase tells *how, when, where, why*, or *to what extent*.

EXAMPLES   The helicopter hovered **over the landing pad.** [The phrase modifies the verb *hovered*, telling *where*.]

Her clothing was black **with soot and mud.** [The phrase modifies the adjective *black*, telling *how*.]

We painted the house completely **except for the window trim.** [The phrase modifies the adverb *completely*, telling *to what extent*.]

An adverb phrase, unlike an adjective phrase, can precede the word it modifies.

EXAMPLE   **During his friend's stay,** Mr. Bruce slept **on the floor in a sleeping bag.** [Each phrase modifies the verb *slept*. *During his friend's stay* tells *when*; *on the floor* tells *where*; and *in a sleeping bag* tells *how*.]

More than one prepositional phrase can modify the same word.

EXAMPLE   The picture **of the author on the book jacket** is quite flattering. [Each phrase modifies the noun *picture*. Both *of the author* and *on the book jacket* tell *which one*.]

EXERCISE 3   **Identifying Adjective and Adverb Phrases**

In the sentences below, underline each adjective phrase once and each adverb phrase twice.

EX.   1.   The greatest number of grasshoppers live in grasslands and semi-arid regions.

 1.   Their colors range from green to brown.

 2.   Markings of red or yellow appear on some grasshoppers.

 3.   Organs for smell are located on a grasshopper's antennae.

 4.   Grasshoppers also have a sense of touch.

 5.   They have feelers on their heads, legs, and abdomens.

 6.   Grasshoppers actually leap through the air, although they do have wings.

 7.   Some grasshoppers lay their eggs on underwater plants.

 8.   The katydid is a type of grasshopper.

 9.   Katydids live on trees and in bushes or grasses.

10.   Many species of katydid look like leaves.

11.   Katydids are known as singers.

12.   Locusts, which can devastate crops when they migrate in swarms, are also grasshoppers.

13.   Locusts fly in the air in swarms when their body temperatures rise.

14.   In 1889, a huge swarm was seen crossing the Red Sea.

15.   Stopping a locust swarm in motion is nearly impossible.

EXERCISE 4   **Revising Sentences Using Prepositional Phrases**

For each of the sentences below, add a prepositional phrase as a modifier. Use at least five adjective phrases and five adverb phrases. Classify each phrase and underline the word each phrase modifies. Write your sentences on your own paper.

EX.   1.   The tree leaves fell.
            1.   The tree leaves fell in the yard. (adverb)

 1.   The woman stepped quickly.
 2.   Is that your camera?
 3.   Let's go.
 4.   Do you still have salamanders?
 5.   I will write them a letter.
 6.   The goats are loose!
 7.   "How many do you want?" Loretta asked.
 8.   That stuff is hers.
 9.   I love tomatoes.
10.   The cat looks quite comfortable.

PARTICIPLES AND PARTICIPIAL PHRASES

A *verbal* is a form of a verb used as a noun, an adjective, or an adverb. The three kinds of verbals are the *participle*, the *gerund*, and the *infinitive*.

A *verbal phrase* consists of a verbal and its modifiers and complements.

12e   A *participle* is a verb form that is used as an adjective.

There are two kinds of participles—the *present participle* and the *past participle*. The perfect tense of a participle is formed with a past participle and the helping verb *having*.

PRESENT   **Smiling**, the two sisters waved to the class. [*Smiling*, a form of the verb *smile*, modifies the noun *sisters*.]

Paco heard something **rustling** outside the tent. [*Rustling*, a form of the verb *rustle*, modifies the pronoun *something*.]

PAST   The **grilled** catfish with lemon tasted delicious. [*Grilled*, a form of the verb *grill*, modifies the noun *catfish*.]

Thrilled and excited, they scrambled into the roller-coaster car. [*Thrilled*, a form of the verb *thrill*, and *excited*, a form of the verb *excite*, modify the pronoun *they*.]

PERFECT   **Having studied** all day, Jessica was ready for her test. [*Having studied*, a form of the verb *study*, modifies the noun *Jessica*.]

Having been soaked by the rain, the cat looked unhappy. [*Having been soaked*, a form of the verb *soak*, modifies the noun *cat*.]

12f   A *participial phrase* consists of a participle and all of the words related to the participle.

EXAMPLES   **Running along the lakefront**, a group of joggers stopped to watch the sunrise. [The participial phrase modifies the noun *group*. The adverb phrase *along the lakefront* modifies the present participle *Running*.]

Eduardo, **delighted immensely by the book**, lent it to his best friend. [The participial phrase modifies the noun *Eduardo*.]

EXERCISE 5   Identifying Participles and Participial Phrases

Underline the participles and participial phrases used as adjectives in the following sentences.

EX.   1.   <u>Having cleaned her room</u>, Gemma went outside for a walk.

1.   Allison, racing down the stairs, dropped her books.

2. Michael's father served baked chicken with wild rice and mushrooms.

3. Waiting for her ride to school, Marie saw a deer leap into the woods.

4. Having written a short story, Andrew asked Carmen to read it.

5. Tuned to perfection, the engine purred.

6. Finding herself alone in the house, Amanda turned up the stereo.

7. The wooden floors, having been rubbed with oil, gleamed.

8. My brother and sister start their cooking lessons next week.

9. We could see shooting stars in the sky.

10. The group of friends, having dined together, sat and talked for hours.

EXERCISE 6   **Identifying Participles and Participial Phrases
and the Words They Modify**

Underline once the participles and participial phrases in the following sentences. Then underline twice the word or words each participle or participial phrase modifies.

EX.   1.   <u>Known as the "Iron Horse,"</u> <u>Lou Gehrig</u> was one of baseball's greatest hitters.

1. Basking in the audience's applause, Mavis took a deep bow.

2. Named after a Bantu word for *okra*, gumbo is a spicy Creole stew.

3. Speaking eloquently, the First Lady captivated the senators.

4. The reward, announced in the newspaper, was a large sum of money.

5. The retriever, known for his gentle nature, played catch with the children.

6. Waving from the car, the O' Shea family left on vacation.

7. In your own words, explain each concept presented in the first chapter.

8. The potluck dinner, grilled chicken and steamed corn, tasted surprisingly good.

9. Having measured and marked the wood, the carpenter began to saw.

10. We heard something tapping on the window.

11. Someone's pager, beeping loudly, alarmed the cockatiel.

12. Can you find the creatures hidden in this picture puzzle?

13. The Parthenon, visited by tourists and scholars, overlooks the city of Athens, Greece.

14. Living on a farm, I always have something to do.

15. My father, writing a book on cacti, teaches in the botany department.

GERUNDS AND GERUND PHRASES

12g A *gerund* is a verb form ending in *–ing* that is used as a noun.

Like nouns, gerunds can be subjects, predicate nominatives, direct objects, or objects of prepositions.

EXAMPLES   **Yodeling** is my favorite type of music. [subject]
One good aerobic sport is **skating**. [predicate nominative]
I do not like **collecting** stamps as much as I used to. [direct object]
In school we heard a lecture on **voting**. [object of a preposition]

Do not confuse a gerund with a present participle used as part of a verb phrase or as an adjective.

GERUND   The teachers have finished **eating** lunch. [*Eating* is the direct object of the verb *have finished*.]

PRESENT   The teachers **are** still **eating** lunch. [*Eating* is part of the verb
PARTICIPLES   phrase *are eating*.]
The teachers **eating** lunch will finish soon. [*Eating* is used as an adjective to modify the noun *teachers*.]

12h A *gerund phrase* consists of a gerund and any modifiers and complements it may have. The entire gerund phrase acts as a noun.

Like gerunds, gerund phrases can be subjects, predicate nominatives, direct objects, or objects of prepositions.

EXAMPLES   **Walking in deep sand** is good for your feet. [The phrase is the subject of the sentence.]
His problem now was **getting the part back into the box**. [The phrase is a predicate nominative.]
I really like **riding my skateboard fast**. [The phrase is the object of the verb *like*.]
You don't need binoculars for **birdwatching from Terry's house**. [The phrase is the object of the preposition *for*.]

NOTE   When a noun or a pronoun comes immediately before a gerund, it is in the possessive form and is considered part of the gerund phrase.

EXAMPLES   **Demi's whistling** woke the baby.
When he's awake, the baby likes **her whistling.**

EXERCISE 7   Identifying Gerunds and Gerund Phrases and Their Uses

Underline the gerunds or gerund phrases in the sentences below. Then on the line before each sentence, identify how each gerund or gerund phrase is used by writing *s.* for *subject, p.n.* for *predicate nominative, d.o.* for *direct object,* or *o.p.* for *object of a preposition.*

EX. ___*o.p.*___ 1. I feel like washing the windows today.

_____ 1. Some people deal with their feelings by talking about them.

_____ 2. Sweeping that barn will take some time.

_____ 3. I don't like being here any more than you do.

_____ 4. Much effort goes into throwing a good party.

_____ 5. "How do you like using your new desk, Jo?"

_____ 6. I'd advise wearing a sweater when you go.

_____ 7. Mom got a ticket for running a red light.

_____ 8. Suturing the incision is one of the last steps in surgery.

_____ 9. The choir was going to the meeting hall for singing and ice cream.

_____ 10. The tar's sticking to Melba's shoe posed a problem.

_____ 11. Printing was invented in Europe in the 1450s.

_____ 12. I like collecting shells and cataloging them.

_____ 13. Do you enjoy working at the clinic?

_____ 14. Reading the newspaper is a daily activity for me.

_____ 15. The pioneer family's dream was owning their own farmland.

_____ 16. He signaled by raising his right hand.

_____ 17. Estimating the number of beans in the jar is almost impossible.

_____ 18. The problem is getting someone to donate furniture for the play.

_____ 19. Phyllis always makes time for reading to the kindergarten class.

_____ 20. There is a renewed interest in raising funds for a new gym.

INFINITIVES AND INFINITIVE PHRASES

12i An *infinitive* is a verb form that can be used as a noun, an adjective, or an adverb. An infinitive usually begins with *to*.

NOUN   **To act** on stage is Melissa's dream.
ADJECTIVE Her first attempt **to act** was a success.
ADVERB   Finally, Melissa moved to New York **to act.**

The word *to*, the sign of the infinitive, is sometimes omitted.

EXAMPLES   Let them [to] **eat** cake.
Make them all [to] **wash** their hands.
You ought not [to] **stand** like that.

12j An *infinitive phrase* consists of an infinitive and all of the words related to the infinitive.

EXAMPLES   Rebecca plans **to move to another neighborhood soon.**
Because of the barking dogs, Lisa was unable **to finish the chapter.**

NOTE   Unlike other verbals, an infinitive may have a subject. Such a construction is called an *infinitive clause.*

EXAMPLE   Luc wanted **Enzo to pour the milk.** [*Enzo* is the subject of the infinitive *to pour.* The entire infinitive clause is the direct object of the verb *wanted.*]

EXERCISE 8   Identifying Infinitives

Underline the infinitives in the following paragraph.

EX.   [1] <u>To learn</u> and <u>to understand</u> Italian cooking, read Marcella Hazan's cookbooks.

[1] In her cookbook's introduction, Ms. Hazan writes that simple, satisfying food has only one objective: to taste good. [2] This cookbook, *Marcella's Italian Kitchen,* lists a few "elementary rules" to teach the basics of making Italian food. [3] Use no other oil but olive oil to dress salads. [4] Grate fresh cheese when you are ready to use it. [5] Other introductory notes teach how to choose and to store olive oil. [6] To have the fresh and vital taste of an Italian dish, fresh tomatoes are required. [7] Ms. Hazan asks us never to forget the fresh, ripe tomato. [8] To keep tomatoes fresh in

winter, hang them in clusters on the vine in an airy, cool, dry place. [9] To compose an Italian menu, begin the meal with a soup or pasta, followed by fish or meat and a vegetable, and then a salad. [10] Some food can be prepared ahead of time, but plan to spend time in the kitchen just before the meal.

EXERCISE 9   Identifying Infinitive Phrases Used as Adjectives and Adverbs

Underline the infinitive phrases in the sentences below. Then, on the line before each sentence, write *adj.* if the phrase is used as an adjective or *adv.* if it is used as an adverb. Circle the word the phrase modifies.

EX.   _adv._   1. Janet (searched) her closet to find the missing button.

_____   1. With his friend Carlos, Juan helped Frank to paint his house.

_____   2. The person to ask for advice is your mother.

_____   3. Was Hannah's attempt to grow asparagus a success?

_____   4. Dad made me sort the recyclables before I could go to play basketball.

_____   5. With their friends, Vanessa and Kim went to the park to ski.

_____   6. Fritz said, "I doubt I'll live to see the day you beat Nashota in tennis."

_____   7. The Bears is the team to watch this year.

_____   8. To play goalie, I need a different stick.

_____   9. Trulia has a plan to revive the Yellow Knights.

_____ 10. The ship offloaded in Bangkok to make room for passengers.

EXERCISE 10   Identifying and Classifying Infinitive Phrases and Infinitive Clauses Used as Nouns

Underline the infinitive phrases and infinitive clauses in the sentences below. Then, on the line before each sentence, identify the function of each phrase by writing *s.* for *subject*, *d.o.* for *direct object*, or *p.n.* for *predicate nominative*.

EX.   _d.o._   1. I've always wanted to play bagpipes.

_____   1. Julio's brother reminded him to drive carefully in the rain.

_____   2. To pick apples is a special pleasure on an autumn afternoon.

_____   3. The office manager wanted Mario to apply for the new position.

_____   4. Kwok often asks his grandfather to tell a story.

_____   5. Alice's dream is to write a book about her grandmother.

REVIEW EXERCISE

A. Identifying Adjective and Adverb Phrases

In the sentences below, classify each italicized phrase. On the line before the sentence, write *adj. phr.* for *adjective phrase* or *adv. phr.* for *adverb phrase.*

EX. __adj. phr.__ 1. The child *in the sunbonnet* played on the beach.

_____ 1. Visiting our classroom, the dentist gave a lecture *about oral hygiene.*

_____ 2. On horseback, the rangers rode along the border *between Mexico and Texas.*

_____ 3. The cardinals flocked *to the special sunflower feeder.*

_____ 4. We attended the pep rally *after school.*

_____ 5. Enjoying her trip to the museum, Andrea hid *behind the marble sarcophagus.*

_____ 6. The neighbors *down the block* play polka music all day long.

_____ 7. *With its long, slinky body,* the snake slithered its way across the short grass.

_____ 8. *After deliberating for days,* the jury reached a decision.

_____ 9. At our favorite Chinese restaurant, Randall ordered chicken *with peanuts and hot pepper sauce.*

_____ 10. Trying to get Andy's attention, Jeremy yelled *across the room.*

B. Identifying Participial, Gerund, and Infinitive Phrases

On the line before each of the following sentences, identify the italicized phrase by writing *part. phr.* for *participial phrase,* *ger. phr.* for *gerund phrase,* or *inf. phr.* for *infinitive phrase.*

EX. __ger. phr.__ 1. By *gathering the suspects together,* the detective heightened the suspense.

_____ 1. *Swimming laps early in the morning* keeps me fit.

_____ 2. *To stop the river from overflowing,* volunteers placed thousands of sandbags along the banks.

_____ 3. *Nodding his head,* the student answered without speaking.

_____ 4. *Sipping a cup of hot jasmine tea* usually relaxes me in the evening.

_____ 5. The dog, *having been lost for a week*, looked shabby, hungry, and completely exhausted.

_____ 6. You'd better get down if you don't want *to fall from there*.

_____ 7. After *breaking the car window*, the emergency rescue team pulled Vlad from the wreck.

_____ 8. Mona listened carefully, *tuning the string* to the exact pitch.

_____ 9. "How did you enjoy *seeing The Nutcracker*, Kishi?"

_____ 10. Where there is smoke, there is not always fire *blazing out of control*.

C.   Using Phrases to Combine Sentences

Combine each group of sentences below into one sentence by changing the italicized sentence into a participial, a gerund, or an infinitive phrase. Use the hints in parentheses to help you. Write the new sentences on your own paper.

EX.   1. Tamara wanted to go to the beach. *She finished her finals on Tuesday.* (participle)

    1. Finishing her finals on Tuesday, Tamara wanted to go to the beach.

1. Robin hiked through part of the Sierra Nevada National Forest. *She stopped at Isabella Lake.* (participle)

2. *She discovered that she is allergic to eggs.* Now she makes salads for breakfast. (participle)

3. Caroline and Jack arrived early for the party. *They helped decorate.* (infinitive)

4. My friend Sheila writes poetry. *She began this while she was still in high school.* (gerund)

5. Cats see well in dim light. *They prowl and hunt at twilight.* (participle)

6. Marvella looked for a paper clip. *She had used the last staple.* (participle)

7. The church group sold homemade sandwiches. *The group was raising money.* (infinitive)

8. J. D. and Phoebe visited an island for their anniversary. *The island lies in the Caribbean Sea.* (participle)

9. The car had a flat tire. *It sat in the parking lot.* (participle)

10. Warren went to the mall. *He bought new shoes.* (infinitive)

APPOSITIVES AND APPOSITIVE PHRASES

12k An *appositive* **is a noun or a pronoun placed beside another noun or pronoun to identify or explain it.**

EXAMPLES Kimiko visited with her, the next-door **neighbor.** [The noun *neighbor* identifies the pronoun *her*.]
Sam Begay, my **neighbor** and best **friend**, won a scholarship to Arizona State University. [The nouns *neighbor* and *friend* explain the noun *Sam Begay*.]

12l **An *appositive phrase* consists of an appositive and its modifiers.**

EXAMPLES Those library books, **the ones that are overdue**, are mine.
For dinner we ate garden-fresh tomatoes and corn on the cob, **two of Luis's favorite foods**.

NOTE An appositive usually follows the word it identifies or explains. For emphasis, however, an appositive may come at the beginning of a sentence.

EXAMPLES Miguel, **the winner of the award,** thanked his parents. [The noun *winner* refers to the noun *Miguel*.]
An African American frontiersman, James Beckwourth discovered an important route through the Sierra Nevada mountains. [The noun *frontiersman* explains the noun *James Beckwourth*.]

EXERCISE 11   Identifying Appositives

Underline the appositive in each sentence. Then circle the word or words the appositive identifies or explains.

EX.   1. Those garden (tools), the ones near the shed, are Mary's.

1. My friends Mary and Hector are helping me plant bulbs and bushes.

2. Hector's wheelbarrow, the one that is bright green, will carry a full load of compost.

3. Yesterday we tilled the back border, the location for the peony bushes.

4. Lemi's favorite flowers, peonies and daffodils, are my favorite flowers, too.

5. Hector, an expert on peonies, has brought me many new varieties.

6. We'll place the boldest colors, magenta and purple, near the porch steps.

7. Whites and pinks, the most subdued colors, we'll place along the border.

8. "Jack Snipe," a variety of narcissus, will surround the peonies in clusters.

9. In March and April, the months for early bloomers, bright yellow daffodil heads will pop up from the soil.

10. Mary and Hector, fellow enthusiasts of spring, are calling for my help.

EXERCISE 12   Identifying Appositive Phrases

Underline the appositive phrase in each sentence. Then circle the word or words the appositive phrase identifies or explains.

EX.   1. Student Council is holding its next meeting on (January 3), the first day after winter break.

1. Hail, ice pellets the size of walnuts, dented the car hood.

2. These fabrics, Egyptian cotton and linen, are cool and comfortable.

3. A translator fluent in five languages, Julia loves her career at the United Nations.

4. A young Pueblo potter, Diego shows a deep understanding of the generations of pottery tradition that have preceded him.

5. At the folk art exhibition we saw many traditional quilt patterns—Flying Geese, Log Cabin, and Dutch Mill.

6. Angela's sisters, owners of a clothing store, hired her to work part time after school.

7. The children were thrilled with the surprise, a calico kitten.

8. Deeply engrossed in a book, Manuel jumped when he heard the knock, a sharp rap on his door.

9. Derek's brother, a two-month-old baby, sleeps most of the time.

10. We gazed in wonder at the snow, a glittering blanket of white.

11. The biggest cow of the lot, the hungry one, is now eating happily.

12. If you are allergic to goldenrod, those tall weeds with yellow flowers, then you'd better stay away from my back yard.

13. I like adobe, that clay used in the Southwest to make houses, mostly because of its color.

14. Did you vote in the election yesterday, the one to choose the commencement speakers?

15. A magazine that comes with our Sunday paper, *Parade* has interesting articles.

CHAPTER REVIEW

A. Identifying Adjective and Adverb Phrases

On the line before each sentence below, identify each italicized phrase by writing *adj. phr.* for *adjective phrase* or *adv. phr.* for *adverb phrase*.

EX. ___adj. phr.___ 1. The almond tree *in front of the window* bloomed all spring.

_____ 1. Early *in the morning,* the courier delivered an urgent package.

_____ 2. The musicians *in the orchestra pit* had already tuned their instruments.

_____ 3. Having a map *of the museum* would be helpful.

_____ 4. In a blur, the cyclist flew *around the corner.*

_____ 5. They discovered his will *in a brittle, old book.*

_____ 6. *Before the huge audience,* Mildred delivered her lines gracefully.

_____ 7. The pair of shoes *under the bed* belongs to Joel.

_____ 8. *After the game* I'll have to finish my college application.

_____ 9. My checking account *at the bank* was closed.

_____ 10. I was *in your garage* fixing your car when the power went out.

B. Identifying Verbal Phrases and Their Functions

On the line before each of the following sentences, identify each italicized phrase by writing *part. phr.* for *participial phrase, ger. phr.* for *gerund phrase,* or *inf. phr.* for *infinitive phrase.* Then identify the function of each phrase by writing *s.* for *subject, d.o.* for *direct object, i.o.* for *indirect object, p.n.* for *predicate nominative, adj.* for *adjective,* or *adv.* for *adverb.*

EX. ___part. phr.–adj.___ 1. Kuri heard something *tapping against the window.*

_____ 1. *Having heard the noise, too,* Kuri's brother Yoshi went to the window.

_____ 2. With her brother, Kuri went outside *to look around.*

_____ 3. A good way to deal with fear is *facing the fear directly.*

_____ 4. *Sitting there listening,* she had many unpleasant thoughts.

_____ 5. *Investigating the noise* required all their courage.

_____ 6. *Having gone outside*, Kuri and Yoshi discovered the cause of their scary noise.

_____ 7. The noise was coming from a branch *scraping against the house.*

_____ 8. *Solving the mystery* gave them some relief.

_____ 9. They decided *to return to the house.*

_____ 10. They postponed *cutting off the branch until the next morning.*

C.   Writing Sentences with Phrases

On your own paper, write ten sentences according to the following guidelines. In each of your sentences, underline the italicized phrase given.

EX.   1.   Use *lost under the porch* as a participial phrase.

    1.   The kitten, <u>lost under the porch</u>, began to meow.

1. Use *humming quietly* as a participial phrase.

2. Use *down the winding road* as an adverb phrase modifying a verb.

3. Use *jogging regularly* as a gerund phrase.

4. Use *to protect the houses* as an infinitive phrase used as a modifier.

5. Use *about her trip* as an adjective phrase.

6. Use *with fresh ingredients* as an adverb phrase modifying an adjective.

7. Use *of apples and oranges* as an adjective phrase.

8. Use *listening to the music* as a participial phrase.

9. Use *to be healthy* as an infinitive phrase used as a noun.

10. Use *a wonderful speaker* as an appositive phrase.

11. Use *disappearing into the fog* as a gerund phrase.

12. Use *to fill the barn with hay* as a modifier.

13. Use *working on the motor* as a gerund phrase.

14. Use *a sleek, shiny car* as an appositive.

15. Use *away from the wasps* as an adverb phrase.

KINDS OF CLAUSES

13a An *independent* (or *main*) *clause* expresses a complete thought and can stand by itself as a sentence.

EXAMPLES **Geoffrey bought a pair of jeans.** [one independent clause]
Malcolm turned on the radio and **Juanita adjusted the antenna.** [two independent clauses joined by *and*]
Many companies are hiring part-time workers; these workers often do not have health insurance. [two independent clauses joined by a semicolon]
It rained all day after the storm arrived. [one independent clause combined with a subordinate clause]

13b A *subordinate* (or *dependent*) *clause* does not express a complete thought and cannot stand alone as a sentence.

Words such as *because, that,* or *whom* usually signal the beginning of a subordinate clause.

EXAMPLES **because** they fixed the furnace
that danced the jitterbug
whom I saw on the roof

Subordinate means less important. The meaning of a subordinate clause is complete only when the clause is attached to an independent clause.

EXAMPLES **Because they fixed the furnace,** we didn't have to replace it.
I hope the couple **who danced the jitterbug** wins the contest.
Do you know **whom I saw on the roof?**

As the preceding examples show, subordinate clauses can be located at the beginning, in the middle, or at the end of a sentence.

EXERCISE 1   Classifying Independent and Subordinate Clauses

In each of the following sentences, classify the italicized clause as independent or subordinate. On the line before each sentence, write *indep.* for *independent* or *sub.* for *subordinate.*

EX.   <u>sub.</u>   1. *Because Harry borrowed the car,* we drove to the dance.

_____ 1. The newspaper article listed the hours of the recycling center, *which opens next Monday.*

_____ 2. *Emilio bought a leather saddle* for a low price at the flea market.

_____ 3. *After they left the movie,* they decided to stop for spring rolls and tea.

_____ 4. My Zeus, *whose bark is deep and loud,* just loves to cuddle and play.

_____ 5. *Kwok made the loaf of millet bread* that is sitting on the counter.

_____ 6. I hope the woman *who played the Schubert piece* wins the piano competition.

_____ 7. Amanda filled the tub with warm water, and *Jerry lifted the dog into the bath.*

_____ 8. *At first the number of ripe tomatoes in the kitchen was overwhelming,* but now I have several jars of canned tomatoes, paste, and sauce.

_____ 9. *Many Americans believe there is a need for national health care,* which was proposed by the Clinton administration.

_____10. The panel of speakers answered several questions about international trade *after introductory comments were made.*

_____11. Paco was very upset when he saw that the boots, *which he had just bought,* had been left in the rain.

_____12. Leah put the bouquet of flowers on the table, and *Mark filled the water glasses.*

_____13. *After the recording session was over,* the musicians stayed in the studio for two hours.

_____14. *Some people freely give advice,* but seldom do they take it.

_____15. Do you know *what the Martinos named their baby daughter?*

_____16. The chef demonstrated *how he makes the dressing for the salad.*

_____17. *Mr. Thompson explained the safety-drill process,* repeating a few points for extra emphasis.

_____18. *When Linda mulched the leaves with the lawnmower,* she asked a neighbor to help.

_____19. The breakfast waffles, *which are made with sunflower seeds and pumpkin,* are Sara's specialty.

_____20. After Sharon read her essay to the class, *the students clapped.*

THE ADJECTIVE CLAUSE

13c   An *adjective clause* is a subordinate clause that modifies a noun or a pronoun.

An adjective clause follows the word or words it modifies and tells *which one* or *what kind*. An adjective clause is usually introduced by a ***relative pronoun***. The relative pronoun relates the clause to the word or words that the clause modifies.

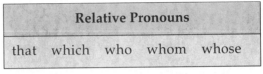

Relative Pronouns
that   which   who   whom   whose

EXAMPLES   Any traveller **who wants to reenter the country** needs a passport. [The clause modifies the noun *traveller,* telling *which one.*]
Kristina's Kitchen, **which serves the best hot cider**, is the place to go to warm up. [The clause modifies the noun phrase *Kristina's Kitchen*, telling *what kind* of restaurant.]

Sometimes the relative pronoun may be left out, but its meaning should be understood.

EXAMPLES   I'll never forget the robins **[that] we used to feed**.
Do you remember the time **[when] we went to Dodger Stadium**?

The relative adverbs *where* and *when* are sometimes used in adjective clauses.

EXAMPLES   That is the place **where the first owner is buried**.
My sister told me about the time **when she piloted an airplane.**

Depending on how it is used, an adjective clause is either essential or nonessential. An *essential clause* provides information that is necessary to the meaning of a sentence. A *nonessential clause* provides additional information that can be omitted without changing the meaning of a sentence. A nonessential clause is always set off by commas.

ESSENTIAL   Swimmers **who have entered the competition** should be in the gymnasium in one hour. [Omitting the adjective clause would change the meaning of the sentence.]
NONESSENTIAL   Sergei, **whose uncle is a composer**, plays the oboe. [The adjective clause gives extra information. Omitting the clause would not affect the meaning of the sentence.]

EXERCISE 2   Identifying Adjective Clauses and the Words Modified

In each sentence below, underline the adjective clause once and the relative pronoun or relative adverb twice. Then circle the word that the clause modifies.

EX.   1. In 1877, (Chief Joseph), who said, "I will fight no more forever," led the Nez Perce on a dramatic flight to Canada.

1. On the Ara River in Japan sits the city of Chichibu, which is known for its annual Shinto shrine festival.

2. I have seen nearly every film that this Italian director has made.

3. Our friends told us about the year when they hiked the Pacific Coast Trail.

4. From 1988 to 1992, our family lived in Texas, where our parents worked for the military.

5. I'm encouraged by volunteers who donate their time and effort.

6. Portugal is a country that I would enjoy visiting.

7. Last night we made a pasta sauce that included artichokes, calamata olives, and tomatoes.

8. Tomás's address book, which was bound in red leather, was nearly full.

9. Is there someone whom I can beat at tennis?

10. The photograph that Alfredo took was the only one taken of his grandfather.

EXERCISE 3   Revising Sentences by Using Adjective Clauses

Revise each of the sentences below by adding an adjective clause to modify the italicized noun. Write the revised sentences on your own paper. Use a variety of relative pronouns and relative adverbs to introduce your adjective clauses.

EX.   1. Helen finally found her *wallet*.

   1. Helen finally found her wallet, which she misplaced last week.

1. After school, Franklin went to the grocery *store*.

2. The broiled *salmon* tasted delicious.

3. The *fans* supported the team.

4. Somehow, Juanita heard about the surprise birthday *party*.

5. The student council *president* called the meeting to order.

THE ADVERB CLAUSE

13d **An** *adverb clause* **is a subordinate clause that modifies a verb, an adjective, or an adverb.**

An adverb clause tells *how, when, where, why, to what extent,* or *under what condition.*

EXAMPLES   Her face looked paler **than it had looked a moment before**.
[The clause modifies the adjective *paler*. It tells *to what extent* her face looked pale.]
You may miss the show **if you eat dinner very late**. [The clause modifies the verb *have*. It tells *under what conditions* you may miss the show.]

An adverb clause that introduces a sentence is set off by a comma.

EXAMPLE   **As soon as you're through,** I'm leaving.

Common Subordinating Conjunctions			
after	as though	since	when
although	because	so that	whenever
as	before	than	where
as if	how	though	wherever
as long as	if	unless	whether
as soon as	in order that	until	while

NOTE   Some subordinating conjunctions may also be used as prepositions.

13e **Part of a clause may be omitted when the meaning can be understood from the context of the sentence. A clause with such an omission is called an *elliptical clause.***

EXAMPLES   Brenda likes me better **than [she likes]** him.
When [he is] walking, he whistles patriotic tunes.

EXERCISE 4   **Identifying Adverb Clauses and the Words They Modify**

In the following sentences, underline each adverb clause once and the word or words it modifies twice.

EX.   1. Tomas took his first chess lesson when he was six years old.

1. Marie will call Patrick as soon as she knows the concert date.

2. The Falcons could win the game if they have a strong second half.

3. We changed our practice time because evening comes an hour earlier.

4. If we start now, we can avoid the seasonal shopping rush.

5. When away on a fishing trip, they call home every night.

6. Wherever they go, Mark and Kathleen take their two children.

7. Aunt Hazel lived with Alex and Kevin until her hip healed.

8. At first, speaking Spanish was embarrassing because I made mistakes.

9. If I eat an apple now, I won't eat popcorn at the movie.

10. Sondra will loan Marta her new dress tonight as long as Marta promises to return it on Sunday.

11. Whenever Ed visits, we drive to the peninsula and fish.

12. After the bolts came loose, the window shutters fell off the house.

13. Mr. Tomasini recycles more materials than anyone else in the neighborhood.

14. Before you leave, come to my office.

15. The young actress felt as though the bright lights were blinding her.

EXERCISE 5   **Building Sentences With Adverb Clauses**

On your own paper, write ten sentences that each contain an adverb clause. To create your sentences, join two clauses from the list below with a subordinating conjunction. Do not use any subordinating conjunction twice. Underline the adverb clauses in your sentences once and the subordinating conjunctions twice.

EX.   1.   the sun was shining; the children played outside

    1. Because the sun was shining, the children played outside.

the baby was asleep	I help him
the storm arrives tonight	Lana thought of her friends
the papers are signed	she whispered softly
someone surprised him	the panel will discuss the issue
Juan solves math problems quickly	the deal is complete
the topic is interesting	it is protected in a glass case
she was traveling	we'll be snowed in tomorrow
the pottery vase is old	he jumped out of his chair

THE NOUN CLAUSE

13f   A *noun clause* is a subordinate clause used as a noun.

A noun clause may be used as a subject, a predicate nominative, a direct object, an indirect object, or an object of a preposition.

SUBJECT	**What Lani told me** helped me a great deal. [The clause is the subject of the verb *helped*.]
PREDICATE NOMINATIVE	That is **where I'd like to be**. [The clause follows the linking verb *is* and identifies the subject *That*.]
DIRECT OBJECT	Louis told us **why he was excited**. [The clause is the direct object of the verb *told*. It tells *what* Louis told.]
INDIRECT OBJECT	Jasper told **whoever would listen** the same story about his pet turtle. [The clause is the indirect object of the verb *told*. It tells *to whom* Jasper told the story.]
OBJECT OF A PREPOSITION	Did they give the food to **whoever asked for it**? [The clause is the object of the preposition *to*.]

Common Introductory Words for Noun Clauses		
how	when	who
if	where	whoever
that	whether	whom
what	which	whomever
whatever	whichever	why

Sometimes the introductory word in a noun clause is omitted.

EXAMPLE   She said **[that] her cold had cleared up**.

EXERCISE 6   Identifying and Classifying Noun Clauses

Underline the noun clause in each of the following sentences. On the line before the sentence, identify how the clause is used. Write *s.* for *subject*, *p.n.* for *predicate nominative*, *d.o.* for *direct object*, *i.o.* for *indirect object*, or *o.p.* for *object of a preposition*.

EX.   _p.n._   1.   That is why I'm always a bit skeptical.

_____   1.   Joy told me that she was nervous.

_____   2.   Ms. Asato, a scientist, explained what ozone depletion is.

171

_____ 3. A motivated captain is what we need for this team.

_____ 4. The Little League coach will give whoever can throw farthest a position in the outfield.

_____ 5. Mrs. Castillo makes seafood paella for whoever asks.

_____ 6. Late for school, Mateo put on whichever shirt was nearest.

_____ 7. Do you know who created the sculpture known as *The Thinker*?

_____ 8. The small country's recently elected leader will announce what the new rationing laws are.

_____ 9. That we need rain is very evident.

_____ 10. The lawyer listened intently to whatever the witness said.

EXERCISE 7   Writing Sentences with Noun Clauses

Write two sentences using each clause below as the two different parts of speech named in parentheses. Underline and label the use of each of the noun clauses. Write your sentences on your own paper.

EX. 1. that Ramon is going to the carnival tonight (*direct object; subject*)

   1. Eliza told me that Ramon is going to the carnival tonight. (direct object)
       That Ramon is going to the carnival tonight is not a secret. (subject)

1. that Stefano is going to play point guard for the basketball team (*direct object; predicate nominative*)

2. what Sondra made for lunch (*subject; object of a preposition*)

3. who announced the contest winners (*subject; predicate nominative*)

4. how they can plant saplings in their yards (*direct object; object of a preposition*)

5. whichever color you like best (*subject; object of a preposition*)

6. whatever she builds (*subject; indirect object*)

7. whoever returns the defective toaster (*indirect object; object of a preposition*)

8. whoever is working today (*indirect object; predicate nominative*)

9. where the sun shines year-round (*object of a preposition; direct object*)

10. why Uncle Jules didn't visit at Thanksgiving this year (*direct object; predicate nominative*)

SENTENCE STRUCTURE

The *structure* of a sentence is determined by the number of independent and subordinate clauses it contains.

13g According to their structure, sentences are classified as *simple, compound, complex,* or *compound-complex.*

(1) A *simple sentence* has one independent clause and no subordinate clauses.

EXAMPLES Uncle Harold threw me into the pool.
I would love to find an evening dress covered with sequins.
Should I go to the prom with Ésteban?

(2) A *compound sentence* has two or more independent clauses but no subordinate clauses.

A compound sentence may be joined by a comma and a coordinating conjunction (*and, but, for, nor, or, so,* or *yet*); by a semicolon; or by a semicolon and a conjunctive adverb (*also, anyway, instead, still, therefore*) or a transitional expression (*as a result, in fact, for example*).

EXAMPLES I went out for milk**, but** the store had already closed.
The rocking horse gathered dust in the attic**;** once it had been her favorite friend.
I do not really enjoy riding the bus**; however,** it is much cheaper than taking a taxi**; also,** it is faster than walking.

(3) A *complex sentence* has one independent clause and at least one subordinate clause.

EXAMPLES Can you believe that I remembered your birthday!
President Carter, after he left office, helped build houses for the homeless.

(4) A *compound-complex* sentence has two or more independent clauses and at least one subordinate clause.

EXAMPLES Isabel, who delivers our newspaper, often comes late, but she never apologizes for it.
Although we enjoy sweets, we avoid eating them, and we try to have fruit for dessert; sometimes we do not have dessert at all.

EXERCISE 8   Classifying Sentences According to Structure

Identify the structure of each of the sentences below. On the line before each sentence, write *simp.* for *simple, comp.* for *compound, cx.* for *complex,* and *cd.-cx.* for *compound-complex.*

EX.   _simp._   1. The Chihuahua, named for the Mexican state of Chihuahua, is the smallest breed of dog.

_____   1. Alice Munro published her first collection of short stories in 1968; the title of that collection is *Dance of the Happy Shades.*

_____   2. After seeing the Lincoln Memorial in Washington, D. C., we stopped at the Vietnam Veterans Memorial.

_____   3. While we were on a class trip to New York City, we visited the Guggenheim Museum, which is shaped like a seashell.

_____   4. The chef said that what they tasted in the pastry crust was a secret ingredient, but he refused to reveal what it was.

_____   5. Covered with layers of straw, compost, and shredded leaves, the garden was ready for the winter.

_____   6. Toya and Derek encouraged me to join the tennis team.

_____   7. Lana never returns the books she borrows; consequently, I don't lend her my books any more.

_____   8. The young designer's collection was presented in the fall and was well received by the fashion critics.

_____   9. The scientific discovery was made in Europe, and it was widely praised there.

_____ 10. A victory over our rival football team would be a spirit booster; moreover, it is necessary if we want to make it to the state championship.

_____ 11. On live camera the news reporter described what he saw, but his account of the incident wasn't very good.

_____ 12. My father, who worked for thirty years, retired in 1992.

_____ 13. When he was congratulated, the young graduate really blushed.

_____ 14. Marcia is a heavy sleeper; she sets three alarm clocks to wake up in the morning.

_____ 15. Carole introduced me to the music of Miles Davis.

CHAPTER REVIEW

A. Classifying Independent and Subordinate Clauses

Classify the italicized clauses in each of the sentences below. On the line before each sentence, write *indep. cl.* for *independent clause, adj. cl.* for *adjective clause, adv. cl.* for *adverb clause,* or *n. cl.* for *noun clause.*

EX. _n. cl._ 1. People in our department check the bulletin board weekly for *whatever messages might be posted.*

_____ 1. *Each year our family harvests and preserves cactus.*

_____ 2. We devised a system *that will promote efficiency and high productivity.*

_____ 3. *The postal carrier delivered the usual stack of junk mail.*

_____ 4. A motivating pep talk is exactly *what we need* before the next track meet.

_____ 5. *As long as we maintain this schedule,* we should meet our deadline.

_____ 6. Do you know *who is bringing the banner to the game?*

_____ 7. Tamara, *who began skiing at the age of five,* organized our high school ski club.

_____ 8. Alano closed the door to his room *so that he could read in peace.*

_____ 9. *Whenever we plan a picnic,* it rains.

_____ 10. The coach said *we could end practice early tonight.*

B. Identifying Sentence Structure

On your own paper, identify the structure of each of the sentences in the following paragraph. Write *simp.* for *simple, comp.* for *compound, cx.* for *complex,* or *cd.-cx.* for *compound-complex.*

EX. [1] Dame Agatha Christie, who was born in 1890 and died in 1976, was an English novelist and a playwright.

1. *cx.*

[1] Dame Christie began writing detective fiction during World War I, when she worked as a nurse. [2] Her two famous detective characters, Hercule Poirot and Jane Marple, appear in many of Christie's novels and short stories, but their personalities and their methods for solving murders

are quite different. [3] Hercule Poirot, who first appeared in *The Mysterious Affair at Styles*, is an odd, selfish, and foolish Belgian. [4] Christie's other famous character, Miss Jane Marple, first appeared in *Murder at the Vicarage.* [5] Miss Marple is an elderly lady; she lives in the English village of St. Mary Mead, where she enjoys gardening. [6] Dame Christie first became famous with her novel *The Murder of Roger Ackroyd*, and this book was followed by many bestsellers. [7] Many of her novels are in series form. [8] *The Mousetrap*, which is a play of Christie's, holds the record for running on stage longer than any other play. [9] Many of her works were made into successful films. [10] One of Christie's stories, which was titled "Witness for the Prosecution," was written over forty years ago, but a film based on the story continues to be popular.

C.   Working Cooperatively to Write Sentences with Varied Structure

Working with a partner, write ten sentences according to the guidelines below. Write these sentences on your own paper.

EX.   1.   a compound sentence with the conjunction *and*

    1. *Donnie put on his pajamas, and I helped put him to bed.*

1. a simple sentence with a compound subject
2. a compound sentence with the conjunction *or*
3. a complex sentence with an adverb clause that modifies a verb
4. a complex sentence with an adverb clause that modifies an adjective
5. a complex sentence with an adjective clause introduced by the relative pronoun *whose*
6. a complex sentence with an adjective clause introduced by the relative pronoun *that*
7. a complex sentence with a noun clause used as the subject of the sentence
8. a complex sentence with a noun clause used as a direct object
9. a complex sentence with an elliptical adverb clause
10. a compound-complex sentence

SUBJECT-VERB AGREEMENT

14a   A verb should agree with its subject in number.

(1) Singular subjects take singular verbs.

EXAMPLE   The duck **swims** for the piece of bread. [The singular verb *swims* agrees with the singular subject *duck*.]

(2) Plural subjects take plural verbs.

EXAMPLE   The ducks **swim** for the piece of bread. [The plural verb *swim* agrees with the plural subject *ducks*.]

Like the one-word verb in each of the preceding examples, a verb phrase must also agree in number with its subject. The number of a verb phrase is indicated by the form of its first auxiliary (helping) verb.

EXAMPLES   My sister **is singing** a folk song. [singular subject and verb phrase]
My sisters **are singing** a folk song. [plural subject and verb phrase]
The artist **has painted** murals. [singular subject and verb phrase]
The artists **have painted** murals. [plural subject and verb phrase]

EXERCISE 1   **Selecting Verbs That Agree in Number with Their Subjects**

For each of the following word groups, underline the verb or verb phrase in parentheses that agrees in number with its subject.

EX.   1.   she (<u>*dances*</u>, *dance*)

1.   Carey (*works, work*)

2.   they (*is driving, are driving*)

3.   pineapples (*grows, grow*)

4.   neighbors (*watches, watch*)

5.   artist (*has woven, have woven*)

6.   politicians (*debates, debate*)

7.   I (*am going, is going*)

8.   guests (*has been eating, have been eating*)

9.   lions (*is roaring, are roaring*)

10.   Raoul (*laughs, laugh*)

11.   you (*has been invited, have been invited*)

12.   student (*performs, perform*)

13.   he (*has left, have left*)

14.   storm (*is coming, are coming*)

15.   mosquitoes (*buzzes, buzz*)

16.   Andrew (*cooks, cook*)

17. choir (*sings, sing*)   19. children (*climbs, climb*)

18. rocks (*has fallen, have fallen*)   20. sun (*is rising, are rising*)

EXERCISE 2   Identifying Verbs That Agree in Number with Their Subjects

For each sentence below, underline the verb or verb phrase in parentheses that agrees in number with its subject.

EX.   1.   That plane (*is, are*) flying low.

1. Marta (*has been reading, have been reading*) books by South American authors.

2. Can we (*swims, swim*) in the pond at the farm?

3. Johnny Appleseed, a real man, (*has become, have become*) a folk hero.

4. Her students (*studies, study*) Spanish.

5. "Do you (*knows, know*) the reason?" Tyrone asked.

6. The musicians (*has been practicing, have been practicing*) daily.

7. Because it snowed last night, the roads (*is, are*) closed this morning.

8. Anaba (*is learning, are learning*) to weave from her grandmother.

9. (*Is, Are*) the children making too much noise?

10. By watching the sky patiently, they (*was, were*) able to see a shooting star.

11. She (*was, were*) delighted by his description of wax festivals in Morroco.

12. In spring, the mountains (*is, are*) covered with wildflowers.

13. Squawking loudly, the blue jays (*scares, scare*) away smaller birds.

14. Mattie (*has won, have won*) the debate.

15. Will you see if the noodles (*is, are*) ready?

16. Mr. Jackson asked, "Why (*does, do*) you like this poem?"

17. The pianist (*is playing, are playing*) my favorite song.

18. Next summer, the Alperts (*plans, plan*) to visit Canada.

19. Here is a list of what we (*needs, need*).

20. "Look!" Mr. Wu called. "Here (*comes, come*) the dragon!"

INTERVENING PHRASES AND CLAUSES

14b **The number of the subject is not changed by a phrase or a clause following the subject.**

EXAMPLES   The **pens are** blue, green, and red.
The **pens** on the table **are** blue, green, and red. [The prepositional phrase *on the table* does not affect the number of the subject *pens*.]

The **actor has** many theater awards.
The **actor** signing autographs **has** many theater awards. [The participial phrase *signing autographs* does not affect the number of the subject *actor*.]

Delia makes wonderful knitted sweaters.
Delia, who has many talents, **makes** wonderful knitted sweaters. [The adjective clause *who has many talents* does not affect the number of the subject *Delia*.]

Prepositional phrases may begin with compound prepositions, such as *together with, in addition to, as well as,* and *along with*. These phrases do not affect the number of the verb.

EXAMPLES   **Estelle,** as well as her brothers, **is interested** in working on a farm. [singular subject and verb]
My **bags,** along with that package, **are** by the door. [plural subject and verb]

EXERCISE 3   Identifying Verbs That Agree in Number with Their Subjects

For each of the following sentences, underline the verb or verb phrase in parentheses that agrees in number with its subject.

EX.   1.   The maple tree at the corner (<u>is turning</u>, *are turning*) beautiful colors.

1.   This stack of books (*is waiting*, *are waiting*) to be shelved.

2.   Did you know that Tena, together with her family, (*is arranging*, *are arranging*) the show of Navajo crafts?

3.   The child, as well as her parents, (*becomes*, *become*) excited about summer vacation as it grows closer.

4.   Ariel, along with her two brothers, (*has been preparing*, *have been preparing*) Seder for Passover.

179

5. Tany said, "The salad, as well as the enchiladas, (*looks, look*) delicious."

6. The group of senior citizens (*is visiting, are visiting*) Guam, the Philippines, and Hawaii.

7. Because the pool at school is closed, the girls on the swim team (*needs, need*) another place to practice.

8. High winds, in addition to a high tide, (*has been, have been*) predicted.

9. The first of the tour groups (*is arriving, are arriving*).

10. The report pointed out that the Comanches, as well as the Sioux, (*lives, live*) on the Great Plains.

EXERCISE 4   Proofreading a Paragraph for Correct Subject-Verb Agreement

In the paragraph below, draw a line through each verb or verb phrase that does not agree with its subject. Write the correct form of the verb or verb phrase in the space above the error. Some sentences may contain no errors in agreement.

EX.   [1] For Mrs. Jackson's class, the students has to write a report on a custom of another country.

[1] Marissa have chosen to write about Umlanga. [2] For the girls in Swaziland, Umlanga is a coming-of-age ceremony. [3] During this week-long event, girls travels to Lobamba, the royal city of Swaziland. [4] They gathers reeds from the riverbank. [5] The sixth day of Umlanga are the time to prepare for a dance. [6] The girls participating in this festival wears necklaces, beaded skirts, and ankle and wrist bracelets. [7] These costumes for the Reed Dance is carefully prepared. [8] In this dance, the girls waves the reeds over their heads. [9] Onlookers, including the Queen of Swaziland, watches the girls' Reed Dance. [10] The festival, in addition to the dances, include a ceremony in which the girls use reeds to repair the fences around the Queen's residence.

AGREEMENT WITH INDEFINITE PRONOUNS

14c **The following indefinite pronouns are singular:** *each, either, neither, one, everyone, everybody, no one, nobody, anyone, anybody, someone,* and *somebody.* **A singular indefinite pronoun takes a singular verb.**

Notice that a phrase or a clause following one of these pronouns does not affect the number of the verb.

EXAMPLES   **Everybody is** invited. [singular subject, singular verb]
Neither of them **has called** me. [singular subject, singular verb]
Anyone who has extra time **is joining** the club. [singular subject, singular verb]

14d **The following indefinite pronouns are plural:** *several, few, both,* **and** *many.* **A plural indefinite pronoun takes a plural verb.**

EXAMPLES   **Several** of my neighbors **have moved** away. [plural subject, plural verb]
A **few** in the school **have participated.** [plural subject, plural verb]

14e **The following indefinite pronouns may be either singular or plural:** *some, all, any, most,* **and** *none.*

These pronouns are singular when they refer to a singular word and are plural when they refer to plural words.

EXAMPLES   **Most** of the garden **has been** planted. [*Most* refers to the singular noun *garden.*]
Most of the people **have** already seen that show. [*Most* refers to the plural noun *people.*]
All of the milk **is** sour. [*All* refers to the singular noun *milk.*]
All of the apples **have** been picked. [*All* refers to the plural noun *apples.*]
Some of the mail **is** opened. [*Some* refers to the singular noun *mail.*]
Some of the branches **are** broken. [*Some* refers to the plural noun *branches.*]

NOTE   The word *none* is singular when it means "not one" and plural when it means "not any."

EXAMPLES   **None** of the clocks **works.** [*Not one* works.]
None of the clocks **work.** [*Not any* work.]

EXERCISE 5   Identifying Subjects and Verbs That Agree in Number.

For each sentence below, underline the verb or verb phrase in parentheses that agrees in number with its subject.

EX.   1.   Most of Frank's photographs (*has been sold, have been sold*).

1.   (*Is, Are*) any of those Polish dumplings left?

2.   Harry said, "It looks as if many of the trails (*was, were*) closed by the landslides."

3.   Several of the volunteers (*has, have*) worked all day.

4.   Most of the people who have signed up for the trip (*plans, plan*) to ski.

5.   Neither of the answers (*is, are*) the right one.

6.   According to this chart, one of the highest mountain peaks in the world (*lie, lies*) in the Himalayas.

7.   Most of these recipes (*calls, call*) for yeast.

8.   All of the participants in the Braemar Highland Gathering (*wears, wear*) kilts.

9.   I was glad that all of Katherine Paterson's books (*was, were*) included on the list.

10.   (*Does, Do*) any of the dancers want to take a break?

11.   Each of Dezba's weavings (*sells, sell*) promptly.

12.   If anyone (*wants, want*) to ask questions, the speaker will stay later to answer them.

13.   All of the islands in that area (*is, are*) atolls.

14.   A few of the people I visit on the reservation (*remembers, remember*) a time when their lives were quite different.

15.   Will both of the bands (*plays, play*) in the festival?

16.   Each girl (*dances, dance*) the Sunrise Dance.

17.   None of the representatives (*agrees, agree*) on a date.

18.   Will everyone who (*wants, want*) a part in the play be at the audition?

19.   Each of her paintings (*tells, tell*) a different legend.

20.   Any winds blowing stronger than 74 miles an hour (*is, are*) considered hurricane force.

THE COMPOUND SUBJECT

A *compound subject* consists of two or more nouns or pronouns that are joined by a conjunction and have the same verb.

14f   Subjects joined by *and* usually take a plural verb.

Compound subjects joined by *and* that name more than one person or thing always take plural verbs.

EXAMPLES   **Marty** and **Angela have been** practicing.
Bread, pickles, and **salad are** on the table.

Compound subjects that name only one person or one thing take a singular verb.

EXAMPLES   My favorite **actor and singer is** my friend Damien. [one person]
Spaghetti and salad is a terrific meal. [one thing]

14g   Singular subjects joined by *or* or *nor* take a singular verb.

EXAMPLES   Neither **Anita** nor **Lucy works** there anymore.
Either **Ms. Chia** or **Mr. Jackson wants** to help.

14h   When a singular subject and a plural subject are joined by *or* or *nor*, the verb agrees with the subject nearer the verb.

EXAMPLES   Neither my **sister** nor my **brothers are** home. [The plural subject *brothers* is nearer the verb.]
Neither my **brothers** nor my **sister is** home. [The singular subject *sister* is nearer the verb.]

EXERCISE 6   Correcting Errors in Subject-Verb Agreement

In each of the following sentences, draw a line through any verb that does not agree in number with its subject. Write the correct form of the verb in the space above the error. Some sentences may contain no errors.

EX.   1.   Either Marta or Kuzem ~~have~~ the books. *has*

1.   A screwdriver and a drill ~~is~~ necessary for the project. *are*

2.   Neither the mangoes nor the pineapples ~~was~~ ripe. *were*

3.   According to our count, Susan and Harley ~~has~~ won the most votes. *have*

4.   Kwam's story and Tammy's poems ~~is~~ in the exhibition. *are*

5. We are hoping that either Mrs. Jackson or Mr. Ortega ~~are~~ *is* on the panel of judges.

6. Mandarin and Catonese ~~is~~ *are* spoken in China.

7. Does either Ima or Yoshi ~~have~~ *has* the information?

8. The writer and the director of the school play ~~are~~ *is* Alison.

9. Joe and Kim ~~works~~ *work* on a dig in Mexico during their summer vacation.

10. We read that a feast and a dance ~~forms~~ *form* part of the ceremony.

11. When ~~is~~ *are* Max and Mickey leaving for Canada?

12. Both the Incan and the Mayan civilizations ~~is~~ *are* covered in Jolene's report.

13. Genghis Khan and Kublai Khan ~~was~~ *were* Mongol leaders.

14. Two dollars and a can of food for the homeless ~~are~~ *is* the price of admission.

15. Neither Lisa nor Cam ~~run~~ *runs* in the 50-yard dash.

16. We think that either the windows or the roof ~~are~~ *is* leaking.

17. The storms and the flooding ~~has~~ *have* caused severe damage.

18. Corn, beans, and avocados ~~is~~ *are* grown in Mexico.

19. Both Earth and Jupiter ~~orbits~~ *orbit* the sun.

20. ~~Has~~ *Have* Marla and Lee demonstrated their experiment yet?

21. Neither the principal nor the teachers ~~enjoys~~ *enjoy* long meetings after school.

22. The best coach and teacher ~~are~~ *is* Ms. Yates.

23. Word processing and spread sheets ~~is~~ *are* covered in the computer course.

24. Rice, noodles, spices, and seafood ~~makes~~ *make* a delicious Thai main course.

25. Either the book or the magazines ~~contains~~ *contain* good information for your report.

EXERCISE 7   Using Verbs That Agree in Number with Compound Subjects

Write five sentences on your own paper. In each sentence, use a compound subject joined by *and, or,* or *nor.* Include one example of two singular subjects joined by *either/or* or *neither/nor* and one singular and one plural subject joined by *either/or* or *neither/nor.* Pay special attention to subject-verb agreement.

EX.   1. My uncle and my two aunts play the piano.

COLLECTIVE NOUNS

14i   Collective nouns may be either singular or plural.

A *collective noun* is singular in form, but it names a group of persons or things.

Common Collective Nouns			
army	club	group	series
assembly	committee	herd	squad
audience	crowd	jury	staff
band	faculty	majority	swarm
choir	family	number	team
class	flock	public	troop

Use a singular verb with a collective noun when you mean the group as a unit. Use a plural verb when you mean the members of the group as individuals.

EXAMPLES   The class **is** planning a picnic. [the class as a unit]
The class **are** discussing the plans with each other. [the class members as individuals]

EXERCISE 8   **Writing Sentences with Collective Nouns**

From the list above, select ten collective nouns. On your own paper, write a pair of sentences using each. Each pair of sentences should show how the collective noun may be either singular or plural.

EX.   flock

1. a.   The flock flies over our house.

    b.   The flock are building nests in the meadow.

REVIEW EXERCISE 1

A. Choosing Correct Verbs in Sentences

In each of the sentences below, underline the verb or verb phrase in parentheses that agrees in number with its subject.

EX. 1. Most of my friends (*likes*, *like*) to read.

1. The house (*seems*, *seem*) empty without the cat.

2. Have you noticed that the birds (*is*, *are*) flying south?

3. The carton of milk (*has*, *have*) spilled.

4. Maggie, who has traveled to many countries, (*collects*, *collect*) coins.

5. Strong winds, in addition to a rough surf, (*makes*, *make*) sailing difficult.

6. My father, as well as my two aunts, (*is*, *are*) coming to the show tonight.

7. Cameron and Asher (*has*, *have*) written a play.

8. The dogs, but not the cat, (*has*, *have*) been fed.

9. (*Was*, *Were*) all of the poems by Gwendolyn Brooks collected into one book?

10. Most of the band members (*plays*, *play*) more than one instrument.

B. Making Verbs Agree with Their Subjects

In each sentence below, underline any verb that does not agree in number with its subject. Then, on the line before the sentence, write the correct form of the verb. If a sentence contains no errors, write C.

EX. _is_ 1. The audience are full of students and teachers.

_____ 1. Antonia and Mark has finished putting up the decorations.

_____ 2. According to this list, Angela and her brothers is coming.

_____ 3. Does anyone has a copy of Mildred D. Taylor's book?

_____ 4. The children enjoys playing with clay.

_____ 5. When the choir sing carols, it always draws a crowd.

_____ 6. As soon as Paul and Jaime arrives, we will begin.

_____ 7. Neither this chemical nor that one are what we need.

_____ 8. The unicorn, as well as the griffin, is a mythological beast.

_____ 9. Everybody who take Mrs. Chavez's class says it's really interesting.

_____ 10. The manager said that this radio, but not those, are on sale.

OTHER PROBLEMS IN AGREEMENT

14j   A verb agrees with its subject, not with its predicate nominative.

EXAMPLES   A great **snack is** fresh tomatoes. [singular subject, singular verb]
Fresh **tomatoes are** a great snack. [plural subject, plural verb]

14k   When the subject follows the verb, make sure that the verb agrees with it.

In sentences beginning with *here* or *there* and in questions, the subject follows the verb.

EXAMPLES   Here **is** the **container** of berries. [singular subject, singular verb]
Here **are** the **berries**. [plural subject, plural verb]
Where **is** that **jar** of peanuts? [singular subject, singular verb]
Where **are** those **peanuts**? [plural subject, plural verb]

NOTE   Contractions such as *here's, there's, how's,* and *what's* include the singular verb *is*. Use one of these contractions only if a singular subject follows it.

INCORRECT   **There's** many **sounds** in the cafeteria. [plural subject, singular verb]

CORRECT   **There's** a **lot** of noise in the cafeteria. [singular subject, singular verb]

CORRECT   There **are** many **sounds** in the cafeteria. [plural subject, plural verb]

14l   An expression of an amount may be singular or plural.

An expression of an amount is singular when the amount is thought of as a unit and is plural when the amount is thought of as many parts.

EXAMPLES   **Six thousand books is** a large stock for that store. [The books are thought of as a unit.]
Six hundred books are in that store. [The books are thought of separately.]

A fraction or a percentage is singular when it refers to a singular word and is plural when it refers to a plural word.

EXAMPLES   About **one third** of the crowd **is** satisfied. [The fraction refers to the singular noun *crowd.*]
About **one third** of the people in the crowd **are** satisfied. [The fraction refers to the plural noun *people.*]

Expressions of measurement (length, weight, capacity, area) are usually singular.

EXAMPLES   **Five and three-tenths inches is** the length of thread he needs.
Three kilometers was the distance to her house.
Four quarts equals a gallon.

NOTE   In the expression *number of*, the word *number* is singular when preceded by *the* and is plural when preceded by *a/an*.

EXAMPLES   The **number of** people buying that product **has decreased**.
A **number of** people **purchase** that product regularly.

14m   The title of a creative work (such as a book, song, film, or painting) or the name of a country (even if it is plural in form) takes a singular verb.

EXAMPLES   *The Winter Trees* **was written** by my friend Gerardo.
The United States celebrates Memorial Day.

14n   Many nouns that are plural in form are singular in meaning.

(1) The following nouns always take singular verbs.

civics	genetics	news
economics	linguistics	physics
electronics	mathematics	

EXAMPLES   The **news is** on television now.
Physics was Marta's favorite subject last year.

(2) The following nouns always take plural verbs.

binoculars	pliers	shears
eyeglasses	scissors	trousers

EXAMPLES   The **pliers are** in the kitchen drawer.
My **trousers were torn** on a tree limb.

NOTE   Many nouns ending in *-ics*, such as *acoustics, athletics, ethics, politics, statistics,* and *tactics,* may be singular or plural.

EXAMPLES   **Athletics is** an area in which Rhonda excels.
Athletics are popular at my school.

If you do not know whether a noun that is plural in form is singular or plural in meaning, look in a dictionary.

14o   The name of an organization, though plural in form, usually takes a singular verb.

EXAMPLES   **Walker Fabrics is** a company in town.
The **United Nations assembles** in New York City.

The names of some organizations, however, may take singular or plural verbs. When the name refers to the organization as a unit, it takes a singular verb. When the name refers to the members of the organization, it takes a plural verb.

EXAMPLES   The **San Diego Padres plays** this Saturday.
The **San Diego Padres are discussing** yesterday's game.

EXERCISE 9   Selecting Verbs That Agree in Number with Their Subjects

In each of the following sentences, underline the verb, phrase, or contraction in parentheses that agrees in number with its subject.

EX.   1. (*Here's, Here are*) the tapes you were looking for.

1. The central character in Willa Cather's novel *O Pioneers!* (*is, are*) a pioneer woman in Nebraska.

2. The number of fish in the pond (*is, are*) unknown.

3. Physics (*attempts, attempt*) to explain matter, energy, and their interactions.

4. The Bahamas (*is, are*) a popular vacation spot.

5. We agreed that two hours (*was, were*) a long time to wait.

6. (*Where's, Where are*) the tables for the pottery display?

7. Civics (*is, are*) offered at summer school now.

8. To see the New Year's parade, a number of people (*was, were*) willing to stand in the rain.

9. A great way to spend afternoons (*is, are*) to go to the Museum of Science.

10. The children all cried, "(*Here's, Here are*) the ponies!"

11. Marilyn discovered that the mumps (*is, are*) contagious.

12. Does Raoul know that his trousers (*has, have*) been sent to the cleaners?

13. There (*is, are*) an astonishing variety of life in a rain forest.

14. The lit candles of St. Lucia's Day in Sweden (*is, are*) a beautiful sight to see.

15. To our delight, the news (*was, were*) all good.

16. *The Crusades* (*gives, give*) quite a lot of information about the Middle Ages.

17. (*Where's, Where are*) that package of tortillas I bought?

18. Takako always insists that economics (*is, are*) not as baffling as it seems.

19. The new store, Downtown Videos, (*is, are*) hiring part-time help for the summer.

20. The Boston Celtics (*travels, travel*) on the same plane as we do to Chicago tomorrow.

21. (*There's, There are*) a big storm brewing at sea.

22. Fresh flowers (*adds, add*) charm to a table setting.

23. The Olympic Games (*has, have*) been held every four years.

24. Rhoda has decided that politics (*is, are*) a field in which she would like to work.

25. "Look," Bart called, "(*there's, there are*) a bear with her cubs in that meadow."

EXERCISE 10   **Proofreading a Paragraph for Errors in Subject-Verb Agreement**

In the paragraph below, draw a line through any verb, phrase, or contraction that does not agree in number with its subject. Write the correct form of the verb in the space above the incorrect word.

EX.   [1] Physics ~~are~~ important in the study of astronomy.
                      is

[1] I didn't know that most of the professional astronomers today has

studied physics until two astronomers came to our school on Career Day.

[2] The number of students waiting to talk to the astronomers were large.

[3] Among the instruments the astronomers demonstrated were a small

telescope. [4] Compared to a telescope, binoculars sees very little. [5] There's

many planets and stars to observe with a telescope.

REVIEW EXERCISE 2

A. Selecting Verbs That Agree in Number with Their Subjects

In each sentence below, underline the verb, phrase, or contraction that agrees in number with its subject.

EX. 1. (*Where's*, *Where are*) the instructions for the computer?

1. All of the planets in the solar system (*orbits*, *orbit*) the sun.

2. *The Tombs of Atuan* (*is*, *are*) part of a trilogy by Ursula K. Le Guin.

3. Who (*delivers*, *deliver*) the packages on Saturday?

4. News of the earthquake (*has*, *have*) worried people who have relatives in that area.

5. The San Francisco 49ers (*is*, *are*) in first place.

6. For bird-watching, binoculars (*do*, *does*) help.

7. Couscous and falafel (*was*, *were*) added to the menu.

8. (*Here's*, *Here are*) the schedules for the Eighth Annual Polish Fest.

9. Every member of the ballet (*practices*, *practice*) daily.

10. *Calvin and Hobbes*, the comic strip, (*entertains*, *entertain*) many parents.

11. A number of my grandfather's roses always (*wins*, *win*) prizes.

12. "(*How's*, *How are*) the weather in your part of the world?" he asked, as the storm howled in the background.

13. *Nine Stories* by J. D. Salinger (*was*, *were*) discussed at our last meeting.

14. My favorite of all of Shakespeare's plays (*is*, *are*) *The Tempest*.

15. Three hours (*seems*, *seem*) too long for a children's party.

16. Traditionally, when some of the Tlingit clans in Alaska (*constructs*, *construct*) a new building, they thank the spirit of the forest for the lumber.

17. Marco's Dairy Products (*makes*, *make*) home deliveries.

18. Four quarters (*equals*, *equal*) one dollar.

19. Measles sometimes (*has*, *have*) serious complications.

20. Did you know that your scissors (*needs*, *need*) sharpening?

B.   Proofreading a Paragraph for Errors in Subject-Verb Agreement

In the paragraph below, draw a line through any verb, phrase, or contraction
that does not agree in number with its subject. Write the correct form of the verb
in the space above the error. Some sentences may contain no errors.

EX.   [1] The Mayan civilization flourished in the area that today ~~are~~ [is] part of
       Mexico, Guatemala, and Belize.

[1] Research show that the Mayan culture was highly developed,
particularly in the areas of architecture and astronomy. [2] Sites of Mayan
ruins is found in the jungles of the Yucatán Peninsula. [3] Perhaps the best
known site are the ruins of Chichén Itzá. [4] The remains of this ancient city
draws many visitors each year. [5] The restored buildings includes a Mayan
astronomical observatory. [6] A massive white stone pyramid called El
Castillo, or the Temple of Kulkulcan, fills the plaza of the city. [7] Towering
over the surrounding landscape, the pyramid measure eighty feet high.
[8] This pyramid, like most Mayan buildings, were constructed according to
strict astronomical guidelines. [9] On El Castillo, each flight of stairs have
ninety-one steps. [10] The total number of steps in the stairways, in addition
to the summit platform, equal 365, the number of days in a year. [11] The
precision of the designs ensure that, during the spring and fall equinoxes, the
setting sun lights up the eastern stairwell. [12] The sun casts a shadow that
leads to the Sacred Cenote, or well. [13] Objects was cast into this well as
part of the religious ceremonies. [14] Archaeologists has found all kinds
of relics here. [15] Gold, silver, and jade has been taken from this well.

PRONOUN AGREEMENT

The word to which a pronoun refers is called its *antecedent*.

14p   A pronoun agrees with its antecedent in gender and in number.

(1) Singular pronouns refer to singular antecedents. Plural pronouns refer to plural antecedents.

EXAMPLES   **Abraham** won **his** bicycle in a contest.
The **swimmers** took **their** gold medals with **them.**

(2) A few singular pronouns indicate gender (*masculine, feminine, neuter*). The singular pronouns *he, him, his*, and *himself* refer to masculine antecedents. The singular pronouns *she, her, hers*, and *herself* refer to feminine antecedents. The singular pronouns *it, its*, and *itself* refer to antecedents that are neuter (neither masculine nor feminine).

EXAMPLES   **Roberto** put **his** coat in the closet.
Shayla has more time than **she** usually does.
Dad watered the **plant** and trimmed **its** leaves.

14q   Singular pronouns are used to refer to the following antecedents: *anybody, anyone, each, either, everybody, everyone, neither, nobody, no one, one, somebody,* **and** *someone.*

To determine the genders of these words, look in the phrases following them.

EXAMPLES   **Each** of the **boys** has offered to do **his** part.
One of the **girls** donated **her** time.

If the antecedent may be either masculine or feminine, use both masculine and feminine pronouns to refer to it.

EXAMPLES   **Everyone** who wants a ride should raise **his or her** hand.
Somebody left **his or her** books behind.

 NOTE   You can often avoid the *his or her* construction by revising the sentence to use the plural forms of both the pronoun and its antecedent.

EXAMPLE   **All** of the **members** have sent **their** dues.

14r   Use a singular pronoun to refer to two or more singular antecedents joined by *or* or *nor*.

EXAMPLES   **Either Ralph or Peter** always walks **his** dog at the park.
Neither Mom nor Aunt Rose thinks **she** can come to the road race on Saturday.

14s   Use a plural pronoun to refer to two or more singular antecedents joined by *and*.

EXAMPLES   If **Monica and Leroy** want to participate, tell **them** to arrive at 7:00 P.M. sharp.
            Cassie, Eduardo, and Liza have turned in **their** projects.

NOTE   Revise awkward constructions caused by antecedents of different genders.

    AWKWARD   Either Crystal or Ben will sing his solo.
    REVISED   Either **Crystal** will sing **her** solo, or **Ben** will sing **his**.

14t   When a relative pronoun (*that, which,* or *who*) is the subject of an adjective clause, the verb in the clause agrees with the word to which the relative pronoun refers.

EXAMPLES   My ballet class, **which meets** on Wednesday, is planning a recital. [*Which* refers to the singular noun *class.*]
            I know people **who build** boats. [*Who* refers to the plural noun *people.*]

NOTE   When preceded by *one of [plural word]*, the relative pronoun takes a plural verb. When preceded by *the only one of [plural word]*, the relative pronoun takes a singular verb.

    EXAMPLES   *Romeo and Juliet* is **one of the plays that are** on our reading list.
                That novel is **the only one of the books on the list that tells** the story well.

EXERCISE 11   Proofreading for Pronouns That Agree with Their Antecedents

In each of the following sentences, fill in the blank with the pronoun (or pair of pronouns) that agrees with its antecedent.

EX.   1.   Uncle Jim planted _____his_____ garden yesterday.

1.   When they had finished, the workers removed _____ equipment.

2.   Somebody has volunteered _____ time to repair the fence.

3.   All of the players have had _____ checkups.

4.   Either Mari will deliver _____ speech or Ben will deliver _____.

5.   The new bicycle lost _____ shiny look after a few weeks.

6.   When Lilia and Ted arrive, tell _____ we are in the darkroom.

7. The debate team, which has a debate scheduled next Friday, will hold _____ first practice on Wednesday.

8. Anyone who wants to express _____ opinion should come to the meeting on Tuesday.

9. We told Robin she should send _____ letter to the newspaper.

10. Mimi's uncle promised to give us _____ recipe for tamales.

11. The Hopi dancers will perform _____ traditional Snake Dance.

12. We know winter is coming when the maple tree in our yard starts to lose _____ leaves.

13. Neither Julie nor Amalia wants to give up _____ place.

14. Mikey, Haley, and Yori have had _____ paintings accepted for the show.

15. One of the boys has received _____ paycheck.

16. When the boat docked, we saw people on the wharf selling _____ baskets.

17. This engine has lost _____ power.

18. When the applause finally stopped, Mrs. Ortega got up to give _____ response.

19. Can he find _____ way in the dark?

20. That company makes most of _____ profits through catalog sales.

21. If you want to meet two basketball players from the Indiana Pacers, you can see _____ at the restaurant tonight.

22. Each weekend, either Barry or Nick skates by on _____ in-line skates.

23. In February, the cross-country skiers will hold _____ race.

24. Each of the girls in the family sews _____ own clothes.

25. Anyone who wants to sing in the chorus may sign _____ name on the list.

EXERCISE 12   Proofreading a Paragraph for Errors in Subject-Verb and Pronoun-Antecedent Agreement

In the following paragraph, draw a line through any errors in subject-verb agreement or pronoun-antecedent agreement. Write your correction in the space above the error. Some sentences may contain no errors.

EX.   [1] One of my best and worst vacations ~~were~~ *was* the first time I went backpacking.

[1] Even now when I tries to describe it, I can't believe I ever did it. [2] The chief problem, in addition to many small complications, were that I didn't really know what I was doing. [3] Neither my friends nor I are what you would call an accomplished athlete. [4] We wanted, however, to go backpacking. [5] Paco, who reads quite a bit, say that books can teach you how to do anything. [6] We all read about how to backpack and then we set off to climb Mount Tam, which are one of the highest mountains in our area. [7] Right away, Jake and Mateo said his feet hurt, but they stopped complaining when they began to look around. [8] The views as you climb this mountain is quite spectacular. [9] As we was admiring the view, however, Paco said, "It looks like there are clouds forming in the west." [10] The storm hit just as we was setting up our camp for the night. [11] We tried to pitch our tent quickly, but we had lost his stakes, and so it was useless. [12] Do you has any idea how hard it is to find a dry shelter during a wild storm? [13] We found a cave, but in our rush, we left our packs of food lying out on the ground. [14] I only hope that the two bears who found the food enjoyed its dinner. [15] As we huddled, cold and hungry in our cave, Paco said, "I'll have to read a few more books before we try this again."

CHAPTER REVIEW

A. Proofreading Sentences for Subject-Verb and Pronoun-Antecedent Agreement

In each of the sentences below, draw a line through any errors in subject-verb agreement and pronoun-antecedent agreement. Then, on the line before the sentence, write your correction. If a sentence contains no errors, write C.

EX. _____have_____ 1. Most of the people that we've invited ~~has~~ accepted.

_____ 1. Here's the ingredients you needed for the chile.

_____ 2. Gillian, but not her brothers, works in her father's shop.

_____ 3. Neither Steve nor Jorge has memorized their lines.

_____ 4. Ten dollars are too much to pay for that print.

_____ 5. Because of the storms, that trail have been closed.

_____ 6. Every table has their assigned display items.

_____ 7. The news are good about funds for the basketball court.

_____ 8. There's a new set of books that arrived this morning.

_____ 9. Toby noticed that your shears is in the box.

_____ 10. Mathematics are a subject that Jamillah understands easily.

_____ 11. Is these roads through the jungle paved?

_____ 12. His ten minutes are up.

_____ 13. Unfortunately, measles are going around the school.

_____ 14. Do you think Cora have a good chance to win the election?

_____ 15. Each of my sisters has their day planned.

_____ 16. The tent and the sleeping bags is packed.

_____ 17. My cats, as well as my dog, needs to go for a walk every day.

_____ 18. That bag of clothes are for the rummage sale

_____ 19. Some of the dishes was chipped.

_____ 20. *The Canterbury Tales* make me laugh aloud at times.

B. Proofreading a Paragraph for Errors in Subject-Verb and Pronoun-Antecedent Agreement

In the paragraph below, draw a line through any errors in subject-verb agreement or pronoun-antecedent agreement. Write the corrections on your own paper. Some sentences may contain no errors.

EX.   [1] One of the most unusual athletic competitions ~~are~~ the Frog Jumping Contest.

    1. is

[1] The event take place each year in the foothills of California. [2] This is the area where gold were discovered in 1849, causing the California Gold Rush. [3] Mark Twain, in addition to many other writers, have written about this exciting time in California's history. [4] Twain wrote a story called "The Celebrated Jumping Frog of Calaveras County." [5] Jim Smiley and his frog is the main characters in this story. [6] Smiley claim his frog can outjump any other frog. [7] The town of Angel's Camp began sponsoring frog-jumping contests after the story were published. [8] Each year now, as many as three thousand frogs participates in this competition. [9] Tourists and residents makes a huge, enthusiastic audience. [10] The frog that jumps the farthest three times in a row win the Grand Finals.

C. Writing a Sales Report

As the assistant manager of the Chop Wok Cafe, you have to write a weekly sales report. On your own paper, use the information below to write a report that has five sentences. Be sure your subjects and verbs agree in number.

EX.   Shrimp with noodles and cashew chicken were the most popular items.

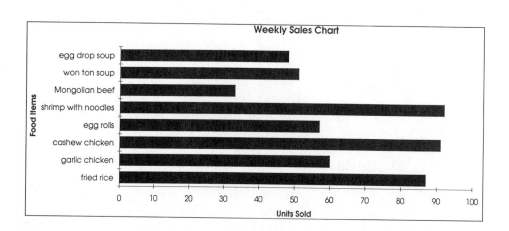

CASE OF PRONOUNS

Case is the form that a noun or a pronoun takes to indicate its use in a sentence. In English, there are three cases: *nominative*, *objective*, and *possessive*.

The form of the noun is the same for both the nominative case and the objective case. For example, a noun used as a subject (nominative case) will have the same form if used as an object (objective case).

NOMINATIVE CASE   The **student** gave her speech. [subject]
OBJECTIVE CASE   Give the **student** your attention. [indirect object]

A noun changes its form for the possessive case, usually by adding an apostrophe and an *s* to most singular nouns and only the apostrophe to most plural nouns.

POSSESSIVE CASE   I enjoyed the **student's** speech. [singular]
I enjoyed the **students'** speeches. [plural]

PERSONAL PRONOUNS		
Singular		
Nominative Case	**Objective Case**	**Possessive Case**
I	me	my, mine
you	you	your, yours
he, she, it	him, her, it	his, her, hers, its
Plural		
Nominative Case	**Objective Case**	**Possessive Case**
we	us	our, ours
you	you	your, yours
they	them	their, theirs

Notice in the chart that *you* and *it* have the same form in the nominative and the objective case. All other personal pronouns have different forms for each case. Notice also that only third person singular pronouns indicate gender.

NOTE   Some teachers prefer to call possessive pronouns, such as *my*, adjectives. Follow your teacher's directions in labeling possessive forms.

EXERCISE 1   Classifying Personal Pronouns

On the line before each sentence below, identify the case of the italicized pronoun by writing *nom.* for *nominative,* *obj.* for *objective,* or *poss.* for *possessive.*

EX.   _poss._   1. We admired *her* photographs.

_____   1. Have you finished *your* report on Guatemala?

_____   2. *We* planted a community garden this year.

_____   3. These seats are *theirs.*

_____   4. When I saw *him* yesterday, Jasper said he would be gone for a week.

_____   5. *They* pointed the telescope at Mars.

_____   6. "Is this *his* project?" the judges asked.

_____   7. Grandma Moses began painting when *she* was in her seventies.

_____   8. In Japan, farmers plant trees in *their* rice fields for good luck.

_____   9. The guard told *us* where to find the room with the Egyptian statues.

_____ 10. Because Wallace is such a good speaker, we have elected *him* our representative.

_____ 11. *Our* ideas for what to do with the vacant lot are on the list of possibilities.

_____ 12. *My* recipe for gazpacho is delicious.

_____ 13. When Asa plays his guitar, *he* always draws a crowd.

_____ 14. The Seminole people have traditionally celebrated *their* new corn crop with the Green Corn Dance.

_____ 15. According to this report, *they* have changed their minds again.

_____ 16. *I* think it's going to rain.

_____ 17. I think that this battery has lost *its* power.

_____ 18. Today *we* are going to hear their speeches.

_____ 19. "The best notes to read are *hers,*" Mrs. Jackson said.

_____ 20. The swimming power of a shark comes from *its* tail.

NOMINATIVE CASE PRONOUNS

15a   The subject of a verb is in the nominative case.

EXAMPLES   **I** organize the file cabinets. [*I* is the subject of *organize*.]
Darnell and she raked leaves. [*Darnell and she* is the compound subject of *raked*.]
They saw that **we** worked hard on the project. [*They* is the subject of *saw*, and *we* is the subject of *worked*.]

A subject may be a compound, with a pronoun appearing in combination with a noun or another pronoun. To help you choose the correct pronoun form in a compound subject, try each form as the simple subject of the verb.

EXAMPLE   (*She, Her*) and (*I, me*) learned to square dance.
Her and *me* learned to square dance. [incorrect use of objective case]
She and *I* learned to square dance. [correct use of nominative case]

ANSWER   **She** and **I** learned to square dance.

15b   A predicate nominative is in the nominative case.

A *predicate nominative* is a noun or pronoun that follows a linking verb and explains or identifies the subject of the sentence. A pronoun used as a predicate nominative always follows a form of the verb *be* or a verb phrase ending in *be* or *been*.

EXAMPLES   The coach of the team is **she.** [*She* follows the linking verb *is* and identifies the subject *coach*.]
The fastest worker has been **he.** [*He* follows the linking verb *has been* and identifies the subject *worker*.]
The third place winners were **he** and **I.** [*He* and *I* follow the linking verb *were* and identify the subject *winners*.]

NOTE   In casual conversation, expressions such as *It's me* and *That's her* are acceptable. Avoid them in more formal speaking situations, such as job interviews. In your written work, do not use them unless you are creating casual conversation in dialogue.

EXERCISE 2   **Using Personal Pronouns as Subjects and Predicate Nominatives**

For each of the following sentences, underline the correct personal pronoun in parentheses.

EX.   1. The best writers are (<u>they</u>, them).

1. (*She, Her*) and I are painting the signs.

2. Have (*they, them*) finished their float for the New Year's parade?

3. Will you see if it is (*they, them*) at the door?

4. Her grandfather and (*she, her*) both play the violin.

5. It was (*he, him*) who recommended that we stop in the Rockies on our way to California.

6. Of course, you and (*he, him*) are invited to the party.

7. If you climb the ladder, (*her, she*) and I will hold it.

8. Like Chim, (*he, him*) was born in Vietnam.

9. Even though I'd lost the map, (*they, them*) and I found our way back through Veracruz to our hotel.

10. Is it (*she, her*) who is going to tell stories about Kwanzaa for the holiday program?

EXERCISE 3   **Proofreading for the Correct Use of Pronouns in the Nominative Case**

In the paragraph below, draw a line through each incorrect pronoun form. Write the correct pronoun in the space above the word. Some sentences are correct.

EX.   [1] When Sam and ~~me~~ go to visit his grandmother, she often tells us about the books she is illustrating.

[1] It was her who drew all the pictures for a popular series of books about American Indian peoples. [2] Right now her project is a book about the Iroquois. [3] The author and her work closely together. [4] She said that she and him talk on the phone several times a day. [5] When Sam and me were at her house last week, we learned that they are working on a chapter about the Midwinter Ceremony of the Iroquois. [6] We saw the drawings that her was making of the masks worn in this ceremony. [7] Sam's grandmother said that when the Iroquois wear these masks, them become "curing spirits." [8] She showed Sam and me some masks that the author and her had borrowed to study. [9] Him and I each had a favorite. [10] Sam tried one on, but I didn't.

OBJECTIVE CASE PRONOUNS

15c   A direct object and an indirect object are in the objective case.

A *direct object* is a noun or pronoun that receives the action of the verb or shows the result of the action.

EXAMPLES   The letter made **her** happy. [*Her* tells whom the letter made happy.]

Lacey reported **it** to the police. [*It* tells what Lacey reported.]

An *indirect object* is a noun or pronoun that tells *to whom* or *for whom* or *to what* or *for what* the action of the verb is done.

EXAMPLES   Mr. Jardim told **them** a wonderful story. [*Them* tells *to whom* Mr. Jardim told a wonderful story.]

Greta brought **him** a map to the stadium. [*Him* tells *for whom* Greta brought a map.]

15d   An object of a preposition is in the objective case.

A noun or pronoun used as an *object of a preposition* comes at the end of a phrase that begins with a preposition.

EXAMPLES   with **her**   next to **me**   beside **you** and **me**

 REFERENCE NOTE: For a list of commonly used prepositions, see page 125.

To choose the correct pronoun in a compound direct object, compound indirect object, or compound object of a preposition, try each form of the pronoun separately in a sentence.

EXAMPLE   Julio surprised him and I.
Julio surprised him. [correct]
Julio surprised I. [incorrect]

ANSWER   Julio surprised **him** and **me.**

EXAMPLE   The man gave directions to them and we.
The man gave directions to them. [correct]
The man gave directions to we. [incorrect]

ANSWER   The man gave directions to **them** and **us.**

EXERCISE 4   Selecting Correct Forms of Objective Case Pronouns

For each sentence below, underline the correct form of the personal pronoun in parentheses.

EX.   1. Kiwa told her and (*I, me*) that the book is good.

1. When it began to rain, Max lent them and (*we, us*) umbrellas for the walk home.

2. Matsuo can sit with (*her, she*) if she needs a translator.

3. The owl surprised Harry and (*he, him*) as it swooped down from the tree.

4. According to the program, they will present the award to (*she, her*) after the band has played.

5. Lani brought pineapples to (*they, them*) when she came back from Hawaii.

6. Ms. Goldstein has encouraged him and (*me, I*) to see that play.

7. Regina said the fireworks frightened the cat and (*she, her*).

8. After Anwar and (*me, I*), you are scheduled to perform.

9. After George had unpacked the dishes, he carefully arranged (*they, them*) on the exhibit table.

10. The police praised Tamara and (*he, him*) for their quick thinking.

11. Will you lend (*we, us*) your dishes for the tea ceremony?

12. He told (*we, us*) the story of Sojourner Truth.

13. "Have you given the package to (*he, him*)?" Tome asked.

14. As they climbed the steps of the old house, Tim fell behind Lily and (*she, her*).

15. In his cooking lesson today, Ken showed (*we, us*) how to fix bean curd.

16. Has anyone else signed up for the backpacking trip with you and (*I, me*)?

17. That letter should be addressed to (*she, her*) as well.

18. Because Ramona worked so hard getting ready for the festival, Mrs. Gutierrez gave (*she, her*) extra tickets.

19. I gave (*they, them*) the guidebooks for the pyramids.

20. Will you tell Franklin that he can ride to the museum with (*I, me*)?

REVIEW EXERCISE

A. Identifying Correct Pronoun Forms

In each of the sentences below, underline the correct pronoun in parentheses. On the line before each sentence, identify the pronoun's use in the sentence. Write *s.* for *subject*, *p.n.* for *predicate nominative*, *d.o.* for *direct object*, *i.o.* for *indirect object*, or *o.p.* for *object of a preposition*.

EX. _____*s.*_____ 1. Mrs. Chen and (*I*, *me*) often walk home together.

_____ 1. Can you give (*we*, *us*) directions?

_____ 2. He and (*I*, *me*) are going to make guacamole for the booth at the fair.

_____ 3. Before the sun had risen, Sanchez had wakened the rest of (*we*, *us*) with the wonderful smells of the breakfast he was cooking.

_____ 4. It was (*I*, *me*) who dropped the keys in the snow.

_____ 5. When a family from Chile moved next door, my mother and (*I*, *me*) decided to call them.

_____ 6. Thanks to (*him*, *he*) we have plenty of flowers for decorations.

_____ 7. The children gave (*she*, *her*) a lantern they had made for the Lantern Festival.

_____ 8. Mrs. Roosevelt entertained (*we*, *us*) with her stories about traveling in foreign countries.

_____ 9. When she left, the villagers thanked (*she*, *her*) for her help with gifts of fruit and seashells.

_____ 10. Didn't you know it was (*I*, *me*) in that costume?

B. Proofreading for Correct Pronouns

In the following paragraph, draw a line through each pronoun that is used incorrectly. Write the correct form in the space above it. Not all sentences contain errors.

EX. [1] U̶s̶ *We* wrote a paper about wolves.

[1] Clay and me wrote to different organizations that are trying to protect wolves today. [2] They sent we quite a lot of information about wolves.

[3] I read that American Indians respect wolves and have learned about survival from them. [4] The Lakota Sioux call they "the animal who looks like

205

a dog but is a powerful spirit." [5] Other people, however, feared wolves and tried to destroy they. [6] Today, wolves are endangered in the United States (except in Alaska and Minnesota), and in many other parts of the world where them once lived. [7] It was me who got the idea to go see some wolves at a nearby wildlife center. [8] Clay thought it was a great idea, although he admitted that he was nervous about being close to a wolf. [9] The director, however, went right into a yard full of they. [10] Clay and I have found that wolves can be both dangerous and shy.

C. Working Cooperatively to Write a Report

You and a partner are co-chairpersons for the See the World Fair that is being held in your school. Work together to write a report of at least fifteen sentences for your class sponsor, explaining your committee's ideas for running the fair. For prewriting, fill in ideas for the categories below. In your report, include one example of each of the three cases of pronouns you have just studied. Underline and label each pronoun (*nom.* for *nominative*, *obj.* for *objective*, or *poss.* for *possessive.*) Write your report on your own paper.

EX.   Games   <u>We</u> will need several different kinds of <u>them</u> for young children.

      nom.   *obj.*

Type of Booth

Decorations for Booth

Shifts for Working at Booth

People for Shifts

Costumes for Workers

Food

Crafts

POSSESSIVE CASE PRONOUNS

15e **The possessive pronouns** *mine, yours, his, hers, its, ours,* **and** *theirs* **are used in the same ways that the pronouns in the nominative and the objective cases are used.**

SUBJECT	Your book and **mine** are getting worn.
PREDICATE NOMINATIVE	That bicycle is **his.**
DIRECT OBJECT	I cleaned **theirs** first.
INDIRECT OBJECT	Please give **ours** a try.
OBJECT OF PREPOSITION	Did I put my coat under **yours?**

15f **The possessive pronouns** *my, your, his, her, its, our,* **and** *their* **are used as adjectives before nouns.**

EXAMPLES **My** hat is ripped.
His water is boiling.
Did you know **our** address changed?

15g **A noun or a pronoun preceding a gerund is in the possessive case.**

A *gerund* is a verb form that ends in *–ing* and functions as a noun. Since a gerund acts as a noun, the noun or pronoun that comes before it must be in the possessive case in order to modify the gerund.

EXAMPLES **Their** careful planning was helpful. [*Their* modifies the gerund *planning*. Whose planning? Their planning.]
I was concerned about **his** jogging on that busy street. [*His* modifies the gerund *jogging*. Whose jogging? His jogging.]

Do not confuse a gerund with a present participle, which is also a verb form that ends in *–ing*. A gerund acts as a noun; a present participle serves as an adjective. A noun or pronoun that is modified by a present participle should not be in the possessive case.

EXAMPLE We watched **people** dancing around the room. [*People* is modified by the participial phrase *dancing around the room*.]

The form of a noun or pronoun before an *-ing* word often depends on the meaning you want to express. If you want to emphasize the *–ing* word, use the possessive form. If you want to emphasize the noun or pronoun preceding the *–ing* word, avoid the possessive form.

EXAMPLES The **Cooking Club's** planning a community dinner received praise. [The emphasis is on the gerund *planning*. *Cooking Club's* modifies *planning*.]
The **Cooking Club** planning a community dinner received praise. [The emphasis is on *Cooking Club*. The participle *planning* modifies *Cooking Club*.]

EXERCISE 5 Using Possessive Nouns and Pronouns

In each of the sentences below, underline the correct noun or pronoun in parentheses. Be prepared to explain why you chose the word you did.

EX.   1. The entire group listened to (*his*, *him*) teachings.

1. After the applause stopped, she began (*her*, *hers*) reading.

2. (*Kwan*, *Kwan's*) cooking always wins praise.

3. "His order and (*your*, *yours*) are ready," the clerk said.

4. (*His*, *Him*) fast driving on the mountain roads made us a little nervous.

5. When it was time for the reports, Ming was the first to read us (*her*, *hers*).

6. To watch my (*grandfather*, *grandfather's*) dancing the tango is a treat.

7. (*Ours*, *Our*) digging resulted in a fine snow cave.

8. The second time we tried (*our*, *ours*) experiment, it worked perfectly.

9. Frank said he was kept awake all night by the (*frogs*, *frogs'*) croaking.

10. (*Their*, *Them*) dancing was the highlight of the program.

11. Someone finally mentioned that (*their*, *them*) giggling disturbed the audience.

12. We watched the (*lights*, *lights'*) twinkling from the dragon boats.

13. Gloomily, we watched the (*bears*, *bears'*) escaping with our fish.

14. Did you hear the (*bells*, *bells'*) ringing at midnight?

15. After looking at all the presents, Maria decided to open (*their*, *theirs*) first.

16. I added my donation to (*her*, *hers*).

17. I tried to count the number of (*lilies*, *lilies'*) floating in the pool.

18. Joel discovered that the books he thought were his were actually (*my*, *mine*).

19. "(*His*, *Him*) giving so much time to this project made all the difference," the speaker said, as he gave the flowers to Mr. Valliere.

20. We admired (*Emily*, *Emily's*) constant practicing.

SPECIAL PRONOUN PROBLEMS

15h **Pronouns used as appositives should be in the same case as the word they refer to.**

An *appositive* is a noun or pronoun used with another noun or pronoun to identify or explain it.

EXAMPLES   The captains, **he** and **she**, should introduce the players. [The pronouns are in the nominative case because they are in apposition with the subject *captains*.]

The award was given to the entire group, **him, her,** and **me.** [The pronouns are in the objective case because they are in apposition with the object of the preposition *group*.]

15i **A pronoun following *than* or *as* in an elliptical construction is in the same case as it would be if the construction were completed.**

An *elliptical construction* is a clause from which words have been omitted.

ELLIPTICAL   Chad was much more careful on the ice **than she.**
COMPLETED   Chad was much more careful on the ice **than she was.**

ELLIPTICAL   The annoying noise bothered Anastasia as much **as him.**
COMPLETED   The annoying noise bothered Anastasia as much **as it bothered him.**

The pronoun form in an elliptical construction determines the meaning of the elliptical phrase or clause. Be sure to use the pronoun form that expresses the meaning you intend. Notice how the meaning of each of the following sentences depends on the pronoun form in the elliptical construction.

EXAMPLES   I have been Carter's neighbor longer **than he.** [I have been Carter's neighbor longer *than he has been Carter's neighbor.*]

I have been Carter's neighbor longer **than his.** [I have been Carter's neighbor longer *than I have been his neighbor.*]

15j **A pronoun ending in *–self* or *–selves* should not be used in place of a simple personal pronoun.**

NONSTANDARD   Wally and **myself** decorated the gym.
STANDARD   Wally and **I** decorated the gym.

EXERCISE 6   Selecting the Correct Pronouns

For each of the following sentences, underline the correct pronoun in parentheses.

EX.   1. She gave the flowers to Winston and (*me, myself*).

1. Rachel has studied Russian longer than (*she, her*).

2. Please give a medal to each of the finalists, Hena and (*he, him*).

3. The two who have been to Kenya, she and (*I, me*), prepared some of the foods we'd eaten there.

4. The captain let the crew, (*he, him*) and me, take a break.

5. The Sherpa guides, both (*she, her*) and he, carried the heavy packs.

6. "Have you been waiting as long as (*I, me*)?" the woman asked worriedly.

7. When we went bird-watching with Derek, no one saw as many birds as (*he, him*).

8. Vanessa gave Troy and (*me, myself*) some photos she'd taken at the ocean.

9. We invited all the neighborhood children, (*they, them*) and their families, to the fair.

10. The best swimmers of the group, you and (*he, him*), should try out for the team.

11. Jeremy and (*I, myself*) plan to explore the caves.

12. Liam was more cautious than (*her, she*) about swimming out too far.

13. The reporter wants to talk to people who saw the accident, (*they, them*) and you.

14. The scientists will demonstrate their experiment for those who are interested, you and (*I, me*).

15. The Robinsons have been living in that neighborhood as long as (*they, them*).

16. Aunt Hannah told us how they, (*her, she*) and her cousins, used to go for sleigh rides in Poland.

17. Those two people, she and (*he, him*), are the authors of the book we've been reading.

18. There have been several articles in the school newspaper about Jamal and (*me, myself*).

19. It takes me twice as long as (*her, she*) to read Chinese.

20. My grandmother likes going to concerts as much as (*I, me*).

21. George has been to Denmark as many times as (*we, us*).

22. The coach gave both teams, them and (*we, us*), the day off.

23. They set off to climb the same mountain, but they went much further than (*we, us*).

24. All of the Guatemalan villagers, (*they, them*) and their prayer leader, participated in the ceremony to protect their crops.

25. Can you lend your notes from history class to Samantha and (*him, himself*)?

WHO *AND* WHOM

Like most personal pronouns, the pronoun *who* (*whoever*) has three case forms.

Nominative	Objective	Possessive
who whoever	whom whomever	whose whosever

15k **These pronouns are called** *interrogative pronouns* **when they are used to form a question. When they are used to introduce subordinate clauses, they are called** *relative pronouns.*

(1) The form an interrogative pronoun takes depends on its use in a question.

Who is used as a subject or as a predicate nominative. *Whom* is used as an object of a verb or as an object of a preposition.

NOMINATIVE **Who** wants to see the show? [*Who* is the subject of the verb *wants.*]

OBJECTIVE With **whom** did you jog? [*Whom* is the object of the preposition *with.*]

NOTE In spoken English, the use of *whom* is gradually disappearing. Nowadays it is acceptable to begin a spoken question with *who* regardless of whether the nominative or the objective form is grammatically correct. In writing, though, it is still important to distinguish between *who* and *whom.*

(2) The form a relative pronoun takes depends on its use in a subordinate clause.

To choose between *who* or *whom* in a subordinate clause, follow these steps.

Step 1: Find the subordinate clause.
Step 2: Decide how the relative pronoun is used in the clause—*subject, predicate nominative, direct object, indirect object,* or *object of a preposition.*
Step 3: Determine the case for this use of the relative pronoun.
Step 4: Select the correct case form of the relative pronoun.

EXAMPLE She is the one (*who, whom*) I met yesterday.
Step 1: The subordinate clause is (*who, whom*) *I met yesterday.*
Step 2: In this clause, the pronoun is the direct object of the verb *met.*
Step 3: As a direct object, the pronoun should be in the objective case.
Step 4: The objective form is *whom.*
ANSWER She is the one **whom** I met yesterday.

EXERCISE 7   Using *Who* and *Whom* Correctly

In the sentences below, underline the correct form of the pronoun in parentheses.

EX.   1.   (*Who*, *Whom*) did you wish to see?

1. Julian Bond is a politician (*who*, *whom*) I admire.
2. We will give a prize to (*whoever*, *whomever*) enters the contest.
3. (*Who*, *Whom*) is in charge of selling tickets?
4. Do you know (*who*, *whom*) the prime minister of Canada is?
5. To (*who*, *whom*) shall we send this letter?
6. William Jay Smith, (*who*, *whom*) was a well-known poet, also wrote about how sounds influenced his writing.
7. After I visited the Sierra Nevada, I began to read about John Muir, (*who*, *whom*) was an early conservationist.
8. We wrote to Mrs. Ramírez, the potter (*who*, *whom*) we met last summer, asking her to visit our school.
9. Can you guess (*who*, *whom*) is going to win the election?
10. Is it Ms. Jefferson (*who*, *whom*) is planning to travel through Africa?
11. The International Club mailed invitations to (*whoever*, *whomever*) had signed up for a language class.
12. I'd really like to know (*who*, *whom*) the artists are.
13. Suni is the only one (*who*, *whom*) got a perfect score on the test.
14. The basketball player (*who*, *whom*) I wrote to sent an autographed photo to sell at our fund-raiser.
15. Flo is going on vacation with the Yamotos, (*who*, *whom*) she has known for several years.
16. The governor said, "I need someone on (*who*, *whom*) I can depend absolutely."
17. The hikers greeted (*whoever*, *whomever*) they passed on the trail.
18. Everyone asked, "(*Who*, *Whom*) is he?"
19. Josie can't decide (*who*, *whom*) she will chose for a partner.
20. "Pardon me," the newcomer said. "To (*who*, *whom*) do I pay my entrance fee?"

Drabble reprinted by permission of UFS, Inc.

CHAPTER REVIEW

A.   Proofreading Sentences for Correct Pronoun Forms

In each of the sentences below, draw a line through any incorrect pronoun forms. On the line before the sentence, write the correct form of the pronoun. If the sentence contains no errors, write C.

EX.   _her_   1. Will you play baseball with Jesse and she?

_____   1. Whom made this painting of the sunset?

_____   2. Leo and myself hope to go to Alaska.

_____   3. Carla went on more rides than him at the carnival.

_____   4. Before the game started, the captains, him and I, shook hands.

_____   5. The winner of the writing contest is she.

_____   6. White Feather told Hy and I stories about his ancestors.

_____   7. Her and Lizzie are going to light the menorah.

_____   8. When we got to the top, we saw that Luna and him were there.

_____   9. Tina, who I saw yesterday, said the rehearsal is at noon.

_____ 10. I wish I practiced as much as him.

_____ 11. Jason and myself are going to audition for parts in the play.

_____ 12. The two who designed the experiment, her and I, will be testing it tomorrow.

_____ 13. Gloria and them are going to the swim meet.

_____ 14. It might have been him who left this message.

_____ 15. We kept the party a secret so that it would surprise her and he.

B.   Proofreading a Paragraph for Correct Pronoun Forms

In the following paragraph, draw a line through each incorrect pronoun form. In the space above it, write the correct form of the pronoun. Not all sentences contain errors.

EX.   [1] Everyone said it was the chance of a lifetime when Tess and me were invited to visit Greenland.

[1] Her uncle is a mountaineer and a man who I admire a lot. [2] It was

quite amazing that he would include Tess and myself in one of his

213

adventures. [3] Tess's mother, who is a photographer, wanted to go with he

and his expedition on their first trip to Greenland. [4] She persuaded him to

include Tess and I. [5] Us three, Tess, her mother and I, worked hard to get in

shape for this trip inside the Arctic Circle. [6] I didn't know anyone whom

had ever gone to Greenland, but I found some books to read about it. [7] First,

we had to fly to Iceland to get a flight to Greenland. [8] While Tess's uncle

made final preparations for the climb, Tess, her mother, and me explored the

town of Ilulissat. [9] Tess and I met an Inuit girl who was not much older

than us. [10] Tess's mom took several photographs of Tess and I with our

new friend.

C.   Writing About Community Service

Your local newspaper wants to interview you, the chairperson of last weekend's
clean-up project at your neighborhood park. On the lines below, write ten
sentences to use as notes during your interview. Include details about people
who helped you and refreshments or tools and supplies they brought. Use
pronouns from all three cases. Also be sure to use forms of *who/whom* and
pronoun appositives. Underline all the pronouns you use.

EX.   My best friends, Paulo and Shannon, who brought rakes and trash bags for us
to use, worked hard all day long.

_____

_____

_____

_____

_____

_____

_____

_____

_____

AMBIGUOUS REFERENCE

A pronoun has no definite meaning in itself. Its meaning is clear only when the reader knows what word it stands for. The word that a pronoun stands for is called the *antecedent* of the pronoun.

16a   A pronoun should always refer clearly to its antecedent.

In the following examples, arrows point from the pronouns to their antecedents.

EXAMPLES   After **Bonny** sang the aria, the audience applauded **her.**

Would a window box help **us** brighten up **our** kitchen?

Tying the **boat** to the mooring, Tiwa said, "**It** should be safe here."

(1) Avoid an *ambiguous reference*, which occurs when a pronoun refers to either of two antecedents.

AMBIGUOUS   Our friends asked the Wongs if they could show them the map. [The antecedents of *they* and *them* are unclear.]

CLEAR   Our **friends** asked if the Wongs could show **them** the map.

CLEAR   Our **friends** asked if **they** could show the map to the Wongs.

AMBIGUOUS   The teacher discussed with Eloise the exercise she had just written on the chalkboard. [The antecedent of *she* is unclear.]

CLEAR   After the **teacher** had written the exercise on the chalkboard, **she** discussed it with Eloise.

CLEAR   After **Eloise** had written the exercise on the chalkboard, the teacher discussed it with **her.**

(2) Avoid a *general reference*, which occurs when a pronoun refers to a general idea rather than to a specific noun.

The pronouns commonly used in making general references are *it, this, that, which,* and *such.*

GENERAL   Raoul could dance, sing, and play the violin. The judges awarded him first prize in the talent show for **this.** [*This* has no specific antecedent.]

CLEAR   Raoul could dance, sing, and play the violin. The judges awarded him first prize in the talent show for **his many abilities.**

CLEAR   **Because Raoul could dance, sing, and play the violin,** the judges awarded him first prize in the talent show.

GENERAL	The team has won every game this season, and we think **it's** terrific. [*It's* has no specific antecedent.]
CLEAR	We think **it's** terrific **that the team has won every game this season.**

EXERCISE 1   Revising Sentences to Correct Ambiguous and General References

On your own paper, rewrite each of the sentences below, correcting the ambiguous or general pronoun references.

EX.   1. Chet was joking with Angelo when he should have been fixing the car.

    1. Instead of joking with Angelo, Chet should have been fixing the car.

1. Jeremy congratulated the chef for his wonderful cooking, which made him quite happy.
2. Mindy waved to Roberta as she came out of the store.
3. We saw jugglers, acrobats, and clowns at the circus, which was very entertaining.
4. Many people disapproved of the candidate's political ideas, and it cost him the election.
5. Albert told Oscar that he'd brought the wrong book.
6. When our lawyer brought the expert to lunch, we asked him to show us the report.
7. Dolores was going to pick up the baby, but then she fell asleep.
8. I sent in three box tops and the answer to the riddle. That could win the contest.
9. The lights went out and we heard a strange sound, which made us jump.
10. Hector and Philip get along well because of his interest in sports.
11. The manager was a smooth talker and a stylish dresser, which everybody knew.
12. Our team raced against the Midvale All-Stars the year they set the league record.
13. We study hard and practice a lot, which is why we're the best.
14. Georgianna heard the news during the bumpy train ride, and it made her feel sick.
15. Choy sent a letter to Ling even though he didn't know him.

WEAK AND INDEFINITE REFERENCE

16b Avoid a *weak reference*, which occurs when a pronoun refers to an antecedent that has not been expressed.

WEAK   We went to the automobile show yesterday, and Dad couldn't decide which of them he liked the best. [The antecedent of *them* is not expressed.]

CLEAR   We went to the automobile show yesterday, and Dad couldn't decide which of the **cars** he liked the best.

WEAK   Ruben was in training to run that marathon, but this year it was cancelled.

CLEAR   Ruben was in training to run that marathon, but this year the **race** was cancelled.

16c In formal writing, avoid the indefinite use of the pronouns *it, they,* and *you.*

An indefinite reference occurs when a pronoun refers to no particular person or thing. Such a pronoun is unnecessary to the meaning of the sentence.

INDEFINITE   In the message it said he should report immediately. [*It* has no clear antecedent in the sentence.]

CLEAR   The message said he should report immediately.

INDEFINITE   In most surveys, they use a balanced sample. [*They* is not necessary to the meaning of the sentence.]

CLEAR   Most surveys use a balanced sample.

INDEFINITE   You aren't shown any of the credits until the end in some modern films. [*You* has no clear antecedent in the sentence.]

CLEAR   Some modern films don't show any credits until the end.

NOTE   The indefinite use of *it* in familiar expressions such as *it is morning, it is raining, it seems,* and *it is warm* is acceptable.

EXERCISE 2   Revising Sentences to Correct Weak and Indefinite References

On your own paper, rewrite each of the following sentences, correcting the weak or indefinite pronoun reference.

EX.   1. High in those mountains, you will discover the air is quite thin.

      1. High in those mountains, the air is quite thin.

1. Sheila is always excited about something, and one of them in particular is basketball.

2. It was a cloudy day, and we thought it might rain if they got any darker.
3. On the radio they said the war was over.
4. On that Caribbean island, you have nothing short of a tropical paradise.
5. Rinaldo was a fine tailor and made sure they were always mended on time.
6. On the back of the carton, it said, "Do not bend."
7. In my garden, they always bloom.
8. We rode in the car for six hours, and it made us tired.
9. Meet me at the train station, and we'll take it home together.
10. In some countries, they already have government-run health-care plans.
11. Frederico was known as the finest swordsman in the land, but he never drew it in anger.
12. The story said that on some planets they had strange creatures.
13. The telephone operator told me to stay on the line, and she would put it through for me.
14. In *The New York Times*, they reported on the peace talks.
15. We often look at the sky at night, but only astronomers using telescopes can always see them.
16. It was mentioned in the newsletter that Ryan had been promoted.
17. They never caught Jesse James.
18. Molly Ringwald is one of my favorite movie stars, but I haven't seen her in any lately.
19. We got to the sailing races just in time to see Jules skipper his in over the finish line.
20. In that math class you have fewer tests.
21. Over the phone they told Peter he had won the raffle.
22. In certain stores in this mall, they always overcharge.
23. You get bored sitting around the house all day.
24. In all of these books they present a true picture of the gypsy life.
25. Maria showed me her butterfly collection and then asked me if I'd like to help her catch one.

CHAPTER REVIEW

A. Correcting Faulty Pronoun References in Sentences

Most of the sentences below contain ambiguous, general, indefinite, or weak pronoun references. On your own paper, revise each incorrect sentence. If a sentence is correct, write C.

EX. 1. Paul is older than Luis and Marek, but he is the tallest.

    1. Paul is older than Luis and Marek, but Marek is the tallest.

1. Rita and Pauline met at the shop.
2. Carlos came in first out of a field of five hundred, which is terrific!
3. After we saw a film about the lifestyles of the British royalty, Oscar said he'd like to tour one of them.
4. In some parts of the country, they'll offer a better price for furniture.
5. He was so gullible he believed me no matter which ones I told him.
6. The senator spoke briefly and to the point, which pleased her audience.
7. I couldn't take drama and dance during the same term, so I dropped it.
8. Sondra's mother explained to her why she didn't have time to see the play.
9. At modeling school, you are taught a new way to walk.
10. I really enjoy the science fiction of Arthur C. Clarke, but my brother hasn't read any of them yet.

B. Proofreading a Paragraph to Correct Faulty Pronoun References

On your own paper, rewrite the following paragraph, correcting any unclear pronoun references. Some sentences may be correct and require no change.

EX. [1] Since 1924, police have used polygraphs to detect lies, but psychologists still question their reliability.

    [1] Since 1924, police have used polygraphs to detect lies, but psychologists still question the reliability of the tests.

[1] The examiner explains to the subject the procedure of the test he is about to take. [2] The subject's wrist and chest are wired to the machine, and this is supposed to measure his emotional responses. [3] Because the subject's pulse, blood pressure, and respiration are unconscious reactions, it's supposed to measure his true feelings. [4] Examiners require special training before they can give them. [5] Control questions like "What is your name?" and "Where do you live?" are asked first, and they provide an example of the subject's normal responses. [6] Any unusual movement

registered by the polygraph may be a reason to think it's a lie. [7] The examiner tries to ask obvious control questions, but it can't really be scientifically exact. [8] When the examiner studies the results, her judgment depends on how much they differ from what is normal. [9] Since the results depend so much on the abilities of the examiner, they aren't admissible in legal testimony. [10] Therefore, they don't use polygraph test results in courts of law.

C.   Working Cooperatively to Write a Letter to a Celebrity

You have been assigned to write a report on a celebrity of your choice. Work with a partner to write a letter to a celebrity whom you would like to know more about. You might ask the person about his or her accomplishments, goals, family, special training, awards, and childhood. Use at least one pronoun in each of your sentences. Underline the pronouns you use.

EX.

410 W. Evans Ave.

Pittsburgh, PA 15239

September 11, 1994

Mrs. Hillary Rodham Clinton
The White House
Washington, DC 20500

Dear Mrs. Clinton,

We have been impressed by your active participation in government and would like to know some more about you. For instance, we know you are interested in many issues, one of which is health care. We would like to know about other public policy issues you intend to work on.

We are also curious about how you manage to be a wife and a mother and the First Lady all at the same time. What do think is your most difficult job, and why?

Mrs. Clinton, please write and tell us about yourself. We hope that you and President Clinton will do great things for our country. We look forward to meeting you one day, and we wish you all the best.

Sincerely yours,

Tama La Croix and April Neiman

REGULAR VERBS

17a **The four principal parts of a verb are the *base form*, the *present participle*, the *past*, and the *past participle*. All other forms of the verb are derived from the base form.**

EXAMPLES   I **walk** the dog. [base form of *walk*]
I **am walking** the dog. [present participle of *walk*]
I **walked** the dog. [past of *walk*]
I **have walked** the dog. [past participle of *walk*]

17b **A *regular verb* is one that forms its past and past participle by adding *–d* or *–ed* to the base form.**

Base Form	Present Participle	Past	Past Participle
call	(is) calling	called	(have) called
gnaw	(is) gnawing	gnawed	(have) gnawed
like	(is) liking	liked	(have) liked
paint	(is) painting	painted	(have) painted
tip	(is) tipping	tipped	(have) tipped
watch	(is) watching	watched	(have) watched

NOTE   A few regular verbs have alternate past and past participle forms ending in *–t*. For example, the past and past participle forms of *burn* are *burned* or *burnt*.

When the present participle and the past participle forms are used as main verbs (simple predicates) in sentences, they always require helping verbs.

EXERCISE 1   Writing the Correct Forms of Regular Verbs

For each of the following sentences, decide what the correct form of the italicized verb should be. Write the correct verb form on the line before the sentence.

EX.   _____liked_____   1. The man *like* his previous job.

_____   1. The kitten purred when Tina *stroke* its head.

_____   2. When Ima is *watch* tennis, she can't hear a word I say.

_____   3. The tiger *jump* over the bar when the lights flickered.

_____   4. My friend is *paint* his bicycle a different color.

_____ 5. Most people have *listen* to different types of music on the radio.

_____ 6. The ancient Greeks *pray* to the many gods that they believed in.

_____ 7. I *call* the store for a price, but no one answered the phone.

_____ 8. My dog would have *gnaw* on the bone instead of licking it.

_____ 9. After Jacques left the mall, he *notice* his wallet was missing.

_____ 10. The contestants have *compete* in every possible game show.

_____ 11. Our eleventh-grade chorus is *visit* the local hospital tomorrow.

_____ 12. We have *wait* long enough for the package to arrive.

_____ 13. Payat *poke* his head into the room to tell us dinner was ready.

_____ 14. The city workers have *continue* to search for the hurricane victims.

_____ 15. The car *screech* to a halt when the traffic light changed.

EXERCISE 2   Proofreading Sentences for Correct Verb Forms

In each sentence below, draw a line through any incorrect verb form, and write the correct verb form before the sentence. If a sentence is correct, write *C*.

EX. _____*chewed*_____ 1. Cary ~~chew~~ the crunchy celery.

_____ 1. This tea taste spicy.

_____ 2. Yesterday, we watch a film about the octopus.

_____ 3. Your uncle fix it, but it could break again.

_____ 4. Stephanie greased the axle carefully.

_____ 5. Bill is phone us at the lodge.

_____ 6. Mrs. Vasquez has convince us that she will complete her college education.

_____ 7. Students have perform the dance well this year.

_____ 8. Many chemicals have polluting our rivers and streams.

_____ 9. The museum presenting a large exhibit of African wildlife.

_____ 10. Has the company refund your money?

IRREGULAR VERBS

17c An *irregular verb* forms the past and past participle in some other way than by adding –*d* or –*ed* to the base form.

Base Form	Present Participle	Past	Past Participle
drive	(is) driving	drove	(have) driven
give	(is) giving	gave	(have) given
sing	(is) singing	sang	(have) sung

NOTE If you are not sure about the principal parts of a verb, look in a dictionary. Entries for irregular verbs give the principal parts.

COMMON IRREGULAR VERBS			
Base Form	**Present Participle**	**Past**	**Past Participle**
be	(is) being	was, were	(have) been
become	(is) becoming	became	(have) become
begin	(is) beginning	began	(have) begun
bite	(is) biting	bit	(have) bitten *or* bit
blow	(is) blowing	blew	(have) blown
break	(is) breaking	broke	(have) broken
bring	(is) bringing	brought	(have) brought
build	(is) building	built	(have) built
burst	(is) bursting	burst	(have) burst
buy	(is) buying	bought	(have) bought
catch	(is) catching	caught	(have) caught
choose	(is) choosing	chose	(have) chosen
come	(is) coming	came	(have) come
cost	(is) costing	cost	(have) cost
do	(is) doing	did	(have) done
draw	(is) drawing	drew	(have) drawn
drink	(is) drinking	drank	(have) drunk
drive	(is) driving	drove	(have) driven
eat	(is) eating	ate	(have) eaten
fall	(is) falling	fell	(have) fallen

COMMON IRREGULAR VERBS

Base Form	Present Participle	Past	Past Participle
feel	(is) feeling	felt	(have) felt
find	(is) finding	found	(have) found
forget	(is) forgetting	forgot	(have) forgotten
freeze	(is) freezing	froze	(have) frozen
get	(is) getting	got	(have) gotten *or* got
give	(is) giving	gave	(have) given
go	(is) going	went	(have) gone
grow	(is) growing	grew	(have) grown
hold	(is) holding	held	(have) held
hurt	(is) hurting	hurt	(have) hurt
keep	(is) keeping	kept	(have) kept
know	(is) knowing	knew	(have) known
lead	(is) leading	led	(have) led
lend	(is) lending	lent	(have) lent
lose	(is) losing	lost	(have) lost
make	(is) making	made	(have) made
meet	(is) meeting	met	(have) met
put	(is) putting	put	(have) put
ride	(is) riding	rode	(have) ridden
ring	(is) ringing	rang	(have) rung
run	(is) running	ran	(have) run
say	(is) saying	said	(have) said
see	(is) seeing	saw	(have) seen
sell	(is) selling	sold	(have) sold
send	(is) sending	sent	(have) sent
show	(is) showing	showed	(have) shown
shrink	(is) shrinking	shrank *or* shrunk	(have) shrunk
sing	(is) singing	sang	(have) sung
sink	(is) sinking	sank *or* sunk	(have) sunk *or* sunken
speak	(is) speaking	spoke	(have) spoken
stand	(is) standing	stood	(have) stood
steal	(is) stealing	stole	(have) stolen
swim	(is) swimming	swam	(have) swum
swing	(is) swinging	swung	(have) swung

COMMON IRREGULAR VERBS			
Base Form	**Present Participle**	**Past**	**Past Participle**
take	(is) taking	took	(have) taken
tell	(is) telling	told	(have) told
throw	(is) throwing	threw	(have) thrown
wear	(is) wearing	wore	(have) worn
win	(is) winning	won	(have) won
write	(is) writing	wrote	(have) written

EXERCISE 3 Writing Past and Past Participle Forms of Irregular Verbs

On the line before each sentence, complete the sentences below by writing the correct past or past participle form of the verb in italics.

EX. _____chose_____ 1. The woman *choose* her new dress.

_____ 1. The children have *speak* their own languages.

_____ 2. The restaurant has *freeze* the fish for later use.

_____ 3. As a result of too much heat, the clothes have *shrink* in the dryer.

_____ 4. Do you realize that your car tires have *wear* thin?

_____ 5. Last year, many people *become* part of our health care group.

_____ 6. The teacher was so busy that she *forget* to correct the papers.

_____ 7. Once everyone agreed on a time, the people *meet* to resolve the remaining issues.

_____ 8. After Anaba had picked a bushel of apples, she picked one for herself and *bite* into it.

_____ 9. The students have *build* a house as a year-long project.

_____ 10. The ancient Romans *get* many of their ideas from Greek culture.

_____ 11. Has everyone *take* her or his shower yet?

_____ 12. Last summer, we *swim* at the YMCA nearly every day.

_____ 13. We *begin* last night's concert with "Respect."

_____ 14. We were disappointed that the store had *sell* all those games.

_____ 15. The phone had *ring* twice by the time I reached it.

——————— 16. The rebel troops had *blow* up the bridge.

——————— 17. Many homes were destroyed when the dam *break*.

——————— 18. Sasha has *keep* busy all morning returning telephone calls.

——————— 19. The audience *leave* quickly after the play was over.

——————— 20. The sunflowers *grow* quite tall last summer.

EXERCISE 4   **Proofreading a Paragraph for Past or**
Past Participle Forms of Verbs

Determine the correct past or past participle form for each of the italicized verbs in the paragraph below. Write the correct form above the verb.

EX.   [1] Ms. Franklin *tell* me about some traditional African sports.
       (told)

[1] She *say* that wrestling has been practiced in the Sudan for thousands of years. [2] In the Ethiopian form of wrestling that she saw, young men from different villages *fight* each other. [3] Also in Ethiopia, she was thrilled when teams *ride* horses in the game Feres Gugs. [4] One team chased the other to tag their opponents with wands when the chasers *catch* them. [5] The riders on the opposing team *hold* circular shields to fight off the wands. [6] A spear-throwing competition *be* particularly popular in Uganda and Zaire when she was there. [7] The winner's spear was the one which was *throw* farthest and fastest. [8] Ms. Franklin also has *see* a langa meet in northern Nigeria. [9] The players *run* into each other to try to knock their opponents off balance. [10] She *say* that the sport requires skill, speed, and a good sense of balance.

LIE AND LAY

17d The verb *lie* means "to rest," "to recline," or "to remain in a lying position." *Lie* never takes an object. The verb *lay* means "to put (something) in a place." *Lay* usually takes an object.

PRINCIPAL PARTS OF *LIE* AND *LAY*			
Base Form	**Present Participle**	**Past**	**Past Participle**
lie (to rest)	(is) lying	lay	(have) lain
lay (to put)	(is) laying	laid	(have) laid

When deciding whether to use *lie* or *lay*, ask yourself two questions.

Question 1:   What do I want to say? Is the meaning "to be in a lying position," or is it "to put something down"?

Question 2:   What time does the verb express, and which principal part is used to show this time?

The examples below show how you can apply these questions to determine which verb—*lie* or *lay*—you should use.

EXAMPLE   The cat (*lay, laid*) on the top shelf, hiding.

Question 1:   Meaning? The meaning is "to be in a lying position." Therefore, the verb should be *lie*.

Question 2:   Principal part? The verb expresses the past, and the sentence requires the past form. The past form of *lie* is *lay*.

ANSWER   The cat **lay** on the top shelf, hiding.

EXERCISE 5   Choosing the Correct Forms of *Lie* and *Lay*

In each of the following sentences, underline the correct form of *lie* or *lay* in parentheses.

EX.   1. The doctor is (*lying, laying*) the instruments on the table.

1. After Robert (*lay, laid*) on the couch, he felt better.

2. When Mother (*laid, lay*) Lana on the quilt, Lana stopped crying.

3. The animals have (*lain, laid*) in the sun for hours.

4. Bricklayers (*lay, lie*) thousands of bricks a year.

5. Where have you (*laid, lain*) the sweater to dry?

6. I would like to (*lay, lie*) my papers over there.

7. (*Lie, Lay*) the box on the dining room table.

8. Have all the students (*laid, lain*) their assignments on the desk?

9. A cloudy mist (*lay, laid*) over the valley.

10. Let's (*lie, lay*) on the beach for a few minutes.

11. The patient is (*lying, laying*) in bed in order to help heal his broken leg.

12. Military officers (*lay, lie*) down rules as helpful guidelines for their troops.

13. He is (*lying, laying*) the new carpet on the floor.

14. Many of the squirrels have (*laid, lain*) acorns beneath the tree.

15. The workers have (*lain, laid*) asphalt the length of the street.

EXERCISE 6   Proofreading Sentences for the Correct Use of *Lie* and *Lay*

In the sentences below, draw a line through each incorrect form of *lie* and *lay*. Write the correct verb form on the line before each sentence. If a sentence is correct, write C.

EX.   ____laid____   1. I have ~~lain~~ the blanket on the bed.

_____   1. After its morning workout, the horse laid in the stall.

_____   2. The customer is laying his money on the counter.

_____   3. Be quiet. My mother is laying on the couch.

_____   4. Khenphet and his brother have lain their coats on the sofa.

_____   5. Queen bees lay fertilized eggs that will develop into new queens.

_____   6. The tigers have laid near the water to keep cool.

_____   7. Monkeys like to lay on the branches of trees.

_____   8. Please lie my sweater on the railing.

_____   9. It is difficult to lie tile correctly.

_____   10. After you have laid in the sun a bit, your swimsuit should be dry.

_____   11. Yesterday, Sam laid in bed for an hour after the game was over.

_____   12. Our neighbor is laying in bed, recovering from her illness.

_____   13. The leather is lying on the rocks to dry.

_____   14. Lay down in your room before you get too tired.

_____   15. The father lay his baby in her crib.

SIT *AND* SET *AND* RISE *AND* RAISE

17e The verb *sit* means "to rest in an upright, seated position." *Sit* almost never takes an object. The verb *set* means "to put (something) in a place." *Set* usually takes an object.

PRINCIPAL PARTS OF *SIT* AND *SET*			
Base Form	**Present Participle**	**Past**	**Past Participle**
sit (to rest)	(is) sitting	sat	(have) sat
set (to put)	(is) setting	set	(have) set

EXAMPLES   Please **sit** down.   **Set** it down gently.
The vase **sat** on the table.   Don't **set** it there.

17f The verb *rise* means "to go in an upward direction." *Rise* never takes an object. The verb *raise* means "to move (something) in an upward direction." *Raise* usually takes an object.

PRINCIPAL PARTS OF *RISE* AND *RAISE*			
Base Form	**Present Participle**	**Past**	**Past Participle**
rise (to get up)	(is) rising	rose	(have) risen
raise (to lift up)	(is) raising	raised	(have) raised

EXAMPLES   I always **rise** before sunup.
Raise that corner just a little more.
Bad weather meant food prices **rose** again.
Have the grocers **raised** their prices yet?

EXERCISE 7   **Proofreading Sentences for Correct Use of**
Sit and Set and Rise and Raise

In the following sentences, draw a line through each incorrect form of *sit*, *set*, *rise*, and *raise*. Write the correct verb form on the line before each sentence. If a sentence is correct, write *C*.

EX.   _____sat_____   1. The hen ~~set~~ on her eggs.

_____   1. We didn't want to set down on the damp ground.

_____   2. The vase of roses is sitting on Mei's desk.

_____ 3. The Mayan farmers rised maize as their primary crop.

_____ 4. Each generation rises its crops a little differently than the previous one.

_____ 5. Ask your brother where he sat the bucket of worms.

_____ 6. House prices dropped for a few years and now are raising again.

_____ 7. Some islands in the Pacific are volcanoes that raise up from the ocean floor.

_____ 8. The Pomo basket set in a prominent place.

_____ 9. People the world over have raised sheep for wool.

_____ 10. How would we survive if the sun never raised again?

_____ 11. I could tell that you looked in the trunk because the lid was slightly risen.

_____ 12. The jurors entered the room and set around the table.

_____ 13. If you're tired of standing, set on a folding chair.

_____ 14. The porter has sat your suitcase by the taxi.

_____ 15. Getting a baby to set still for a photograph is no easy job.

_____ 16. Set the piano down gently, please.

_____ 17. Kate had risen her hand and was waving it wildly.

_____ 18. Has the bread raised yet?

_____ 19. We won't leave the tent until the sun has risen.

_____ 20. When Pang heard his name called, he set up straighter.

_____ 21. When Mr. March enters a room, he rises his walking stick and nods.

_____ 22. Steam was rising from the kettle on the stove.

_____ 23. As the lava cools, the ground level actually raises.

_____ 24. I could sit through this film again and again.

_____ 25. If that paper sets in the rain any longer, it will be unreadable.

REVIEW EXERCISE

A. Using the Past and Past Participle Forms of Verbs

On the lines provided, complete the paragraph below by writing the correct past or past participle form of the verb given in parentheses.

EX. [1] Flax has been ____raised____ (raise) for many centuries to make clothes and rope.

[1] People have_____(make) linen, yarn, and rope from flax since at least 8000 B.C. [2] The ancient Egyptians_____(wear) linen clothes and wrapped mummies in linen. [3] Linen cloth_____(become) part of domestic life around the Mediterranean long before the Christian era. [4] Some early linen fabrics_____(is) extremely fine, with five hundred threads to the inch. [5] In the ninth century, Charlemagne_____(set) up centers for linen weaving in Flemish cities. [6] By the late Middle Ages, many Europeans _____(weave) cloth made of wool and linen. [7] At that time, most European monasteries_____(produce) flax for their own use. [8] By the mid-eighteenth century, Ireland had_____(become) a center of linen weaving. [9] The early colonists_____(take) flax with them to North America. [10] A fabric made from linen and wool_____ (is) the main clothing material in the colonies.

B. Using the Past and Past Participle Forms Correctly

For each of the following sentences, decide whether the italicized verb is correct. If it is not, write the correct verb form on the line before the sentence. If a sentence is correct, write *C*.

EX. ____rose____ 1. A small tree *raised* up from the rock.

_____ 1. The stock market had *raised*.

_____ 2. Mr. Ito *set* on the board of trustees for the library.

_____ 3. Dr. Johnson has *call* for you twice.

_____   4. Bright and smooth, the new patchwork quilt *lay* on the sleigh bed.

_____   5. Surprisingly, silkworms have *became* incapable of surviving on their own in nature.

_____   6. Without our paddles, we nearly *wash* out to sea during the storm.

_____   7. You *sample* the eggplant salad for Mother, didn't you?

_____   8. Where have you *lay* that Russian history book you were reading?

_____   9. Having a party together nearly *ruin* Shing's and Yori's friendship.

_____   10. What *happen* during Cinco de Mayo, a Mexican holiday?

C.   Proofreading a Paragraph for the Correct Use of Irregular Verbs

Most of the sentences in the paragraph below contain an error in the use of irregular verbs. Draw a line through each error, and write the correct verb form above the error. Some sentences may have no errors.

EX.   [1] In our family, my first camping trip will never be ~~forgot~~. *forgotten*

[1] Lanie and I been seven when we decided to camp near the stream behind my house. [2] We spent an hour setting up the tent about a hundred yards from the house. [3] Lanie had bringed essential supplies of apples and popcorn. [4] My older brother Parnell told us scary stories all evening. [5] Then we gone out with our flashlights to the tent. [6] We made shadows on the tent walls until our batteries run out of power. [7] After we stopped talking, the night sounds taken over. [8] An animal nosing around the tent, probably smelling the popcorn, maked us panic. [9] Be it a skunk or a rat? [10] We wished Lanie had thought fresh batteries were more important than fresh popcorn.

VERB TENSE

17g The time expressed by a verb is called the *tense* of the verb.

(1) The *present tense* expresses an action (or a state of being) occurring now. The present tense is also used to show a customary or habitual action (or state of being); to convey a general truth, something that is always true; and to summarize the plot or subject matter of a literary work (such use is called the *literary present*).

EXAMPLES   In the evenings, I **run** laps at the track. [customary action]
In "Goldilocks and the Three Bears," a child **learns** about respecting others' privacy and property. [literary present]

(2) The *past tense* expresses an action (or a state of being) that occurred in the past and ended.

EXAMPLE   I **ran** an extra lap last night.

(3) The *future tense* expresses an action (or a state of being) that will occur but has not yet occurred. The future tense is formed with *will* or *shall* and the base form.

EXAMPLE   Next week I **will run** in my first race.

NOTE   A future tense verb may also be expressed by using the present tense of *be* followed by either *going to* or *about to* and the base form of a verb.

EXAMPLES   My best friends **are going to visit** Austin in September.
Dr. Steele **is about to announce** the winner.

(4) The *present perfect tense* expresses an action (or a state of being) that occurred at some indefinite time in the past. The present perfect tense always includes the helping verb *have* or *has*.

EXAMPLE   I **have** not **run** in a race before.

(5) The *past perfect tense* expresses an action (or a state of being) that occurred in the past and was completed before some other past occurrence. The past perfect tense always includes the helping verb *had*.

EXAMPLE   I **had run** for eight months before I decided to enter the race.

(6) The *future perfect tense* expresses an action (or a state of being) that will be completed in the future before some other future occurrence. The future perfect tense always includes the helping verbs *will have* or *shall have*.

EXAMPLE   By the time I leave the track, I **will have run** twelve laps.

Each of the tenses also has a progressive form, which expresses a continuing action (or state of being). It consists of a form of the verb *be* plus the present participle of a verb. The progressive is not a separate tense but an additional form of each of the six tenses.

Form	Examples
Present Progressive	am, is, are running
Past Progressive	was, were running
Future Progressive	will (shall) be running
Present Perfect Progressive	has been, have been running
Past Perfect Progressive	had been running
Future Perfect Progressive	will (shall) have been running

EXERCISE 8   **Identifying Verb Tense**

For each of the sentences below, identify the tense of the italicized verb. On the line before each sentence, write *pres.* for *present, past* for *past, fut.* for *future, pres. perf.* for *present perfect, past perf.* for *past perfect,* or *fut. perf.* for *future perfect.* Include *prog.* for *progressive form* where appropriate.

EX.   _past prog._   1. George *was trying* to get tickets to the concert.

_____   1. Every month, Virgil *calculates* the interest earned by his savings account.

_____   2. I'm afraid that I *will* never *see* an alien spaceship.

_____   3. The refrigerator *had been running* nonstop for three days.

_____   4. Kuri *brought* home the new <u>Webster's New World Dictionary</u> and <u>Roget's Thesaurus</u>.

_____   5. Kaloma *is* not *carrying* your groceries home again.

_____   6. I *had seen* the amazing running of Emmitt Smith before.

_____   7. *Will* you *have bought* a car by this time next year?

_____   8. Archaeologists *have found* some Mayan temples by studying Landsat photographs from space.

_____   9. Vladimir Nabokov *saw* colors in connection with letters of the alphabet.

_____   10. The waves *have been pounding* this shore for a million years.

SEQUENCE OF TENSES

17h **When describing events that occur at the same time, use verbs in the same tense.**

EXAMPLE   The car **zoomed** by and dust **flew** into the air.

17i **When describing events that occur at different times, use verbs in different tenses to show the order of events.**

EXAMPLE   Kip **plays** the tuba, but years ago he **played** the trumpet. [Kip plays the tuba now, so *plays* is in the present tense. He used to play the trumpet, so *played* is in the past tense.]

17j **Avoid the use of *would have* in "if clauses" that express the earlier of two past actions. Use the past perfect tense.**

NONSTANDARD   If I would have studied more, I would have done better in history.

STANDARD   If I **had studied** more, I would have done better in history.

EXERCISE 9   Using Tenses Correctly

In the sentences below, draw a line through each incorrect verb form, and write the correct form above it.

EX.   1. Hallie ~~blows~~ the dust off and read the inscription.
               blew

1. The clock fell and breaks into several pieces.

2. We stand in line forty minutes or so before we could buy tickets.

3. I had eaten the entire fish before I see the bowls of vegetables.

4. If I sunk this shot, I will have made nineteen out of twenty.

5. If the team would have practiced more, it would have won the game.

6. Have the stores closed for the holiday, or were they open until five?

7. Lara had sung for sixteen years before she gets her first career break.

8. If you would have closed the window tightly, the rain would not have ruined the wallpaper.

9. Mario hummed softly while he is wrapping up the romano cheese.

10. Because Hans injures his knee, he no longer skates.

17k The *present infinitive* expresses an action (or a state of being) that follows another action or state of being.

EXAMPLE   Julianne wants **to ride** with me. [The action expressed by *to ride* follows the action expressed by *wants*.]

17l The *present perfect infinitive* expresses an action (or a state of being) that comes before another action or state of being.

EXAMPLE   They hoped **to have been** here by now. [The state of being expressed by *to have been* comes before the action expressed by *hoped*.]

17m The *present participle* expresses an action (or a state of being) that occurs at the same time as another action or state of being.

EXAMPLE   **Smiling** through the glass, her mother waved to her. [The action expressed by *Smiling* occurs at the same time as the action expressed by *waved*.]

17n The *present perfect participle* expresses an action (or a state of being) that precedes another action or state of being.

EXAMPLE   **Having finished** his sculpture, he began to clean up. [The action expressed by *Having finished* comes before the action expressed by *began*.]

EXERCISE 10   Revising Sentences for Correct Verb Tense

Draw a line through the incorrect verb forms in the sentences below. On your own paper, write the correct forms.

EX.   1. The ball signaling the new year was supposed to ~~drop~~ by now.

    1. to have dropped

1. Fighting back a smile, Lucas will give back the toddler's toy.
2. The girls scattered to have hidden from Bernice.
3. Hitting the clock, the startled cat jumped off the mantlepiece.
4. Freyda expected to hand in her resignation by now.
5. Winning the National Book Critics Circle Award, Maxine Hong Kingston became well known for her writings about the Asian American experience.
6. To have sung at the Met is what she wants most of all.
7. Deciding to take a drawing class, Rene registered at the Art Institute.
8. After a tough day like today, it is hard not to have asked, "Why me?"
9. Waiting for the bus yesterday, I nearly freeze.
10. The Luttrells had wanted to have been there by noon.

ACTIVE VOICE AND PASSIVE VOICE

Voice is the form a transitive verb takes to indicate whether the subject of the verb performs or receives the action.

17o   A verb in the *active voice* expresses an action done by its subject. A verb in the *passive voice* expresses an action done to its subject.

ACTIVE VOICE   Trina and Luis **washed** the car. [The subject, *Trina and Luis*, performed the action.]

PASSIVE VOICE   The car **was washed** by Trina and Luis. [The subject, *car*, received the action.]

A transitive verb in the active voice often has an indirect object as well as a direct object. Either object can become the subject or can remain a complement in the passive construction.

	S	V	I.O.	D.O.
ACTIVE VOICE	Grandpa	gave	each of us	a two-dollar bill.

PASSIVE VOICE   Each of us was given a two-dollar bill (by Grandpa).

PASSIVE VOICE   A two-dollar bill was given to each of us (by Grandpa).

In the preceding examples, the direct object *two-dollar bill* in the active construction becomes the complement in the first passive construction, and the indirect object *each* becomes the subject. In the second passive construction, *two-dollar bill* is the subject, and *each* is the object of the preposition. A complement in a passive construction is called a ***retained object***, not a *direct object* or an *indirect object*.

17p   Avoid using the passive voice except in special circumstances.

(1) Use the passive voice when you do not know who or what performed the action.

EXAMPLES   Did you know that this sweater **was made** by hand?
            I heard that a new bookstore **had been opened** at the mall.

(2) Use the passive voice when you do not want to reveal who or what performed the action.

EXAMPLES   Many mistakes **were made** in today's game.
            The museum **will be given** one million dollars.

(3) Use the passive voice when you want to emphasize the receiver of the action.

EXAMPLES   **Were** you absolutely **soaked** by the rain?
            Some fabulous antiques **were found** in the attic.

EXERCISE 11   **Classifying Voice in Sentences**

Classify each verb in the sentences below as active or passive. Write *act.* for *active* or *pass.* for *passive* on the line before each sentence.

EX.   _act._   1. The team carried the coach down the field.

_____   1. Several moths were attracted to the light.

_____   2. Sometime during the night, the store windows had been broken.

_____   3. Hortense Powdermaker made connections between psychoanalysis and anthropology.

_____   4. In the Book of Job, a good man is persecuted for a long time.

_____   5. Who was handing out pamphlets at the transfer station?

_____   6. The wet mail was delivered by an equally wet carrier.

_____   7. You may donate canned goods for the food drive at the supermarket.

_____   8. The snow will soon be shoveled from the driveway.

_____   9. The relay team passed the baton smoothly after each lap.

_____   10. Vivian was singled out for high praise.

EXERCISE 12   **Revising Sentences in the Passive Voice**

On your own paper, rewrite each of the sentences below to change passive voice verbs to the active voice.

EX.   1. My newspaper is delivered by a man driving a 1978 Ford.
    1. A man driving a 1978 Ford delivers my newspaper.

1. Witch hazel was used by the Cherokees to make a medicinal tea.

2. My lawn mower was tuned up last spring by Emma, who does odd jobs in the neighborhood.

3. The old cellar was filled in by a construction worker driving a bulldozer.

4. After being directed to the ticket office by the conductor, we found our way to the correct gate.

5. Water may be saved by the use of low-flow faucets.

6. Around 1700 B.C., each city of Canaan was ruled by a king.

7. Mary's favorite novels were written by Naguib Mahfouz.

8. When we were overlooked by the host, Bo stepped up and wrote her name on the waiting list.

9. Should laws that apply only to women be written by women?

10. In 1935, the Nobel Prize in chemistry was shared by Frédéric and Irène Joliot-Curie.

MOOD

Mood is the form a verb takes to indicate the attitude of the person using the verb. Verbs may be in one of three moods: the *indicative,* the *imperative,* or the *subjunctive.*

17q   The *indicative mood* expresses a fact, an opinion, or a question.

EXAMPLES   We **went** to the circus Saturday.
I **think** the clowns were terrific.
Will you come with us next year?

17r   The *imperative mood* expresses a direct command or request.

EXAMPLES   **Get** off my toe!
Hand me that wrench.

17s   The *subjunctive mood* expresses a suggestion, a necessity, a condition contrary to fact, or a wish.

EXAMPLES   It is requested that everyone **arrive** before 9:00 A.M.
If I **were** a sailor, I would sail about Chesapeake Bay.

(1) The *present subjunctive* expresses a suggestion or a necessity.

EXAMPLES   Dad suggested we **build** a TV table.
It is important that I **visit** Aunt Willoughby.

(2) The *past subjunctive* expresses a wish or a condition contrary to fact.

EXAMPLES   I wish I **were** taller.
He bossed us as if he **were** king.

EXERCISE 13   Classifying the Mood of Verbs

Classify the mood for each of the italicized verbs in the following sentences. Write *ind.* for *indicative,* *imp.* for *imperative,* or *subj.* for *subjunctive* on the line before each sentence.

EX.   _imp._   1. Look out for the boom!

_____   1. If you *were* president, how would you change the budget?

_____   2. The Dorset people *used* stone lamps to light the dark Arctic winters.

_____   3. Please *accept* my apologies for not writing sooner.

_____   4. *Take* two aspirin to ease the pain in your knee.

_____ 5. This plane *will take* three hours to get to Dallas.

_____ 6. Our boss insisted that we *wear* safety helmets.

_____ 7. Home to the Algonquian and Athapaskan peoples, the Subarctic *has* always *been* sparsely *populated.*

_____ 8. First, *thread* the needle with fishing line.

_____ 9. Helia guessed that the hummingbirds *migrate* each spring and fall.

_____ 10. It is impossible that Marty *visit* his uncle in Rome.

_____ 11. At that instant, Rosa wished she *were* anyplace else.

_____ 12. If you *do* not *have* a hook and line, you can't go fishing.

_____ 13. Bison *provided* many necessities to the American Indians of the Plains.

_____ 14. Before dinner, *take* this key over to Mercedes' house.

_____ 15. Hoa suggested that I *call* my brother.

_____ 16. *Is* there a word for someone who has lost the sense of smell?

_____ 17. If I *were* the cook, I would add spice to the chili.

_____ 18. Quick, *hand* me the pliers!

_____ 19. Mr. Poe asks that all club members *be* present to vote.

_____ 20. *Listen* carefully; you might learn something.

_____ 21. *Write* your answers on the back of the page.

_____ 22. I should have asked if Yuan *were* the last one on board.

_____ 23. Contrary to common belief, snakes *are* not slimy.

_____ 24. *Try* on this old dress, and take a look in the mirror.

_____ 25. A whippoorwill is a bird that sounds as if it *carries* a megaphone.

Shoe, by Jeff MacNelly, reprinted by permission: Tribune Media Services.

CHAPTER REVIEW

A. Proofreading Sentences for Correct Verb Usage

Identify the errors in verb usage in each of the sentences below. Draw a line through each incorrect verb form, and write the correct form of the verb above it. Some sentences may be correct.

EX. 1. Aviva ~~hear~~ *heard* that she got the job.

1. The two tourists ride the elevator to the seventieth floor and saw the city sparkling below.

2. Set down on that sofa, and I'll bring you some my mother's curried eggs.

3. Ms. Chiago laid the unfinished frame on top of the canvas.

4. By the time we arrive, I have finished reading your letter.

5. Chim has worked on that coconut-shell carving since Monday.

6. Jobelle pumps gas at the crossroads, but last summer she works at the station near Route 60.

7. If Jacy would have received a scholarship, he would have gone to college.

8. Around here, the flag is risen at sunup each day.

9. The receptionist suggested that everyone keeps a schedule on the computer.

10. I wish it were a nice summer day instead of a rainy fall one.

11. We rise in the morning and start on our chores.

12. Since last Monday we have not losed a single game.

13. It looks as though your sari has shrank in the dryer.

14. Lian has studied every night before last week's test, and it showed.

15. Jo is very polite, although he used to have been less courteous.

B. Proofreading a Paragraph for Correct Verb Usage

Identify the errors in verb usage in the following paragraph. Draw a line through each incorrect verb form, and write the correct form of the verb above it. Some sentences may be correct.

EX. [1] Have you ever imagined you ~~are~~ *were* traveling through someone else's body as a microscopic being?

[1] *Fantastic Voyage,* a novel by Isaac Asimov, describe what traveling inside a human might be like. [2] Having liked the book, I decided that I would imagine being inside a jellyfish. [3] This decision may rise a few eyebrows among you readers. [4] However, those of you who have float on an inner tube, pushed along by a mild sea breeze, will understand the idea's appeal. [5] Some jellyfish that drift in tropical seas be so large that I wouldn't have to shrink much to fit inside. [6] Also, some jellyfish are colonies builded of several kinds of members. [7] I hope this spirit of cooperation would allow the colony to temporarily accept a stranger like me. [8] I made up my mind to have spent a quiet day in a tropical jellyfish when an idea striked me.

[9] Jellyfish caught smaller animals by stinging them with tentacles. [10] How could I get through the tentacles without being stinged?

C.   Writing Notes for a Presentation

You are one of the leaders for a Wilderness Club troop of boys and girls from eleven to twelve years old. You have been asked to give a presentation on first aid at the next meeting. To prepare for your presentation, write your notes so that you can study them.

First, choose an emergency that you could give instructions for, such as a burn, sprain, cut, nosebleed, bee sting, or broken bone. Research the first-aid steps in Red Cross manuals, health books, encyclopedias, or other reference materials. On your own paper, write the first-aid steps in proper sequence, using complete sentences. Use the active voice, and be sure to use correct verb forms in your sentences.

EX.

First Aid for a Sprained Ankle

The symptoms of a sprained ankle are pain, swelling, and bruising. Start treating a sprained ankle by sponging it with cold water or by applying ice to it. You should wrap the ice in a cloth before putting it on bare skin. After that, wrap the ankle in an elastic bandage to give it support. The bandage manufacturers enclose instructions and diagrams on how to apply these bandages properly. Now, I'll demonstrate how to bandage a sprain.

USES OF MODIFIERS

18a   A *modifier* is a word that limits the meaning of another word. The two kinds of modifiers are *adjectives* and *adverbs*.

(1) An *adjective* limits the meaning of a noun or a pronoun.

EXAMPLES   **a light** breeze   **an** orangutan   **the best** movie

(2) An *adverb* limits the meaning of a verb, an adjective, or another adverb.

EXAMPLES   dances **beautifully**   **well** written

exceptionally smart   quite **far**

NOTE   Most modifiers with an *–ly* ending are adverbs. Many adverbs, such as *beautifully* and *hopefully*, are formed by adding *–ly* to adjectives, such as *beautiful* and *hopeful*. However, some modifiers ending in *–ly*, such as *daily* and *early*, may be used as adjectives. A few modifiers, such as *hard, far,* and *long,* have the same form whether used as adjectives or as adverbs.

18b   Use an adjective to modify the subject of a linking verb.

A linking verb is often followed by a ***predicate adjective,*** a word that modifies the subject.

EXAMPLES   Those sunflowers grew **tall.** [*Tall* follows the linking verb *grew* and modifies the subject, *sunflowers.*]
The accident on the commuter rail was **scary**. [*Scary* follows the linking verb *was* and modifies the subject, *accident.*]

☞   **REFERENCE NOTE:** For a list of common linking verbs, see page 119. For more information about predicate adjectives, see page 143.

18c   Use an adverb to modify an action verb.

Action verbs are often modified by adverbs that tell *how, when, where,* or *to what extent* an action is performed.

EXAMPLE   The eagle flew **high** above us. [*Flew* is an action verb. The modifiers following it are the adverb *high* and the prepositional phrase *above us.*]

Some verbs, such as *grow, appear, feel, look, sound, smell,* and *taste,* can be used as linking verbs or as action verbs. To determine whether a verb is a linking verb or an action verb, replace the verb with a form of *seem.* If the substitution sounds reasonable, the original verb is a linking verb. If not, it is an action verb.

EXAMPLES   Emilio looked **nervous.** [*Emilio seemed nervous* makes sense. Therefore, *looked* is a linking verb and is modified by the adjective *nervous.*]
Emilio looked **nervously** around the room. [*Emilio seemed nervously around the room* doesn't make sense. Therefore, *looked* is an action verb and is modified by the adverb *nervously.*]

EXERCISE 1   Selecting Modifiers to Complete Sentences

Complete the sentences below by writing appropriate modifiers on the lines provided. In parentheses after the modifier, identify each modifier by writing *adj.* for *adjective* or *adv.* for *adverb.*

EX.   1. Gregory Hines danced _____gracefully (adv.)_ .

1. The music is too _____ .

2. Last night we saw a _____ sunset.

3. Cicely Tyson is a _____ talented actress.

4. _____ winds raced through the forest.

5. The kung pao shrimp smells _____ .

6. The algebra test seemed _____ .

7. That wastebasket is _____ full.

8. You look very _____ today.

9. After I read the paper, I cut out a _____ article.

10. The rabbit ran _____ into the thicket.

11. We are _____ coming to the end of this unit of study.

12. The reception for the Japanese authors was _____ planned.

13. The pole-vaulter leaped _____ and cleared the beam.

14. Do you know all the words to this _____ song?

15. "I'm not wearing that _____ costume!" Ben shouted.

SIX TROUBLESOME MODIFIERS

18d *Bad* **is an adjective.** *Badly* **is an adverb. In standard English, only the adjective form should follow a linking verb.**

NONSTANDARD   If the punch tastes badly, we'll have to make some more.
STANDARD   If the punch tastes **bad,** we'll have to make some more.

18e *Good* **is an adjective.** *Well* **may be used as an adjective or as an adverb. Avoid using** *good* **to modify an action verb. Use** *well* **as an adverb meaning "capably" or "satisfactorily." As an adjective,** *well* **means "in good health" or "satisfactory in appearance or condition."**

NONSTANDARD   Conchetta sings very good, don't you think?
STANDARD   Conchetta sings very **well**, don't you think?
STANDARD   After taking the medicine given him by the doctor, Mario felt **well** again.

18f *Slow* **is an adjective.** *Slowly* **is an adverb. Avoid the common error of using** *slow* **to modify an action verb.**

NONSTANDARD   The waiter moved so slow that we thought he must be extremely tired.
STANDARD   The waiter moved so **slowly** that we thought he must be extremely tired.

EXERCISE 2   Choosing Correct Modifiers

In the following sentences, underline the correct modifier in parentheses.

EX.   1. Isabella looks (*good, well*) with her new hairdo.

1. Turtles and snails are two animals that move rather (*slow, slowly*).

2. Don't feel (*bad, badly*) if you lose the game; just play as hard as you can.

3. The artist Monet had an unusually (*good, well*) eye for light and shadows.

4. Harley didn't feel (*good, well*), so he went to see the nurse in the school infirmary.

5. This bus is quite (*slow, slowly*) because it stops at almost every corner.

6. Some young players have difficulty learning to be (*good, well*) losers.

7. I'm afraid I sang that song (*bad, badly*); may I try again?

8. The truck went (*slow, slowly*) down the icy hill.

9. The sauce tasted (*good, well*) after Ramon added a little parsley.

10. The special effects were done so (*good, well*) that the alien spaceship seemed totally realistic.

11. The car drove (*good, well*) after Regina had the tires rotated.

12. When I was baby-sitting, little Peter was cheerful, but his sister acted (*bad, badly*) all afternoon.

13. The honey oozed out of the bottle (*slow, slowly*).

14. "I don't know my lines (*good, well*) enough yet," the actor admitted.

15. The cat crept (*slow, slowly*) along the path, watching the birds.

16. "Drive (*slow, slowly*) so that we don't miss our turn," Al said.

17. Don't eat the fruit if it is (*bad, badly*).

18. Ever since Helena moved away, Emma has missed her (*bad, badly*).

19. If the next song is a (*slow, slowly*) one, I hope that Ossie asks me to dance.

20. Marissa paints as (*good, well*) as a professional artist.

21. We'll win today's game if our luck continues to be (*good, well*).

22. Without enough sun or water, the plants suffered (*bad, badly*).

23. Do you think that this perfume smells (*good, well*)?

24. "You will look (*good. well*) again once the marks from the chickenpox fade," the doctor assured the young boy.

25. The day at the beach passed (*slow, slowly*), and we finished our books.

FOX TROT

by **Bill Amend**

Fox Trot, copyright 1989 Bill Amend. Reprinted with permission of Universal Press Syndicate. All rights reserved.

COMPARISON OF MODIFIERS

18g *Comparison* **refers to the change in the form of an adjective or an adverb to show increasing or decreasing degrees in the quality that the modifier expresses.**

There are three degrees of comparison: *positive, comparative,* and *superlative.* The *positive degree* of a modifier is used to modify a single thing. The *comparative degree* is used to describe one of two things. The *superlative degree* is used to describe one of three or more things.

POSITIVE   Nico keeps his room **neat.**
COMPARATIVE   Nico's room is **neater** than Susan's.
SUPERLATIVE   Nico's room is the **neatest** one in the whole house.

(1) Most one-syllable modifiers form the comparative and superlative degrees by adding *–er* **and** *–est.*

EXAMPLE   The gray horse is **fast,** the black one is **faster,** and the white one is the **fastest** of all.

(2) Some two-syllable modifiers form the comparative and superlative degrees by adding *–er* **and** *–est.* **Other two-syllable modifiers form the comparative and superlative degrees by using** *most* **and** *more.*

Positive	Comparative	Superlative
simple	simpler	simplest
freely	more freely	most freely

(3) Modifiers of more than two syllables form the comparative and superlative degrees by using *more* **and** *most.*

Positive	Comparative	Superlative
efficient	more efficient	most efficient
skillfully	more skillfully	most skillfully

(4) To show a decrease in the qualities they express, all modifiers form the comparative and superlative degrees by using *less* **and** *least.*

Positive	Comparative	Superlative
proud	less proud	least proud
reasonably	less reasonably	least reasonably

(5) Some modifiers do not follow the regular methods of forming the comparative and superlative degrees.

Positive	Comparative	Superlative
bad	worse	worst
well/good	better	best
many/much	more	most
little	less	least

EXERCISE 3   Forming the Degrees of Comparison of Modifiers

On your own paper, write the forms for the comparative and superlative degrees of the following modifiers. Write the comparative and superlative degrees with *less* and *least*, too.

EX.   1. happily   *more (less) happily, most (least) happily*
      2. slow   *slower, less slow; slowest, least slow*

1. carefully
2. importantly
3. quick
4. beautiful
5. joyful
6. tall
7. lazy
8. fashionable
9. terrifically
10. soothing
11. loudly
12. easy
13. sincere
14. nervous
15. hungry
16. absent-minded
17. direct
18. clearly
19. brave
20. grainy

EXERCISE 4   Using Comparison Forms of Adjectives

On your own paper, write a sentence comparing each of the pairs below. Use the comparative form of adjectives in your sentences.

EX.   1. the sun and the moon
      1. *The sun is larger than the moon.*

1. summer and winter
2. writing and revising
3. movies and television
4. dogs and cats
5. sandals and moccasins
6. lying and telling the truth
7. ice-skating and roller-skating
8. mountain climbing and spelunking
9. computer games and board games
10. plastic flowers and real flowers

USES OF COMPARATIVE AND SUPERLATIVE FORMS

18h **Use the comparative degree when comparing two things. Use the superlative degree when comparing more than two.**

COMPARATIVE | This computer is **faster** than that one.
Of the two players, Paco is the **more skillful**.
This radio is **less expensive** than yours was.

SUPERLATIVE | This computer is the **fastest** of all the models on the market.
Of the three players, Paco is the **most skillful**.
This radio is the **least expensive** one of those I have seen.

NOTE | In everyday conversation, people sometimes use the superlative degree in comparing two things: *Put your best foot forward.* In your writing, however, you should use the comparative degree when comparing two things.

18i **Include the word *other* or *else* when comparing one thing with others in the same group.**

NONSTANDARD | Andrea can sing better than anyone in the choir. [Andrea cannot sing better than herself.]

STANDARD | Andrea can sing better than **anyone else** in the choir.

18j **Avoid double comparisons. A double comparison is incorrect because it contains both *-er* and *more* (or *less*) or *-est* and *most* (or *least*).**

NONSTANDARD | The first book was more longer than the second one was.
STANDARD | The first book was **longer** than the second one was.

NONSTANDARD | What state has the most coldest weather?
STANDARD | What state has the **coldest** weather?

EXERCISE 5 Revising Sentences by Correcting Modifiers

In each of the following sentences, draw a line through the incorrect modifiers. On the line before each sentence, write the correct comparative or superlative form. Write *C* if the sentence is correct.

EX. ___sicker___ 1. The doctor was ~~more sicker~~ than I was.

_____ 1. Great Danes are more bigger than collies.

_____ 2. This is the most best grapefruit that I have ever tasted.

_____ 3. Of all the planets, Mercury is closer to the sun.

_____ 4. In your opinion, who is the most fastest athlete today?

_____ 5. Georgio's joke was most humorous than mine.

_____ 6. To me, a poem is harder to write than any piece of literature I have attempted.

_____ 7. Mama's roghan josh is less spicier than Grandma's.

_____ 8. Which country has the largest population, China or India?

_____ 9. Out of all the contest entries, yours was better.

_____ 10. This television set is the least expensive one in the store.

_____ 11. Texas is more larger than any other state, except Alaska.

_____ 12. He felt least enthusiastic before the game than he did once the Phillies got a home run.

_____ 13. Of all the movies I've seen, this one was the absolute worse for dialogue.

_____ 14. I think you need to try on a more smaller size; those shoes are too loose.

_____ 15. The climate of Maine is least warm than that of Florida.

_____ 16. Are pigs really more smarter than dogs?

_____ 17. I think Amsterdam is more beautiful than any city I have visited in the world.

_____ 18. She found rugby more challenging than lacrosse.

_____ 19. Of the Jewish holy days, Yom Kippur is one of the more important.

_____ 20. The new monorail travels most quickly than the old train.

_____ 21. It is more easier to get there than to get back.

_____ 22. Winter is the most bad time to visit Sven.

_____ 23. I like the desert more better than Louis does.

_____ 24. Their house is the most colorful on the block.

_____ 25. Who spoke most eloquently, Paula or Abraham?

CHAPTER REVIEW

A. Using Modifiers Correctly

In the sentences below, draw a line through each incorrect modifier. Write the correct modifier on the line before the sentence. If a sentence is correct, write C.

EX. _____*best*_____ 1. Of all the Dutch cities, Leiden is probably the ~~better~~ one to visit if you want to see fields of tulips.

_____ 1. In the sixteenth century, Carolus Clusius brought the most earliest tulip bulb to the Netherlands from Turkey.

_____ 2. Ever since then, tulips have grown good in the Netherlands.

_____ 3. Today, tulips are among the Netherlands' most biggest exports.

_____ 4. They also happen to be one of the country's popularest tourist attractions.

_____ 5. Naturally, of all the seasons, spring is the better time to visit if you want to see flowers.

_____ 6. One of the easiest ways to see the tulips is to ride the train.

_____ 7. As the train passes slow through Leiden, you can see the vast tulip fields.

_____ 8. The fields look well, covered with blocks of flowers in many vivid colors.

_____ 9. Near Leiden, farther west, are the most largest flower gardens in the world.

_____ 10. Named the Keukenhof Gardens, they are truly beautifully.

_____ 11. You'd feel badly if you went all the way to Leiden and failed to see them.

_____ 12. More flowers grow there than in any garden in the world.

_____ 13. Tulips bloom more later in the spring than some other flowers.

_____ 14. More earlier in the year, daffodils and hyacinths bloom.

_____ 15. Of the three kinds of flowers, I feel the tulips are the more dramatic.

B. Proofreading a Paragraph for Correct Use of Modifiers

In the paragraph below, draw a line through each incorrect modifier . Write the correct modifier above the error. Some sentences have no errors.

EX. [1] The city of Honfleur lies ~~quiet~~ *quietly* on the coast of Normandy, a region in northern France.

[1] Unlike Le Havre, a much largest city nearby, Honfleur looks like a fishing village of long ago. [2] Honfleur is the birthplace of Erik Satie, one of the more creative composers who ever lived. [3] In the early 1900s, Satie wrote least complicated music than other composers wrote. [4] Satie wrote long ballet scores and more shorter pieces for the piano. [5] He also worked as a pianist in Paris, France's capital and larger city. [6] His critics treated him badly. [7] Perhaps critics would have treated Satie more kinder if he hadn't given his pieces such strange names. [8] One of his most earliest works was called *Truly Flabby Preludes for a Dog.* [9] He wrote even more humorouser performance directions. [10] Of all of them, the most funniest was "to be played like a nightingale with a toothache."

C. Writing a Memo

You are on the staff of a major television network. You must decide which two of the four possible new series below you will recommend for the new fall season. On your own paper, write a memo of at least ten sentences to your boss, explaining the reasons for your choices. Use modifiers correctly to explain your choices.

1. *Space Pioneers:* a series about such prominent figures as Russian cosmonaut Yuri Gagarin, the first person in space, and American astronaut Mae C. Jemison, the first African American female in space

2. *Strange Pets:* a series about famous people and their strange pets. First episode: Abraham Lincoln and his White House pet, a turkey named Jack

3. *Deep Trouble:* a comedy about a modern family that lives on a submarine

4. *A Stitch in Time:* a science fiction adventure about a tailor who journeys to other time periods, both historic and futuristic

EX. To: Iris Shaw, Program Manager
From: Charles Mills, Program Assistant
Date: October 21, 1995
Re: Fall season recommendations
One of the most popular topics today is space travel. For this and other reasons, I think *Space Pioneers* is a good choice for a new series.

MISPLACED MODIFIERS

A modifying phrase or clause that sounds awkward because it modifies the wrong word or group of words is called a *misplaced modifier.*

19a   Avoid using a misplaced modifier.

To correct a misplaced modifier, place the phrase or clause as close as possible to the word or words you intend it to modify.

MISPLACED   Ms. Sims saw the cat jump off the roof while gardening.
CLEAR   **While gardening,** Ms. Sims saw the cat jump off the roof.

19b   Avoid placing a phrase or clause so that it seems to modify either of two words. Such a misplaced modifier is often called a *two-way,* or *squinting, modifier.*

MISPLACED   The teacher said when class met she would explain the talent contest.
CLEAR   **When class met,** the teacher said she would explain the talent contest.
CLEAR   The teacher said she would explain the talent contest **when class met.**

EXERCISE 1   Revising Sentences by Correcting Misplaced or Squinting Modifiers

Revise each of the following sentences by underlining the misplaced or squinting modifier. Then insert a caret (∧) to show where the modifier should be placed.

EX.   1.   ∧We stopped to see the quaint old house <u>on the way to school.</u>

1. My friend said during intermission she almost always liked comedies. ∧

2. The tired explorers noticed a herd of elephants eating <u>as they rode their jeeps across the savannah.</u>

3. Mildred and Jenny overheard the aliens planning a surprise attack <u>on the roof today.</u>

4. Carlos and I listened intently to the commentator on the radio <u>drinking lemonade.</u>

5. There is a watch in the bureau upstairs <u>that is over fifty years old.</u>

6. ∧Returning home on the ferry, <u>a whale was seen by the tourists.</u>

7. The legislator running for reelection last night admitted in his speech he had made some mistakes.

8. Tamara decided she'd like to visit the West Indies while reading a brochure.

9. The circus was quite exciting, but I watched the motorcyclists crossing the high wire nervously.

10. The teacher asked Bill after class to take another exam.

11. Every morning, Carrie made certain she fed her pet goldfish wanting to be responsible.

12. To do all sorts of interesting tricks, Don liked to hire magicians for the entertainment of his party guests.

13. Rita promised when it started to snow she would buy a new winter coat and mittens.

14. They were silent as they witnessed the northern lights sitting on their porch.

15. After lifting weights for six months, we noticed that Kiyoshi had some new muscles.

16. I agreed on Tuesday I would help Sheila.

17. The lifeguard made sure to tell the swimmers to get out of the water before taking a break.

18. Shimmering in the golden afternoon sunlight, the vacationers enjoyed the view of the city.

19. The cowhands wondered on the second night of the cattle drive where fifteen steers went.

20. Joachim had finally learned how to do a double-flip off the high board bursting with pride.

21. Don't forget to write every point of the treaty down on paper that will end this conflict.

22. Tell your sister before she leaves for the party I need to see her.

23. We were amazed after we read we had passed our exams with all A's on the bulletin board.

24. The men crossing the desert on foot were grateful when they encountered the merchants, having empty canteens.

25. The wind blew down the fence that reached a speed of fifty miles per hour.

DANGLING MODIFIERS

A modifying phrase or clause that does not sensibly modify any word or words in a sentence is called a *dangling modifier*.

19c   Avoid using a dangling modifier.

You may correct a dangling modifier in one of two ways.

(1) Add a word or words that the phrase or clause can sensibly modify.

(2) Add a word or words to the phrase or clause itself.

DANGLING   Handing out papers, the teacher's pencil slipped from her hand.
 [Whose hand was it?]
CLEAR   **Handing out papers,** the teacher let her pencil slip from her hand.

DANGLING   After climbing to the mountaintop, it was too cloudy to see very far. [Who was climbing?]
CLEAR   **After climbing to the mountaintop,** we found that the weather was too cloudy to allow us to see very far.

DANGLING   While working at the shop, news arrived of his brother's wedding. [Was the news working at the shop?]
CLEAR   **While Alejandro was working at the shop,** news arrived of his brother's wedding.

 NOTE   A few dangling modifiers have become standard in idiomatic expressions.

EXAMPLES   **Generally speaking,** it doesn't snow here until mid-to-late February.
To be perfectly frank, the speech was quite dull.

☞   **REFERENCE NOTE:** For more information about using commas after introductory words, phrases, and clauses, see page 291.

EXERCISE 2   **Revising Sentences by Correcting Dangling Modifiers**

On your own paper, revise each sentence to eliminate the dangling modifier.

EX.   1.   After four days of camping, the home-cooked meal tasted great.

1.   *After four days of camping, the boys thought the home-cooked meal tasted great.*

1.   Having purchased fishing equipment, a trip to the lake was taken.

2.   Before calling directory assistance, the telephone book is a good place to look.

3. Thrilled by all the attention, Sallie's ~~face~~ lit up in a smile.
   I heard
4. The sound of many cars honking their horns ~~was heard~~ while making a
   ^
   slow left turn.
5. To earn a place in the school orchestra, daily practice is necessary.
   I saw
6. While waiting for the phone to ring, an interesting program was on
   ^
   television.
   I saw
7. Relaxing on the beach, dark storm clouds appeared.
8. Surprised by the sudden sound of the alarm, the rescue trucks were
   ^
   hastily driven to the scene of the accident.
9. For the benefit of the audience, replacing the old seats was his first task as
   theater manager.
   someone must
10. To help the candidate win the election, many signs ~~must be made.~~
    ^
11. After sitting in the sun for a while, the lotion was applied.
    the ~~boat~~
12. Driving the boat too fast, from shore Dad shouted at me to slow down.
    ^ ^
    I I have heard
13. Before leaving town, the hotel bill ~~needed to be paid.~~
    ^ *I had enjoyed*
14. Encouraged by the favorable reviews his first play received, another
    ^
    one was written almost immediately.
    She wrote
15. While making room on the desk for the new computer, the box of pencils
    fell to the floor.
    I threw

EXERCISE 3   Writing Sentences with Modifiers

On your own paper, write complete sentences, using each of the modifiers given
below as the introductory element of the sentence. To be sure you include a word
or words the modifier can sensibly refer to, underline the word or words modified.

EX.   1. after class
      1. After class, <u>we</u> all walked to the store.

1. before practicing the piano, *I came home*
2. jumping high into the air, *I scream for joy*
3. delighted by the beautiful weather, *I went outside*
4. to help his brother understand the problem better, *I gave him a hint*
5. while rummaging through the basement, *I found toys*
6. after years of hard work, *I went to college*
7. filled with pride, *I accepted the award*
8. having read the article, *I laughed*
9. skating circles around Fred, *I laughed*
10. laughing softly, *started to cry*

CHAPTER REVIEW

A. Revising Sentences by Correcting Misplaced Modifiers

For each of the sentences below, underline the misplaced or squinting modifier. Then insert a caret (^) to show where the modifier should be placed.

EX. 1. ∧We saw it was going to be quite a year for sports <u>reading our school newspaper.</u>

1. My brother Carlos assured me after breakfast the school was going to be a ∧contender in almost every sport.

2. Sometime in the spring the paper said that Pearl Chen, last year's shot put champion, will be trying out for the nationals. ∧

3. My brother said we had to be at every football game right after reading the article. ∧

4. We remembered when the coach told the fullback he would have to play on both defense and offense in the middle of the Glendale game.

5. This year the paper informed us there is a new person playing fullback.

6. The article talked about Chris Evler which was very positive.

7. Carlos said during the season that the new fullback would probably win several awards. ∧

8. We were happy to see the girl's hockey team practicing on the way to school. ∧

9. Carlos and I watched Ingrid Swanson make a tricky goal while walking through the park. ∧

10. We lingered by the rink to watch the game admiring Ingrid's skill.

11. Carlos reminded me the sports writers had predicted that the basketball team would be state champions for two more years right after last spring's playoffs. ∧

12. Carlos, who played center on the team, was waiting for the basketball season to begin quite impatiently. ∧

13. Carlos had often told me on the basketball court anyone can figure out how to pass and shoot the ball. ∧

14. What makes the game interesting is that one player has to outmanuever the other player while trying to make a basket. ∧

15. I finally admitted to Carlos that after the baseball season began I would be happy. ∧

B. Revising Sentences by Correcting Dangling Modifiers

On your own paper, rewrite each sentence to correct the dangling modifier.

EX.   1. Having seen *Superman: The Movie*, it was amazing how Christopher
          Reeve, playing Superman, could perform all those incredible acts.

    1. Having seen <u>Superman: The Movie</u>, we were amazed at the way Christopher
        Reeve, playing Superman, could perform all those incredible acts.

1. To make a good fantasy like *Superman: The Movie*, solutions to technical
    problems must be provided.
2. Suspended by two wires from a pole, the flying really seems to occur.
3. Photographers sometimes tried trick photography using models of New
    York City's streets.
4. Superman's cape swirled in the wind which was operated by remote
    control.
5. To keep Reeve from crashing into the studio wall, a net was placed at the
    end of the track.
6. The director said it is difficult to create the effect of a character flying after
    working with *Superman: The Movie.*
7. When creating animated films, fantastic scenes are as easy to draw as
    ordinary scenes.
8. When shoving a big boulder off a mountain, however, it must be played
    by a real person.
9. The boulder and the mountain were built in miniature size on which it
    stood.
10. Thinking that Superman was really standing on the mountain, the final
    scene was quite effective.

C. Collaborating to Write a Story Starter

You and a partner are writing a science fiction story. As prewriting, you have
jotted down the phrases and clauses below. On your own paper, work together
to use five phrases or clauses to begin the story. Make sure that you don't have
any dangling or misplaced modifiers.

EX.   speeding through the galaxy at a breakneck speed

       Speeding through the galaxy at a breakneck speed, the crew suddenly
       noticed the ship was running low on rocket fuel.

landing with a bump on the distant planet
to make sure the pressure suits contained enough oxygen
after checking for alien life forms
before reaching for her laser rifle
having an extremely large head and what seemed to be a purple tail
running out of food
boasting that he knew better than the rest how to survive in space
relieved when they saw the strange, blue sun vanish from the screen
while it sounded like a meteorite had hit the hull
turning to face them with a grim expression

AFFECT / BEING AS, BEING THAT

This chapter contains a **glossary,** or alphabetical list, of common problems in English usage. Throughout the chapter, examples are labeled *standard* or *nonstandard.* **Standard English** is the most widely accepted form of English. **Nonstandard English** is language that does not follow the rules and guidelines of standard English.

affect, effect   *Affect* is a verb meaning "to influence." *Effect* used as a verb means "to bring about." Used as a noun, *effect* means "the result of some action."

EXAMPLES   Years of playing in a rock-and-roll band **affected** Brian's hearing.
The principal has **effected** changes in lunchroom schedules.
The medicine had no **effect** on my cold.

all the farther, all the faster   Avoid these expressions. Use *as far as* and *as fast as*.

NONSTANDARD   Eighty miles per hour is all the faster that electric car can go.
    STANDARD   Eighty miles per hour is **as fast as** that electric car can go.

allusion, illusion   An *allusion* is a reference to something. An *illusion* is a mistaken idea or a misleading appearance.

EXAMPLES   Literature is full of **allusions** to the Bible and to Shakespeare.
This book of magic tricks will teach you how to create many popular **illusions.**

alumni, alumnae   *Alumni* is the plural of *alumnus* (a male graduate). *Alumnae* is the plural of *alumna* (a female graduate). As a group, the graduates of a coeducational school are usually called *alumni.*

EXAMPLES   The women's college planned a conference for its **alumnae.**
All of these **alumni** were once members of the men's chorus.
Alumni often wear T-shirts with their colleges' names on them.

 In informal usage the graduates of a women's college may be called *alumni.* However, *alumnae* is preferred in formal situations.

anyways, anywheres, everywheres, nowheres, somewheres   Use these words without the *s* at the end.

EXAMPLE   We couldn't find the keys **anywhere.**

as, as if   See **like, as, as if.**

at   Do not use *at* after *where*.

EXAMPLE   Where did you find Tanya?[not *find Tanya at*]

because   In formal situations, do not use the construction *reason . . . is because*. Instead, use *reason . . . is that*.

NONSTANDARD   The reason for the ordinance against washing cars is because we have a water shortage.
STANDARD   The **reason** for the ordinance against washing cars **is that** we have a water shortage.

being as, being that   Avoid using these expressions. Use *because* or *since* instead.

NONSTANDARD   Being as Carol was the best candidate, we voted for her.
STANDARD   **Because** Carol was the best candidate, we voted for her.

EXERCISE 1   Identifying Correct Usage

For each sentence below, underline the correct word or words in parentheses.

EX.   1.   Your shoe is (*somewheres, somewhere*) in the living room.

1.   The sad song on his latest CD (*affected, effected*) my mood.

2.   (*Being as, Because*) Lawrence draws well, we had him design the brochure.

3.   The colors on my wall were part of an optical (*allusion, illusion*).

4.   The reason for playing soft music is (*because, that*) customers like it.

5.   That bad weather had an (*affect, effect*) on my driving.

6.   Three hundred miles is (*all the farther, as far as*) I can travel.

7.   The (*effect, affect*) of the changes in the test schedule was obvious.

8.   Where is that (*puppy at, puppy*)?

9.   Joaquín made (*allusions, illusions*) to his favorite stories in that essay.

10.   Zora looked (*everywheres, everywhere*) for her keys.

11.   Franklin Roosevelt's New Deal (*affected, effected*) great changes in the United States.

12.   The (*alumni, alumnae*), both men and women, donated money for a women's studies center.

13.   Thirty miles an hour was (*all the faster, as fast as*) the train could travel.

14.   (*Being that, Because*) we were tired, we called it a night.

15.   The (*alumni, alumnae*) of the girls' school all went to college.

COULD OF / OFF, OFF OF

could of Do not use *of* with the helping verb *could*. Use *have* instead. Also avoid *had of, ought to of, should of, would of, might of,* and *must of*.

EXAMPLE   I **could have** been a contender. [not *could of*]

effect, affect See **affect.**

emigrate, immigrate *Emigrate* means "to leave a country or region to settle elsewhere." *Immigrate* means "to come into a country or region to settle there." Remember that *emigrate* always takes *from* and *immigrate* always takes *to*.

EXAMPLES   How many people have **emigrated** from Ireland?
Many Irish **immigrated** to Boston.

everywheres See **anyways,** etc.

he, she, it, they Avoid using a pronoun along with its antecedent as the subject of a verb.

NONSTANDARD   My brother, he won the fifty-yard dash.
STANDARD   My **brother** won the fifty-yard dash.

illusion See **allusion.**

kind of, sort of In formal situations, avoid using *kind of* for the adverb *somewhat* or *rather*.

INFORMAL   Otto was kind of unhappy when he did not make the swimming team.
FORMAL   Otto was **somewhat** [or **rather**] unhappy when he did not make the swimming team.

kind of a, sort of a In formal situations, omit the *a*.

INFORMAL   What kind of a pet would you like?
FORMAL   What **kind of** pet would you like?

like, as, as if *Like* is a preposition. In formal situations, do not use *like* for the conjunctions *as, as if,* or *as though* to introduce a subordinate clause.

INFORMAL   You look like you need some help.
FORMAL   You look **as if** [or **as though**] you need some help.

nowheres See **anyways,** etc.

off, off of Do not use *off* or *off of* in place of *from*.

NONSTANDARD   You can get a train schedule off of that conductor.
STANDARD   You can get a train schedule **from** that conductor.

EXERCISE 2   Identifying Correct Usage

For each sentence below, underline the correct word or words in parentheses.

EX.   1.   Leslie (*could of, could have*) helped you with your project.

1.   My ancestors (*emigrated, immigrated*) from Italy many years ago.

2.   Gina was (*kind of, somewhat*) unhappy that she did not receive a part in the play.

3.   It looks (*like, as if*) we'll go to the grand opening of the mall.

4.   My friend Kayla (*isn't, she isn't*) happy about the plan to move her desk across the room.

5.   Did you buy a stamp (*from, off*) the woman at the post office on Main Street?

6.   I would like to formally introduce Delia, who plays her violin (*as, like*) a professional does.

7.   The evening bus for commuters is usually (*sort of, rather*) crowded.

8.   You (*might have, might of*) warned me about this problem.

9.   Did you receive an invitation (*off of, from*) Elsie?

10.   If you want to learn the basics about computers, it doesn't matter what (*kind of a, kind of*) computer you have.

EXERCISE 3   Proofreading a Paragraph to Correct Usage Errors

For each sentence in the paragraph below, draw a line through the error in usage. Then write the correct usage in the space above each word.

EX.   [1] I could not ~~of~~ picked a more interesting topic for my report.
have

[1] I borrowed off of the town library a science book that describes this kind of insect. [2] As you might of guessed, moths and butterflies are related but difficult to tell apart. [3] However, this book, it says that moths usually fly around in the evening and at night, while butterflies are usually seen in the daytime. [4] When resting on a plant, moths don't hold their wings upright like butterflies do; instead, they lay their wings down flat. [5] It is sort of fascinating to learn that there are over 100,000 kinds of moths but only 17,000 types of butterflies.

OR, NOR / WHO, WHOM, WHICH, THAT

or, nor   Use *or* with *either;* use *nor* with *neither.*

EXAMPLES   We can **either** go to a movie **or** simply walk in the park.
Neither Alexandra **nor** Alfonso will forget to deliver the important package.

reason . . . is because   See **because.**

some, somewhat   Use *somewhat* to mean "to some extent."

INFORMAL   After reading the long letter, Karl's mood brightened **some.**
FORMAL   After reading the long letter, Karl's mood brightened **somewhat.**

somewheres   See **anyways,** etc.

sort of   See **kind of.**

sort of a   See **kind of a.**

than, then   *Than* is a conjunction used in comparisons. *Then* is an adverb telling when.

EXAMPLES   I don't know anyone who sleeps more soundly **than** I do.
The violinist tightened the bow, **then** tuned the strings.

this here, that there   Avoid using *here* or *there* after *this* or *that.*

EXAMPLE   **That** automobile looks like a June bug [not *That there*]

type, type of   Avoid using *type* as an adjective. Add *of* after *type.*

NONSTANDARD   Cherese, do you still prefer this type running shoe to the other type?
STANDARD   Cherese, do you still prefer this **type of** running shoe to the other type?

when, where   Do not use *when* or *where* to begin a definition.

NONSTANDARD   Alliteration is when the beginning sounds of words are repeated.
STANDARD   Alliteration is **a figure of speech in which** the beginning sounds of words are repeated.
NONSTANDARD   Estimating is where you make a guess about the size or quantity of something.
STANDARD   Estimating is **a problem-solving technique** used to guess the size or quantity of something.

---

who, whom, which, that   *Who* and *whom* refer to persons only. *Which* refers to things only. *That* may refer to either persons or things.

EXAMPLES   Was it Don Marquis **who** wrote "The Lesson of the Moth"?
That poem, **which** appears in the book *Archy and Mehitabel,* is one of my favorites.
It is a poem **that** I think about often.
The person **that** showed me the poem was Kimberly.

EXERCISE 4   Identifying Correct Usage

For each sentence below, underline the correct word or words in parentheses.

EX.   1. After the training session, the puppy's behavior improved (*some, somewhat*).

1. Neither Pedro (*or, nor*) Collin feels strongly about the issue.

2. Who can run that race faster (*than, then*) Marlena can?

3. That (*type, type of*) guitar is quite expensive.

4. The woman (*who, which*) painted our house did a wonderful job.

5. Aponi shucked the corn and (*then, than*) filled a pot with water.

6. Please call either Jason (*nor, or*) Pauli as soon as possible.

7. The wind died down (*somewhat, some*), so cycling was easier.

8. A collage (*is when a person pastes, involves pasting*) different objects and papers together to form a picture.

9. Mary watered (*that, that there*) garden yesterday afternoon.

10. The window screen (*which, who*) ripped in the storm is being replaced.

EXERCISE 5   Proofreading a Paragraph to Correct Usage Errors

In the sentences below, draw a line through each error in usage. Then write the correct usage in the space above the word. Some sentences may be correct.

EX.   [1] ~~That there~~ table in the library is made out of marble.

[1] Marble is when limestone is compressed and made very hot. [2] This here

rock in its purest form is white. [3] Most marble has either one substance nor

another in it that gives it different colors. [4] Because it is somewhat easy to shape,

marble is often used for statues. [5] The best type sculpting marble comes from Italy.

THE DOUBLE NEGATIVE

A *double negative* is a construction in which two or more negative words are used where one is enough.

NONSTANDARD	Herbert never has no time to relax any more.
STANDARD	Herbert **never** has time to relax any more.
	or
	Herbert has **no** time to relax any more.

the contraction *n't* Do not use the contraction *n't,* meaning *not,* with another negative word.

NONSTANDARD	There isn't no tread on those tires.
STANDARD	There isn't **any** tread on those tires.

barely, hardly, scarcely Do not use *barely, hardly,* or *scarcely* with another negative word.

NONSTANDARD	There aren't hardly any tickets left for the concert.
STANDARD	There are **hardly** any tickets left for the concert.

no, none, not, nothing Do not use any of these negative words with another negative word.

NONSTANDARD	Yolanda asked for some correction fluid, but I don't have none.
STANDARD	Yolanda asked for some correction fluid, but I do**n't** have **any.**
NONSTANDARD	"I didn't do nothing," said the suspect.
STANDARD	"I did**n't** do **any**thing," said the suspect.

EXERCISE 6   Correcting Errors in Usage

In each of the following sentences, draw a line through the error in usage. Write the correct form above the error. [Note: There may be more than one way to correct each error.]

EX. 1. There isn't ~~no~~ *any* reason to be afraid.

or

1. There isn't no reason to be afraid. *is*

1. I couldn't barely hear my baby brother crying for his bottle.

2. Giorgio didn't have no papers on his desk during the exam.

265

3. I heard her say that she didn't do nothing wrong.

4. Doris doesn't have no more time to practice her trumpet.

5. We hadn't scarcely enough orange juice for the family at breakfast yesterday.

6. I looked for clues concerning his disappearance but didn't find nothing for several weeks.

7. "I don't want no more trouble," the frustrated shopkeeper exclaimed at the town meeting.

8. I haven't never seen no marsupials, even on television.

9. My grandmother Sánchez hasn't never left her beautiful homeland of Puerto Rico.

10. Soon-Yi doesn't have no easy answers to that complicated problem.

11. Do you think it's true that sailors never really saw nothing like a true mermaid?

12. I couldn't hardly complain about my convenient work schedule.

13. Diane wanted some popcorn, but we didn't have none in the pantry.

14. There aren't no more potatoes in the sack.

15. I don't know nothing about fixing clogged drains.

16. "I don't want no dessert," the diner said to the server.

17. Before last night, I hadn't never seen a shooting star.

18. I can't believe they still haven't done nothing about that leak.

19. Do not give no money to that phony organization.

20. Jasper wanted to sing campfire songs, but we didn't know none.

EXERCISE 7   Creating a Safety Poster

As a student in the food preparations program, you have been asked to create a poster of ten safety rules. On your own paper, write the ten rules that students should follow as they work. In at least five of the sentences, be sure you use a negative expression correctly.

EX.   1. Do not use the meat slicer without the blade guard in place.

CHAPTER REVIEW

A. Identifying and Correcting Errors in Usage

In each of the following sentences, draw a line through the error in usage. Then write the correct usage in the space above the word. Some sentences may be correct.

EX. 1. The drought ~~effected~~ *affected* this season's corn crops.

1. We reached a dead end and realized that this was all the farther we could go.

2. In my poem I made an illusion to the Persian Gulf Conflict.

3. The engraved invitation was to a party for the alumni of a girls' prep school.

4. Marta couldn't find her dance shoes anywheres.

5. Where did you find those South American instruments at?

6. The reason for the dress code is because company employees need to look presentable to customers.

7. Being that it was getting quite cold, we decided to move the party inside.

8. The soprano soloist sounded like she had a head cold.

9. You should of put air in the tires before putting them on the car.

10. What kind of a hockey stick are you using?

11. My brother he is learning to speak Swahili, an African language.

12. That kind of a dog makes an excellent playmate for children.

13. I want to study law just like my mother did.

14. You can get a hall pass off of the teacher.

15. Someone left a vase of flowers at the door, but neither María or I saw who did it.

16. Hanging art prints on the wall improved the appearance of the room some.

17. My grandmother immigrated from the Soviet Union in 1972.

18. This here colt comes from a long line of champion thoroughbreds.

19. Emilio enjoys horror films, but I have never liked that type of movie.

20. Panning is when you move the camera slowly from one side of a scene to another.

21. No one prepares Chinese food better than my father does.

22. Even though it was the first time Lee had skied downhill, he was kind of pleased.

23. The increases in enrollment effect the number of available dormitory rooms.

24. Six miles per hour is all the faster that this old car can go.

25. Have you finished folding that there laundry, Tom?

B.   Proofreading a Paragraph for Errors in Usage

In the paragraph below, draw a line through the errors in usage. Then write the correct usage in the space above the word. Some sentences may be correct.

EX.   [1] Sarah Winnemucca is an American Indian woman ~~which~~ *whom* we learned about in our history class.

[1] When she was young, there weren't hardly any European Americans in her part of Nevada. [2] Soon, however, white settlers arrived, and Sara's people, the Paiutes, were moved from their land onto a reservation. [3] Because the Paiutes, they were hungry on the reservation, they took some of the settlers' cattle. [4] This here action was unacceptable to the whites, who raided the Paiute camp. [5] Later, Sarah Winnemucca wrote a book about these experiences in which she was kind of blunt about broken agreements made between the U.S. government and the Paiute people.

C.   Writing a Newspaper Article

You and some other students have just toured a factory that is making a new car that runs on electricity instead of gasoline. Your science teacher has asked you to describe your experience for the school newspaper. On your own paper, write a brief article about electric cars. Include why you think they are or are not worth building. In your article, use at least ten of the following expressions correctly.

affect	illusion	nowhere	kind of
effect	anyway	reason . . . is that	neither . . . nor
as far as	anywhere	could have	somewhat
as fast as	everywhere	than	type of

EX.   kind of
      This kind of car gives off less pollution.

PEOPLE AND PLACES

21a   Capitalize the names of persons.

EXAMPLES   Ella Fitzgerald, Sandra Day O'Connor, Ed Loomis

Some names contain more than one capital letter. Usage varies in the capitalization of *van, von, du, de la,* and other parts of many multiword names. Always verify the spelling of a name with the person, or check the name in a reference source.

EXAMPLES   La Fontaine   McEwen   O'Conner   Van Doren
            Yellow Thunder   Ibn Ezra   Villa-Lobos   van Gogh

21b   Capitalize geographical names.

Type of Name	Examples
towns, cities	Madison, Augusta, Topeka, Springfield
counties, states	Litchfield County, Wayne County, Alaska, Idaho
countries	Australia, Portugal, Romania, Peru, Mali
islands	Java, Madagascar, Tasmania, Iceland, Florida Keys
bodies of water	Pacific Ocean, Bay of Bengal, Lake Superior
forests, parks	Bryce Canyon National Park, Constitution Gardens
streets, highways	New Jersey Turnpike, Route 128, Interstate 93
mountains	Himalayas, Rocky Mountains, Andes
continents	Africa, South America, Europe, Asia
regions	the South, the Midwest

NOTE   Words such as *east, west, north,* and *south* are not capitalized when they indicate direction.

EXAMPLES   I traveled north for one hour.
            Joni lives west of the school.

NOTE   In a hyphenated street number, the second part of the number is not capitalized.

EXAMPLE   East Seventy-eighth Street

EXERCISE 1   **Correcting Errors in Capitalization**

For each sentence below, correct the errors in capitalization by drawing a line through each incorrect word. Write your corrections on the line before each sentence.

EX. _Sleepytime Drive_ 1. We moved to <u>sleepytime drive</u>.

_____ 1. My sister found the indian ocean on the map.

_____ 2. Have you dreamed of climbing mount everest, which is located on the eastern border of nepal?

_____ 3. Who was the first European to see the amazon river?

_____ 4. The caspian sea is fed by eight different rivers.

_____ 5. The aguilar family wants to visit the cayman islands, which are 150 miles South of cuba.

_____ 6. My class went to the kenai fjords national park.

_____ 7. Our friend pascal enjoyed his visit to albany, New York.

_____ 8. The principal, fran washington, worked at a school in the midwest last year.

_____ 9. Travel north on route 1 to essex county.

_____ 10. "How long is the missouri river?" Ty asked.

EXERCISE 2   **Proofreading Sentences for Correct Capitalization**

In the sentences below, underline the words that should be capitalized, and write the corrections above the words. Some sentences may be correct.

EX.   1. Repairs are being made on <u>Interstate</u> 84.

1. I would like to visit lake tahoe in california.

2. I think boston, the capital of massachusetts, is a beautiful city.

3. Whenever I travel to the south, I visit cypress gardens, florida.

4. My older sister gertie lives at west fifty-sixth street.

5. I enjoy the view of the adirondack mountains from lake george.

6. The group travelled north along the eastern slope.

7. The danube river travels through the major cities of eastern europe.

8. Kings's Canyon national park is in the sierra nevada range.

9. Is Australia a Continent or an Island, or is it both?

10. To get to buffalo, new york, from syracuse, take the new york state thruway, or interstate 90, west.

SCHOOL SUBJECTS, FIRST WORDS, PROPER ADJECTIVES

21c Do *not* capitalize the names of school subjects, except for names of languages and course names followed by a number.

EXAMPLES   art   chemistry   algebra   music
               Spanish   English   Geometry I   History II

21d Capitalize the first word in every sentence.

EXAMPLES   I crocheted a sweater. It was a gift for Lee.

The first word of a sentence that is a direct quotation is capitalized even if the quotation begins within a sentence.

EXAMPLE   Dora said, "My aloe plant is on the windowsill."

Traditionally, the first word in a line of poetry is capitalized.

EXAMPLES   Sunflowers filled the ragged front yard
               And faced the street, as if to stand guard.

The pronoun *I* and the interjection *O* are capitalized whether or not they are the first words of sentences. The common interjection *oh* is capitalized only when it begins a sentence or is part of a title.

EXAMPLES   I replaced the flat tire; then I got back on the freeway.
               Sherry titled her essay "O the Way West: Oh the Things We Saw."

21e Capitalize proper nouns and proper adjectives.

A *common noun* names any one of a group of people, places, or things. A *proper noun* names a particular person, place, or thing. A *proper adjective* is formed from a proper noun.

Proper Nouns	Proper Adjectives
Brazil	Brazilian dance
Queen Victoria	Victorian house
Irish	Irish literature

NOTE   Proper nouns and proper adjectives may lose their capitals after long use.

EXAMPLES   sandwich   china   diesel

EXERCISE 3   Using Capital Letters Correctly

For each sentence below, correct the errors in capitalization by drawing a line through each error and writing the correct form in the space above it.

EX.   1.   Adrian said, "~~my~~ shoes are wet."
        M

1.   I think my latin class will help me in my future studies.

2.   Since we moved, we often miss the beautiful hawaiian weather.

3.   Marcus and Lydia are going to wait until the spring of the next school year to take algebra II, i heard.

4.   One of Rodney's most interesting poems begins with the line, "rain fell on the roof."

5.   Cousin Elena made delicious spanish rice for the town banquet.

6.   how long did it take you to learn the art of making paper?

7.   Katrina received a long letter from her japanese pen pal yesterday.

8.   Sadly, my grandmother lost some antique China during that earthquake.

9.   My uncle said, "the cat and the dog need fresh water and food before we leave."

10.   We were all wondering if Leonardo's new italian restaurant attracted a lot of business.

11.   In Art class, Rita made earrings with colorful wooden beads and copper wires, and oh, are they lovely!

12.   I was moved by the poem that opened with the line, "the child's smile lit up her grandfather's face."

13.   The mayor said, "o city! you should be proud!"

14.   I've heard that history III focuses on the twentieth century.

15.   Ed told them that ethiopian food is available on Tremont Street.

16.   We read wonderful short stories in my english class this year.

17.   I would like to interview our property owner. she is armenian.

18.   Mariah said, "my favorite color is purple."

19.   do you understand why i had to do that?

20.   I love my father's french onion soup.

GROUPS, ORGANIZATIONS, AND RELIGIONS

21f Capitalize the names of teams, organizations, businesses, institutions, buildings, and government bodies.

Type of Name	Examples
teams	Montreal Canadiens, Indiana Pacers, New York Giants
organizations	Wilderness Society American Heart Association
businesses	Family Car Care Dragon Light Restaurant
institutions	Louisiana State University, World Trade Center, Lahey Clinic
buildings	Rialto Theater, Sears Tower
government bodies	Internal Revenue Service, U.S. Air Force, U.S. Postal Service

NOTE The names of organizations, businesses, and government bodies are often abbreviated as a series of capital letters.

EXAMPLES Federal Bureau of Investigation **FBI**
Environmental Protection Agency **EPA**
Commission on Civil Rights **CCR**

 REFERENCE NOTE: Do not capitalize words such as *building*, *hotel*, *theater*, *college*, *high school*, *post office*, and *courthouse* unless they are part of a proper name. For more discussion about the differences between common and proper nouns, see page 113.

21g Capitalize the names of nationalities, races, and peoples.

EXAMPLES Asian, Hispanic, African American, Caucasian, Inuit, Chinese, Italian, Polish

21h Capitalize the names of religions and their followers, holy days, sacred writings, and specific deities.

EXAMPLES Taoism, Judaism, Easter, Ramadan, Old Testament, Koran, Torah, God, Allah, Buddha

EXERCISE 4   Identifying Correct Capitalization

Write the letter *C* on the line before each phrase that is capitalized correctly.

EX.   _____ 1. a. north shore linen service
       __C__   b. North Shore Linen Service

_____ 1. a. the Chinese   _____ 6. a. Scott's Auto clinic

_____   b. the chinese   _____   b. Scott's Auto Clinic

_____ 2. a. Endicott college   _____ 7. a. Children's Hospital

_____   b. Endicott College   _____   b. a Children's Doctor

_____ 3. a. a Seattle Fishery   _____ 8. a. c. i. a.

_____   b. Seattle Mariners   _____   b. CIA

_____ 4. a. National Guard   _____ 9. a. the holy spirit

_____   b. National Defense   _____   b. the Holy Spirit

_____ 5. a. hinduism   _____ 10. a. the russians

_____   b. Hinduism   _____   b. the Russians

EXERCISE 5   Proofreading Sentences for Correct Capitalization

For each sentence below, correct the errors in capitalization by drawing a line through each error and writing the correct form above it. Some sentences may contain no errors.

EX.   1. Most participants in s̶hintoism are a̶sian.

1. I think the coast guard has issued a warning.

2. My father has worked at giovanni's barbershop for eleven years.

3. On christmas Pastor Reeves read several passages from the new testament.

4. Meredith read about the royal astronomical society of canada.

5. We ate a good breakfast of English muffins and fresh fruit before going to the new england patriots game.

6. The U.S. department of health and human services sent a memo.

7. They towed the car to tony's house of tires.

8. Dana volunteers at Yale-new haven hospital every week.

9. We will celebrate the jewish holiday yom kippur.

10. I would like to work in the theater.

OBJECTS, EVENTS, AND AWARDS

21i **Capitalize the brand names of business products.**

EXAMPLES   Borden milk, Bridgestone tires, Neutrogena soap

21j **Capitalize the names of historical events and periods, special events, and calendar items.**

EXAMPLES   Civil War, Middle Ages, Olympics, New Year's Day, Ching Ming Festival, Friday, June

21k **Capitalize the names of ships, monuments, awards, planets, and any other particular places, things, or events.**

Type of Name	Examples
ships, trains	USS *Nautilus*, Express Metroliner
aircraft, spacecraft, missiles	Concorde, *Atlantis*, *Apollo 11*
monuments, memorials	Fort Frederica, Statue of Liberty
awards	Caldecott Medal, Tony Awards
planets, stars, constellations	Neptune, Sirius, Ursa Major

EXERCISE 6   Proofreading Sentences for Correct Capitalization

For each sentence below, correct the errors in capitalization by drawing a line though the incorrect word. Write your corrections on the line before each sentence. If a sentence is correct, write C.

EX.   _____Venus_____ 1. Cam saw the planet ~~venus~~ through a telescope.

_____ 1. The united states marine corps war memorial in Washington, D.C., is also known as *Iwo Jima.*

_____ 2. The tanker *grand zenith* sank off Cape Cod, Massachusetts, January 11, 1977.

_____ 3. St. lucia's day is a late-december celebration worth attending.

_____ 4. My report on the louisiana purchase is due next wednesday.

_____ 5. I had coupons for progresso bread crumbs and tender vittles cat food.

_____   6. My grandfather received one medal, a purple heart, because he was injured in the line of duty.

_____   7. Can you see the north star or the big dipper?

_____   8. "I will be describing the cenozoic era in history," the teacher said.

_____   9. My mother, a respected poet, has won a guggenheim fellowship.

_____   10. Jethro saw photographs of the plane *graf zeppelin*.

_____   11. Miles would love to win a "young artist auditions" scholarship.

_____   12. That book explains the spanish-american war.

_____   13. Can Rafael distinguish a boeing 747 from other types of planes?

_____   14. That space museum has a display on project apollo, the space program.

_____   15. Jacob and I think saturn must be the most interesting planet to see.

_____   16. During the ice age, large portions of the earth were covered with ice.

_____   17. On monday we will watch a long filmstrip about *sputnik II*.

_____   18. Will the olympics this winter feature figure skating?

_____   19. If you study the harlem renaissance, you will surely read about the writer Zora Neale Hurston.

_____   20. The star you saw saturday night may have been betelgeuse.

_____   21. Arlo Guthrie wrote a song about a train ride on the *city of New Orleans*.

_____   22. One of the few constellations I recognize is orion.

_____   23. My stepbrother is a fighter jet test pilot in France.

_____   24. Pablo's lifelong dream was to win the national book award.

_____   25. If I never travel to mars, I won't be surprised.

TITLES

21l   Capitalize titles.

(1) Capitalize the title of a person when the title comes before the name.

EXAMPLES   My doctor, **D**r. Rivera, was on call last night.
I saw **G**overnor Weicker at the event.

(2) Capitalize a word showing a family relationship when the word is used before or in place of a person's name but not when preceded by a possessive.

EXAMPLES   We prepared dinner for **D**ad and **U**ncle Oscar.
Has my **a**unt Millie met your **g**randmother?

(3) Capitalize the first and last words and all important words in titles of books, newspapers, magazines, poems, short stories, historical documents, movies, television programs, and works of art and music.

Unimportant words in titles include articles (*a, an, the*), coordinating conjunctions (*and, but, for, nor, or, so, yet*), or prepositions of fewer than five letters (*at, for, from, with*).

NOTE   An article (*a, an,* or *the*) before a title is not capitalized unless it is the first word of the title.

Type of Title	Examples
books	*Walden, Roots*
newspapers	*Baltimore Sun, Detroit News*
magazines	*Discovery, Gourmet, Essence*
poems	"**A B**lessing", "**T**he **R**ed **W**heelbarrow"
short stories	"**M**ana **S**eda", "**S**plit **C**herry **T**ree"
historical documents	the **M**agna **C**arta
movies	*La Bamba, Batman, Jurassic Park*
television programs	*Evening Shade, Sixty Minutes*
works of art	*Autumn Rhythm, Pieta*
works of music	*We Can't Dance, Peer Gynt Suite*

EXERCISE 7   Proofreading for Correct Capitalization

For each sentence below, correct the errors in capitalization by drawing a line through the error and writing the correct form in the space above it. Some sentences may be correct.

EX.   1.   Hoping to become ~~s~~enator Ferraro, Geraldine Anne Ferraro
       ran against Alfonse D'Amato of New York.

1.   Our science teacher read to us a passage from Edward O.
     Wilson's book *the diversity of life.*

2.   Lois Rosenthal edits a magazine called *story.*

3.   Did your Sister Susan write a thank-you note to uncle Emilio?

4.   Have you read "aardvark," Julia Fields' poem about Malcolm X?

5.   Maika says that the *oakland tribune* is her favorite newspaper.

6.   Between 1980 and 1989, *the cosby show* was the third most
     popular show on television.

7.   The best-selling nonfiction book in 1990 was Charles Kuralt's
     a life on the road.

8.   You need to make an appointment to see the doctor.

9.   Was the longest-running television program in history *the
     wonderful world of disney*?

10.   I love Auguste Rodin's sculpture *the thinker.*

11.   Lincoln issued the emancipation proclamation on January 1, 1863.

12.   I thought the movie *parenthood* was quite funny.

13.   In school we read the book *ragtime* by E. L. Doctorow.

14.   My neighbor, professor Rivera, teaches Mexican history.

15.   The *tacoma morning news tribune* is published in Washington state.

16.   In 1783, the treaty of paris ended the American Revolution.

17.   Will aunt Dolores be traveling to Paraguay again this year?

18.   Haruki Murakami wrote the story "the little green monster."

19.   I have long admired the Nez Perce leader chief Joseph.

20.   Didn't Vincent van Gogh paint that wonderful work called *the
     starry night*?

CHAPTER REVIEW

A. Correcting Errors in Capitalization

For each sentence below, correct the errors in capitalization by drawing a line through the error and writing the correct form in the space above it.

EX. 1. Mom's best friend, ~~dr.~~ ~~rutkowski~~, teaches at a junior college. (D R)

1. "have you ever seen a cincinnati team play?" asked Rolf.
2. sally and matt ate at a thai restaurant called bow thai.
3. The offices of the united nations children's fund are located at three un plaza, new york, new york.
4. Do you really think that Uncle Maxwell once worked for the cia?
5. We saw mary cassatt's painting *the boating party* at the national gallery of art in washington, d. c.
6. aunt harriet is writing a book called *how to be a kid till the day you die.*
7. I wanted to buy some of Jackson's piccadilly brand herbal tea, so I went to cape ann market on eastern avenue.
8. on valentine's day we visted the petrified forest national park in arizona; then we returned home on a southwest airlines flight.
9. Chandra looked for a copy of Helene Chirinian's book *camping out* at the chicago public library.
10. My brother showed me a poem called "choices," written by nikki giovanni; he had read it in an english class at gordon college.

B. Proofreading for Correct Capitalization

On your own paper, correct the capitalization errors in the paragraph below. Some sentences may be correct.

EX. [1] Two large islands, north island and south island, make up most of the country of new zealand.
[1] North Island; South Island; New Zealand

[1] We were told this and many other interesting facts about new zealand history and geography by dr. Flo Marino. [2] She gave a lecture

at the downtown library yesterday. [3] Dr. marino teaches cartography

at the university but spends all of her free time in the south pacific.

[4] Besides the two main islands, the country includes stewart island and

several other small islands. [5] Large cities in new zealand include

auckland, manukau, wellington, and christchurch. [6] Located in the

south on the tasman sea is fiordland national park. [7] Through this park

runs part of the mountain range known as the southern alps. [8] New

Zealand has many rivers, including the waikato river in the north and the

clutha river in the south. [9] The islands were first settled by a polynesian

people known as the maoris. [10] Dr. marino said that her frequent trips

to New Zealand give her the opportunity to explore her maori heritage.

C.   Writing a Letter

You've just started writing to a teenager in India. You and your pen pal are
eager to learn more about each other's cultures. Write a letter of at least ten
sentences to your pen pal. Describe some custom or practice that is unique to
United States culture or special to your family. In your letter, apply five of the
rules of capitalization given in this chapter.

EX.   April 3, 1995

    Dear Amit,

        How are things in Bombay? I really enjoyed your last letter,
    especially the part about the trip that you took with your family to
    Varanasi on the Ganges River.

        My family has never made a pilgrimage, but we do have special
    celebrations and traditions. Perhaps you have heard of Thanksgiving
    Day? On this day in November, we try to remember and to be grateful
    for all the good things in our lives. Thanksgiving Day celebrates a time
    in early American history when American Indians helped the English
    colonists and then shared with them a special meal. So, on
    Thanksgiving, we eat special meals and remember that time in our
    history.

                        Write again soon,

                        Emily

END MARKS

End marks—periods, question marks, exclamation points—are used to indicate the purpose of a sentence.

22a   A statement (or declarative sentence) ends with a period.

EXAMPLES   Yoshi is feeding the dog**.**
Elaine went to the market**.**

22b   A question (or interrogative sentence) ends with a question mark.

EXAMPLES   Have you washed the dishes yet**?**
Who was that boy I saw you talking to**?**

(1) Do not use a question mark after a declarative sentence stating an indirect question.

DECLARATIVE   Stevie wondered who would win**.**
INTERROGATIVE   Do you think you will win**?**

(2) Commands and requests are often put in question form even when they aren't actually questions. In that case, they may be followed by either a period or a question mark.

EXAMPLES   Will you please state your name**.**
Will you please state your name**?**

(3) Place a question mark inside the closing quotation marks when the quotation itself is a question. Otherwise, place a question mark outside the closing quotation marks.

EXAMPLES   He asked, "Where is my Garth Brooks CD**?"**
Did you say "Garth Brooks CD"**?**

22c   An exclamation ends with an exclamation point.

EXAMPLES   How disgusting**!**   I don't believe it**!**   Hey**!**

Place an exclamation point inside the closing quotation marks when the quotation itself is an exclamation. Otherwise, place the exclamation point outside the quotation marks.

EXAMPLES   At the graduation exercises the class cheered, "Yea, Carlos**!"**
I thought you said "Time's up"**!**

22d   An imperative sentence may end with either a period or an exclamation point.

EXAMPLES   Please hand me that wrench**.** [request]
Give me that**!** [a command]

Sometimes a command is stated in question form. However, since its purpose is to give a command or make a request, it may be followed by a period or an exclamation point.

EXAMPLES   Will you get off my foot!   May we get through, please.

EXERCISE 1   Correcting Sentences by Adding End Marks

Add the proper end mark to each of the following items. Some items may have more than one correct answer.

EX.   1. Are we going now?

1. Where are you

2. Walter renewed his driver's license

3. Stop right now

4. Running barefoot through the grass can be fun

5. Do students go to school during Ramadan

6. What an incredible film

7. Don't say a word

8. Where I come from, cricket is a very popular sport

9. Go, Patriots, go

10. Why do you think so

11. Believe it or not, Sergio wrote me a letter

12. Please don't go out after dark

13. Move over there

14. We knew she was already here

15. Watch out

16. Tell me if everyone has accepted the invitation

17. Have you ever been to the *Carnaval* parade in Veracruz

18. Are you kidding

19. A magnet attracts metal

20. How are the driving conditions today

ABBREVIATIONS

22e An abbreviation is usually followed by a period.

Abbreviations with Periods	
Personal Names	Susan B. Anthony, W. C. Fields
Titles Used with Names	Dr., Jr., Sr., Mr., Mrs., Ms.
States	N.Mex., Ga., Conn., Wash.
Organizations and Companies	Co., Inc., Corp., Assn.
Addresses	St., Rd., Ave., P.O. Box, Blvd.
Times	A.M., P.M., A.D., B.C.
Abbreviations without Periods	
Government Agencies	FBI, CIA, FDA, NASA
State Abbreviations Followed by ZIP Code	Jackson, AL 36545 Willows, CA 95988
Units of Measure	cm, kg, ml, oz, ft, yd, mi, lb
Widely Used Abbreviations	VCR, PTA, NAACP, UNICEF, TV

NOTE Two-letter state codes are used only when the ZIP Code is included. These state codes are not followed by periods.

EXAMPLE Springfield, **MA** 01101

NOTE In most cases, an abbreviation is capitalized only if the words that it stands for are capitalized. If you are unsure whether to use periods with an abbreviation or whether to capitalize it, check a dictionary.

EXERCISE 2 Proofreading for Correct Punctuation of Abbreviations

In the items below, add or delete any periods where needed. Some items may be correct.

EX. 1. Dr. Jane R. Otis

1. 1-hr. service
2. NFL
3. Dr. Ana P Carr
4. 50 m.m.
5. Concord, NH 03301
6. Freeyklund Construction Co
7. Orlando, Fla
8. 12 $\frac{1}{2}$ Davis St
9. 3:00 P M sharp
10. 50-yd. dash

REVIEW EXERCISE

A. Proofreading Sentences for Correct Punctuation

In the sentences below, add punctuation where needed. Some sentences may be correct.

EX. 1. I hear Constance caught a 6-in. fish.

1. When did Roberto leave for the Main St station

2. We thought it unusual that he signed his name D T R Parker

3. Was it really 10:00 A M before they arrived

4. Don't debate about the Panama Canal

5. Sometimes the newscasters on CBS, NBC, and ABC refer to former presidents as FDR, JFK, and LBJ.

6. I can't believe he actually ran 50 ft. that fast

7. The letter was addressed to Dr Manuel T Clemente

8. What famous person was born at 5:00 P M in 40 B C

9. They mailed the 4-lb. package to a P O Box in Honolulu

10. Pitcairn Island in the South Pacific measures 1.5 sq mi

B. Writing Dialogue for a Cartoon

You are a syndicated cartoonist. You are writing the dialogue for the illustrations below. On your own paper, write at least two sentences for each frame of the cartoon. Use each of the four types of sentences—declarative, interrogative, imperative, and exclamatory—at least once in your dialogue. Be sure to use correct punctuation. (Your dialogue will eventually be placed in word balloons, so you do not need to use quotation marks.)

EX. 1. I'll see you when I finish playing, Mom.

Calvin and Hobbes   by **Bill Watterson**

Calvin & Hobbes copyright 1986 Watterson. Reprinted with permission of Universal Press Syndicate. All rights reserved.

284

COMMAS IN A SERIES

22f **Use commas to separate items in a series.**

WORDS   I am going to the riverside cleanup day with Marcie, Latrice, Betty, and Dominic.

PHRASES   We looked for the glasses in my bedroom, in the car, in my hall locker, and in my gym locker.

CLAUSES   Mr. Hartry said that we had worked hard, that we had improved immensely, and that we would put on a terrific show.

NOTE   Some paired words—such as *macaroni and cheese* or *shoes and socks*— may be considered a single item.

EXAMPLE   Shimon put on his pants, shoes and socks, and jacket.

22g **If all items in a series are joined by *and, or,* or *nor*, do not separate them with commas.**

EXAMPLES   Washington **and** Oregon **and** Idaho are three states I'd like to visit next summer.

Do you swim in the upper pond **or** the lower pond **or** the creek?

22h **Use commas to separate two or more adjectives preceding a noun.**

EXAMPLES   Marge had a wonderful, happy, exciting day with her uncle.
Ulna is an imaginative, expressive, determined artist.

EXERCISE 3   Proofreading Sentences for the Correct Use of Commas

In the following sentences, insert commas where needed. Draw a line through any unnecessary commas. If the sentence is correct, write *C* on the line before the sentence.

EX.   _____ 1.   Bring forks, knives, spoons, and napkins/to the picnic.

_____ 1.   Joachim won the talent show by singing well being polite and dressing appropriately.

_____ 2.   By the end of the game, the basket seemed two inches around one thousand yards away and ten miles high.

_____ 3.   These hats come in black, and green, and brown.

_____ 4.   Red blue and yellow are the primary colors.

_____ 5.   His favorite foods are potatoes, corn and peas.

_____ 6. My sister enjoys all the holidays: Christmas Easter Thanksgiving and Valentine's Day.

_____ 7. Ricardo and Bill and Consuela and Sam were elected class officers.

_____ 8. "What a marvelous wonderful terrific incredible day!" she enthusiastically exclaimed.

_____ 9. Who doesn't know about Happy Dopey Grumpy Sleepy Doc and the rest of the dwarves?

_____ 10. Lunch consisted of both ham and cheese and peanut butter and jelly sandwiches.

_____ 11. Neither rain, nor snow, nor dark of night stopped the fearless explorers.

_____ 12. Thanks for the flowers and candy for the kind words and for everything else you did during that long week.

_____ 13. Pick any direction: north or south or east or west.

_____ 14. Nobody knew who the burglars were when exactly they had broken in what they took or where they went.

_____ 15. Thank you good luck and goodnight.

_____ 16. It's Halloween, but I'm not sure if we're going trick-or-treating.

_____ 17. Visiting the Washington Monument the Jefferson Memorial and the White House was a remarkable experience.

_____ 18. Domingo was amazed that he wasn't winded grateful that his feet didn't hurt and delighted that he'd won.

_____ 19. You can get a ticket by going over the speed limit double-parking failing to use the turn signal or driving without proper registration.

_____ 20. Rudolph was finally accepted by Donner Blixen Comet and Cupid.

_____ 21. These musicals were written by the well-known teams of Rodgers and Hammerstein and Lerner and Loewe.

_____ 22. Go over the hill cross the plain walk through those pines find the cave and you'll see the underground waterfall.

_____ 23. Neither Lulu nor Susan nor Bianca could stand to wear the turquoise sweater.

_____ 24. Hopeful cautious and ready, we waited.

_____ 25. The last ones to rent scuba gear were Marie Che Marge and Don.

COMMAS WITH INDEPENDENT CLAUSES

22i Use commas before *and, but, for, nor, or, so,* and *yet* when they join independent clauses.

EXAMPLE   Morgan threw the baseball hard**,** and Hu caught it.

NOTE   Before *for, so,* and *yet* joining independent clauses, always use a comma. However, before *and, but, nor,* and *or,* the comma may be omitted if (1) the clauses are very short and (2) there is no possibility of misunderstanding either clause.

CORRECT   I talked **but** nobody listened.
INCORRECT   I talked to Sam and Jens and Rita danced.
CORRECT   I talked to Sam**,** and Jens and Rita danced.

Do not confuse a compound sentence with a simple sentence that has a compound verb.

SIMPLE SENTENCE   I folded my clothes **and** put them away. [one independent clause with a compound verb]
COMPOUND SENTENCE   I folded my clothes**,** and I put them away. [two independent clauses]

22j Independent clauses in a series are usually separated by semicolons. Short independent clauses, however, may be separated by commas.

EXAMPLES   On our vacation we drove through the woods**;** we hiked up a mountain**;** and we swam in the Pacific Ocean.
On our vacation we drove**,** we hiked**,** and we swam.

EXERCISE 4   Correcting Punctuation in Sentences

For each of the following sentences, insert commas where needed. If a sentence is correct, write *C* on the line before the sentence.

EX.   _____   1.   Flags are used to represent nations**,** but they are also used to send messages.

_____   1.   Flags may be placed in various arrangements on a line or they can be held by a signaler, using a method known as semaphore.

_____   2.   Semaphore was invented in the late 1700s and it was widely used until the arrival of the telegraph.

_____   3.   The distance between the semaphore posts still is often great and the signalers use telescopes to read each other's messages.

_____   4.   Each signaler holds two flags, one in the left hand and one in the right.

_____ 5. The signalers send messages over water and they use red and yellow flags; but over land the signal colors are red and white.

_____ 6. One can read a message from the pattern of the flags and send an answer back right away.

_____ 7. Some flag positions represent letters but others stand for numbers.

_____ 8. People used semaphore less after the 1830s for about that time Samuel Morse invented the electric telegraph.

_____ 9. Morse developed the telegraph and created a code to go with it.

_____ 10. Various patterns of dots and dashes represent numbers and letters.

_____ 11. These dots and dashes don't correspond to the colors or positions of flags; but with this code signalers can send messages much farther.

_____ 12. Telegraphy is a more efficient way to send messages yet even it has disadvantages.

_____ 13. During a sea battle two friendly ships may be able to trade messages rapidly but the radio signals might also give away their position to the enemy.

_____ 14. "Be silent or be sunk" might be the rule in some situations.

_____ 15. The code may be sophisticated but it still can be intercepted.

_____ 16. Morse code and similar systems are now the standard everywhere for the old-fashioned way of using flags to send messages has been replaced for the most part.

_____ 17. The international flag code consists of twenty-six flags and each flag stands for a different letter of the alphabet.

_____ 18. The sailors on ships may not be able to speak one another's languages but they can still communicate using the flag code.

_____ 19. Single flags can sometimes stand for an entire message so the letter "V" may mean "I need assistance."

_____ 20. Ship flags can carry coded messages or they can be national flags that identify the ship's native country.

_____ 21. On merchant ships, flags can be national flags or merchant flags.

_____ 22. National flags usually show one or more of the following colors: yellow, green, white, black, blue, red, and orange.

_____ 23. Flags of ships from Muslim countries often have a crescent and star and many flags from Christian countries have crosses on them.

_____ 24. On Britain's flag, the red cross stands for England the white cross stands for Scotland and the blue field stands for Ireland.

_____ 25. The national flag of the United States also uses red white and blue; but the stripes represent the original thirteen states and the stars represent the modern fifty states.

COMMAS WITH NONESSENTIAL ELEMENTS

> **22k Use commas to set off nonessential participial phrases and nonessential clauses.**
>
> EXAMPLES   The woman, exhausted by the heat, took a drink of water.
> My new stepfather, who works in a bank, is named Edward.
>
> A *nonessential* (or *nonrestrictive*) phrase or clause is one containing information that is not needed to understand the main idea of the sentence.
>
> NONESSENTIAL PHRASE   The critic, pleased with our performance, wrote a good review of our show.
> NONESSENTIAL CLAUSE   Our class party, which we have been planning, will take place this Saturday afternoon.
>
> An *essential* (or *restrictive*) clause or phrase is one that cannot be omitted without changing the meaning of the sentence.
>
> ESSENTIAL PHRASE   The man **carrying the luggage** was walking slowly.
> ESSENTIAL CLAUSE   The team **that fills the most garbage bags** will win a trip to Mount Rushmore.
>
> NOTE   Adjective clauses beginning with *that*, like the one in the last example above, are nearly always essential.

EXERCISE 5   Correcting Sentences by Adding Commas

For each of the following sentences, identify the italicized phrase or clause by writing *e.* for *essential* or *n.e.* for *nonessential* on the line before the sentence. Insert commas where needed.

EX.   __n.e.__   1. Our uncle Ben, *who played for the Phillies*, came for the holidays.

_____   1. We picked up Cousin Mathilda at the exact time *that she had requested in her letter*.

_____   2. Rodrigo *skeptical of airplanes* always took the train.

_____   3. Ali *having worked for the city of Tucson for thirty years* had just retired.

_____   4. The tour group watched as the three seals *no longer interested in watching the people from the rocks* plunged back into the water.

_____   5. Carl *proud of his accomplishment* bragged a little.

_____   6. He was one of those rolling stones *that gathers no moss*.

_____ 7. Nobody *who met Dixie* could help liking her.

_____ 8. Send the forty pounds of paper to that manufacturer *who will recycle it.*

_____ 9. The students *excited by the arrival of the guest speaker* filed into the auditorium.

_____ 10. The actors *enjoying the moment* smiled and bowed to the audience.

_____ 11. The jockey *who had crossed the finish line first* received the trophy.

_____ 12. Anoki's store *which features original handmade prints* opened yesterday.

_____ 13. The agent *unnoticed by the crowd* quietly left the room.

_____ 14. Kim *who brought the tomatoes* sat down to make the salad.

_____ 15. I don't know what I'd do without that clock *which helps me to be on time.*

_____ 16. The children *hoping to see their favorite clown again* returned to the circus.

_____ 17. Ring the bell *that has the name "Martinez" printed next to it.*

_____ 18. Mrs. Thompson *noticing the students' restlessness* dismissed the class early.

_____ 19. Do you know *who did it?*

_____ 20. There were rumors that Mr. Cleburne *whom we all knew to live on North Street* had recently moved.

_____ 21. Only the soldiers *carrying the equipment* were allowed to rest.

_____ 22. Tell Max *which one to take.*

_____ 23. The store was advertising that new brand of soap *which nobody had tried yet.*

_____ 24. The skier *racing down the hill recklessly* almost hit a tree.

_____ 25. Emilio was determined to learn how to play tennis, a sport *that had always interested him.*

COMMAS WITH INTRODUCTORY ELEMENTS

22l   Use a comma after certain introductory elements.

(1) Use a comma after interjections such as *hey, oh, well,* **and** *why,* **and after other introductory words such as** *yes* **and** *no.*

EXAMPLES   **Well,** this is rather surprising.
Hey, what are you doing here?
No, thank you, I do not want more rice now.

(2) Use a comma after an introductory participial phrase.

EXAMPLES   **Turning to me,** she asked where the dining hall was.
Covered with rust, the antique trunk refused to open.

(3) Use a comma after two or more introductory prepositional phrases.

EXAMPLES   **At the beginning of the day,** I feel energetic.
In the top drawer of the dresser near the door, you'll find the key.

(4) Use a comma after an introductory adverb clause.

An introductory adverb clause may appear at the beginning of a sentence or before any independent clause in the sentence.

EXAMPLES   **If we leave now,** we won't be late.
I told Lin that I cannot work on the yearbook anymore; yet**,**
whenever he sees me, he asks me to work on it.

EXERCISE 6   Correcting Sentences by Adding Commas

For each of the following sentences, insert commas where needed. If a sentence is correct, write *C* on the line before the sentence.

EX. _____ 1. In the cool of the morning, we walked to the shore.

_____ 1. Please I need to use the telephone.

_____ 2. Getting right to the point the coach drew a line across the center of the board.

_____ 3. Until you came along I didn't think anyone could do it.

_____ 4. In a pleasant valley across the snowcapped mountains they finally found water.

_____ 5. You may be leaving now; but wherever you go I'll be sure to write to you.

_____ 6. Yes they'll be back in an hour.

_____ 7. Singing the same old song, they sauntered slowly across the sand.

_____ 8. Until the break of day not a sound was heard in the cabin.

_____ 9. Reliable as ever the pilot steered the ship through the storm.

_____ 10. Decked out in several layers of clothing my cousins attended the New Year's Day parade.

_____ 11. No I don't want you to do that!

_____ 12. Curious as to what had made the noise Rachel opened the door.

_____ 13. They waited until everyone had left; and, before the moon rose, they made their escape.

_____ 14. Wait nobody move!

_____ 15. Having said what he needed to say Cornelius stopped talking.

_____ 16. Up the stairs to the right, there's a closet.

_____ 17. Thanking the two boys she left.

_____ 18. No matter how much you want to go you should think it over first.

_____ 19. Boy it's hot!

_____ 20. Almost more quickly than the eye could see the deer sprang across the road.

_____ 21. Maybe but let's vote on it.

_____ 22. Sticking the insect repellent in her pack Bea headed up the trail.

_____ 23. David said, "Well I guess I should have looked first!"

_____ 24. In the middle of the night, we watched the lunar eclipse.

_____ 25. When he answered the phone he was still half asleep.

COMMAS WITH SENTENCE INTERRUPTERS

22m Use commas to set off elements that interrupt the sentence.

(1) Commas are usually used to set off appositives and appositive phrases.

An *appositive* is a noun or pronoun that follows another noun or pronoun to identify or explain it. An *appositive phrase* consists of an appositive and its modifiers.

EXAMPLES   Team sports, **especially soccer,** are quite popular.
Julio, **the boy in the first row,** works for a repair shop.

Sometimes an appositive is so closely related to the word preceding it that it should not be set off by commas. Such an appositive is called a *restrictive appositive*.

EXAMPLES   My friend **Gar** helped me.
The publisher **Penguin Books** produces paperback books.

(2) Use commas to set off words used in direct address.

EXAMPLES   **Dad,** have you seen my toast?
Your briefcase, **Stella,** is in the rack by the door.
You played that ballad very well, **Rodney.**

(3) Use commas to set off parenthetical expressions.

Parenthetical expressions are remarks that add incidental information or relate ideas to each other.

Commonly Used Parenthetical Expressions		
after all	I believe (hope, etc.)	naturally
at any rate	incidentally	nevertheless
by the way	in fact	of course
consequently	in general	on the contrary
for example	in the first place	on the other hand
for instance	meanwhile	that is
however	moreover	therefore

EXAMPLES   **On the contrary,** I have done it many times.
My whole-grain bread is, **in fact,** quite delicious.
I made two of those goals, **I believe.**

> **NOTE**
>
> A contrasting expression introduced by *not* or *yet* is parenthetical and must be set off by commas.
>
> EXAMPLES   It was Franklin Roosevelt**, not Theodore,** who met Stalin and Churchill at Yalta.
> Hockey is similar to**, yet slightly different from,** lacrosse.

EXERCISE 7   Proofreading Sentences for Correct Use of Commas

For each of the sentences below, insert commas where needed. If a sentence is correct, write *C* on the line before the sentence.

EX.   _____ 1. By the way, have you seen my camera?

_____ 1. My sister Phoebe got me to join the camera club.

_____ 2. She said, "Rick you need a hobby."

_____ 3. Consequently I joined the group.

_____ 4. My first camera just a small black box made fairly good pictures.

_____ 5. I still have the photograph I took of my cousin's horse Florence.

_____ 6. Of course the background of the picture is a little dark.

_____ 7. On the other hand I was just a beginner.

_____ 8. Naturally after a while I got a new camera one that made better pictures.

_____ 9. The camera club meets every Thursday afternoon at the home of Vicky Morales the club president.

_____ 10. Most of the time the meetings are informal not businesslike.

_____ 11. Nevertheless Rob Samuelson the club secretary occasionally takes notes for us.

_____ 12. Last month a debate began between Phoebe and Warner Hopkins an ace photographer.

_____ 13. Incidentally the discussion was over having a photo contest.

_____ 14. Phoebe said, "You just want to have a contest Warner because you know you'll win."

_____ 15. In fact we had the contest; and Phoebe my surprised sister won.

OTHER USES OF COMMAS

22n   Use a comma to separate items in dates and addresses.

EXAMPLES   On Sunday**, January 1, 1995,** I'm having a party.
Reply to 92 Keystone Crossings**, Indianapolis,** IN 46240.

NOTE   Commas are not placed between the month and the day, between the house number and the street name, or between the two-letter state code and the ZIP Code.

22o   Use a comma after the salutation of a friendly letter and after the closing of any letter.

EXAMPLES   Dear Luis**,**   Yours truly**,**

22p   Use a comma before an abbreviation such as *Jr., Sr.,* or *M.D.* following a name and also after the abbreviation when the name and the abbreviation are used together in a sentence.

EXAMPLES   Felice Wilson**, J.D.**
Isn't that John F. Kennedy**, Jr.,** in that car?

22q   Do not use unnecessary commas.

Use a comma only when a rule requires one or if the meaning is unclear without one.

INCORRECT   The girl in my homeroom who plays bass with the orchestra, is from Kiev. [*Girl,* the subject, must not be separated from its verb *is.*]

CORRECT   The girl in my homeroom who plays bass with the orchestra is from Kiev.

EXERCISE 8   Proofreading Sentences for Correct Use of Commas

For each of the following sentences, insert commas where needed, and draw a line through any commas that are misplaced. If a sentence is correct, write *C* on the line before the sentence.

EX.   _____ 1. The winner/of the award/was Alex Wong, CPA.

_____ 1. The movie credits listed the hero's name as "King Kong Sr."

_____ 2. End the message, "Yours truly Renata."

_____ 3. On Saturday April 24 1995, we're having a class reunion.

_____ 4. I sent congratulations to Shirley Draper Ph.D.

_____ 5. John Craig lived at 15 Cedar Street Colorado Springs Colorado.

_____ 6. The type of string that works best with this kite is sold here.

_____ 7. Mail twenty-five cents and the coupon to the cereal company in Battle Creek Michigan.

_____ 8. Bill Jr. looks just like Bill Sr.

_____ 9. The invitation began, "Dear Remi Can you come . . . ."

_____ 10. During the 1980s one of the fastest growing U.S. cities, was Yuma Arizona.

_____ 11. Someone whom you know arrived today.

_____ 12. A researcher sent the results to Los Angeles Harbor College Wilmington CA 90744.

_____ 13. The sign on the door, Frederick Hong M.D. was freshly painted.

_____ 14. She sent a letter to the Moon Institute of Technology 84 Crescent View, Solar System 203, Milky Way.

_____ 15. We attended the graduation of Susan Sakamoto J.D.

_____ 16. On July 4 1989, I saw the best fireworks display of my life.

_____ 17. The toothpaste that I like the most is in my suitcase.

_____ 18. Our school is located at Roger Williams Avenue Highland Park IL 60035.

_____ 19. The car that Bart was driving, crossed the finish line first.

_____ 20. The show first aired at 9:30 P.M. on Thursday March 31.

_____ 21. The return address read 34 Main St. Mobile AL 36601.

_____ 22. We're going to a wedding on the ninth of May.

_____ 23. An attorney needs a J.D., to practice in this state.

_____ 24. The notebook with the blue ribbon on it, is mine.

_____ 25. The card was signed, "Best wishes Helen, Sen, and Carlita Armstrong."

CHAPTER REVIEW

A. Proofreading Sentences for Correct Punctuation

For each of the sentences below, insert commas, periods, and other end marks where needed, and draw a line through any commas that are misplaced. If a sentence is correct, write *C* on the line before the sentence.

EX. _____ 1. Quick, bring me the 35-ft rope!

_____ 1. Dr Pines lived at 59 Sagebrush Ave Tucson Ariz

_____ 2. Lonato played the drums Motega played the xylophone and Kibbe played the flute

_____ 3. The fourteen people, who hadn't known they would be, chosen stood up.

_____ 4. Were you born at 5:00 A M or 10:00 P M

_____ 5. She ended the letter, "Sincerely yours Karen Q O'Connell."

_____ 6. Katya planted lilacs daisies and daffodils but Bruno preferring trees planted ten 5-ft maples.

_____ 7. After hiking in the winter, they huddled by the fireplace.

_____ 8. Get out of that rain Shawn before you catch cold

_____ 9. The batter swung connected and hit the pitch over the center field wall

_____ 10. Did you watch the special on PBS the Public Broadcasting System?

_____ 11. She bet that no one would believe it and they didn't

_____ 12. Before you could blink your eye the lemonade was gone

_____ 13. Ms Jackson the grocer's wife sometimes gave out free soda on Sundays; so we were always sure to be there just in case

_____ 14. Limping along, Claude was glad the hike was over.

_____ 15. Yikes what a fish

_____ 16. Proud of their new boat Jeff and Walter named it, the J W Flash

_____ 17. Naturally you can ask Masako; but Akio who was there earlier may be able to tell you more about it

_____ 18. Happy enthusiastic energetic we set out on the long voyage

_____ 19. Lionel catch that falling plate of tamales before they are ruined

_____ 20. Tired from a long day in the woods the lumberjack in the heavy plaid jacket sat down to speak to his friend Jody

B.   Correcting Punctuation in a Paragraph

In the paragraph below, add end marks and commas where needed. Draw a line through any punctuation marks that are misplaced.

EX.   [1] Did you know that sculptures can be made from clay, stone, wood, or metal?

[1] Some artists make sculptures by building them out of various materials, and others create them, by carving them out of solid blocks of stone wood or other hard substances. [2] The earliest known sculptures were made in the Stone Age about thirty thousand years ago [3] By 3000 B C sculptors, in Middle Eastern civilizations, were making fine stone carvings *in relief* that is, with the figures standing out a bit from a flat background. [4] During the time of the ancient Greeks and Romans sculptors made statues of their gods and goddesses; but they also sculpted men women athletes soldiers and lawmakers. [5] Modern sculptors who tend to emphasize shape rather than reality in their work have used moving parts to add a whole new dimension to the art form.

C.   Working Cooperatively to Write a Letter

You are living in the year 2820 on the planet Discor. You can speak and write in English, and you have a new pen pal on Earth. Work with a partner to write a letter describing a sports event you have recently attended on Discor. Create an explanation of the rules, setting, and equipment for one of the games listed below. Or you may devise a game of your own. Remember that what you describe will be totally unknown to your pen pal, so you'll have to use restrictive and nonrestrictive phrases and clauses in your explanation of the game. Be sure to use end marks and commas correctly.

Speed Rings	Combat Ball	Star Words	Crater Hop
Planet Diving	Star Chase	Moon Zoom	Warp Walk

EX.   Crater Hop
      Dear Ricardo,
          Last week, I saw a Crater Hopping Contest, a game that is popular here on Discor. In this game, for young and old alike, players compete with each other by bouncing from one crater to another.

SEMICOLONS AND COLONS

23a **Use a semicolon alone between closely related independent clauses if they are not joined by** *and, but, for, nor, or, so,* **or** *yet.*

EXAMPLE Joyce's favorite group was coming to town**;** she was standing in line to buy concert tickets.

23b **Use a semicolon between independent clauses joined by conjunctive adverbs or transitional expressions. Also use a semicolon (rather than a comma) between independent clauses joined by a coordinating conjunction when the clauses contain commas.**

EXAMPLES Joleen decided not to take the shop class**; instead,** she would take the auto mechanics class.

Frank arrived early at the office**; for this reason,** he received the first interview appointment.

Jefferson washed the dog and the cat**;** he rinsed out the tub and mopped the floor**;** then he took a nap.

23c **Use a colon before a list of items, especially after such expressions as** *as follows* **and** *the following.*

EXAMPLES For her birthday, Kay received several things she had been wanting**:** a new dress, the latest CD by her favorite group, a red hat, and a silver bracelet.

Hall monitors are responsible for the following**:** picking up all trash, reporting hazards, and directing fire drills.

NOTE Do not use a colon before a list that directly follows a verb or a preposition.

EXAMPLE My favorite cartoonists are Robb Armstrong, Cathy Guisewite, Garry Trudeau, and Charles Schultz.

23d **Use a colon before a long, formal statement or quotation.**

EXAMPLE Grady stood at the podium before the town council and began his speech**:** "I am a citizen of this country. I am a resident of this state. I have lived in this town for seventeen years."

23e **Use a colon between independent clauses when the second clause explains or restates the idea of the first.**

EXAMPLE Jacques decided to walk**:** he wanted to learn his way around the new neighborhood.

EXERCISE 1   Proofreading Sentences for Correct Use of Semicolons and Colons

Use a caret (∧) to show where a semicolon or colon is needed in each sentence below. Some sentences are correct.

EX.   1. Krista's boss asked her to order the following office supplies∧ a box of felt-tip pens, two reams of copy paper, twenty-five floppy diskettes, and staples.

1. Lydia's father is a master chef he oversees the kitchen at a five-star restaurant.

2. That magazine contains articles on the Olmec people of Mexico, the Red Sea, Kodiak Island in Alaska, and Taiwan.

3. The mystery writer's latest book is sold out in all the neighborhood bookstores however, I was able to order a copy from the publisher.

4. The mayor concluded the debate with this statement "My worthy opponent, you have indeed presented a persuasive argument."

5. Carlotta asked for a large glass of ice water she was extremely thirsty after her run.

6. Tina was surprised when she was selected to play the lead in the junior class play she had expected only a minor role.

7. The arrow is an important part of traditional Crow culture older Crow men teach the younger men how to make and shoot the arrows.

8. In his backpack, Jaimie had the following items his notebook, a few pens and pencils, a baseball mitt, two tennis balls, a half-eaten pretzel, an empty box of raisins, and one sock.

9. Monroe ran into the house and sped up the stairs he took a shower and dressed then he ran down the stairs and out of the house.

10. Steve went to his room right after dinner he needed some time to be alone.

Nancy reprinted by permission of UFS, Inc.

DASHES, PARENTHESES, AND BRACKETS

23f   Use a dash to show an abrupt break in thought.

EXAMPLES   And then Arnold showed up—what luck!
Cameron, I want to tell you—and I really mean this—you've
been a great friend.

**23g   Use a dash to mean *namely*, *in other words*, *that is*, and similar
expressions that come before an explanation.**

EXAMPLE   I left for the reason I told you—I had to meet Cynthia to return
her keys to her.

**23h   Use parentheses to enclose informative or explanatory material of
minor importance. Be sure that the material can be omitted without
losing important information or changing the basic meaning of
the sentence.**

EXAMPLES   On our way to Amarillo (the only city anywhere near us), we
stopped every twenty minutes.
My nephew Neil (my sister's son) is directing the school play.

NOTE   A parenthetical sentence that falls within another sentence should
not begin with a capital unless it begins with a word that should
always be capitalized. It also should not end with a period but may
end with a question mark or exclamation point.

EXAMPLE   Rosemary Apple Blossom Lonewolf **(have you heard of her?)** is a
talented Native American potter.

**23i   Use brackets to enclose informative or explanatory material within
quoted material.**

EXAMPLE   The doctor was yelling, "Get him two units [of blood], stat [fast]!"

EXERCISE 2   Using Dashes, Parentheses, and Brackets Correctly

In each of the following sentences, use a caret (∧) to add dashes, parentheses,
and brackets where needed.

EX.   1.   Our new neighbors ∧actually, they moved in six months ago∧ are
from Santiago, Chile.

1.   My math teacher Mrs. Penta did you have her for math, too? expects all of
us to be as excited and enthusiastic about equations as she is.

2. Two years after the first commercial radio station KDKA in Pittsburgh, Pennsylvania went on the air in 1920, five hundred stations were broadcasting across America.

3. Flo will do as you asked she will pick you up at the train station at exactly six o'clock.

4. Peter yelled up the stairs to Nina, "Toss me my mitt on the shelf in the closet, please."

5. Many of his friends actually, only two of them agree with his opinion about longer school days.

6. My sister Ellie whose real name is Elvira Maria was named for my great-grandmother who immigrated to America from Italy in the early 1900s.

7. The winner of the acoustic guitar competition there were more than 150 contestants was Paul Hunter.

8. Zimbabwe formerly known as Rhodesia, Southern Rhodesia, and Zimbabwe-Rhodesia is in the eastern half of southern Africa.

9. Instead of waffles my favorite breakfast food I ordered whole-grain muffins.

10. Some prepositions look at the list in Chapter 10 are compound.

11. People with *joie de vivre* literally, "joy of living" get enormous pleasure out of their lives.

12. Samuel Clemens 1835–1910, wrote under the pen name of Mark Twain worked as a riverboat pilot, a newspaper reporter, and a printer.

13. The door swung open and Marianna walked in what a shock!

14. There was a rumor going around school rumors spread like wildfire in a small town like this that Spike Lee was going to film a movie in our town.

15. The dog's barking although harmless seems endless.

16. We overheard Franco say, "Today his wedding day is the happiest day of my life."

17. The pages of the diary packed in a trunk for seventy-five years had yellowed and become brittle.

18. In 1846, The Know-Nothing Party it got its name because its members responded "I know nothing" to questions about the party was a secret organization that tried to keep foreign-born people from holding political office in America.

19. French physicist Marie Curie who was married to Pierre Curie won a Nobel Prize for chemistry and one for physics.

20. Jenna, I want to explain and I really hope you will understand why I missed your party.

UNDERLINING (ITALICS)

Italics are printed characters that slant to the right. Use **underlining** to indicate italics in handwritten or typewritten work.

23j **Underline (italicize) titles of books, plays, periodicals (magazines and newspapers), films, television programs, works of art, long musical compositions, trains, ships, aircraft, and spacecraft.**

Type of Name	Examples
Books	*Anything Goes, Julie of the Wolves*
Plays	*Oedipus the King, Annie Warbucks*
Periodicals	*Tucson Star, Popular Photography*
Films	*Home Alone, Free Willy*
Television Programs	*Designing Women, What's Happening*
Works of Art	*The Night Watch, The Cry*
Long Musical Compositions	*C-Minor Piano Trio, Turandot*
Trains	*Renaissance, TGV Atlantique*
Ships	*America, Intrepid*
Aircraft	*Kitty Hawk, Air Force One*
Spacecraft	*Soyuz 11, Columbia*

NOTE Italicize the title of a poem only if the poem is long enough to be published as a separate book. Such long poems are usually divided into titled or numbered sections. The titles of these sections are enclosed in quotation marks.

23k **Italicize (underline) foreign words and letters, words, and figures referred to as such.**

EXAMPLES   The *q.v.* in an encyclopedia stands for the Latin words *quod vide,* meaning "which see."
There are four *i*'s in *Mississippi.*
Make that *6* more readable if you can.

EXERCISE 3   Correcting Sentences with Underlining (Italics)

For each sentence below, underline the word or item that should be italicized.

EX.   1.   This mystery story takes place on a train called the <u>Orient Express</u>.

1. The painting by Aaron Douglas on page 422 and the poem by James Weldon Johnson on the next page have the same title, which is <u>The Creation</u>.

2. His last name has every vowel in it except an <u>a</u>.

3. Do you know which actor played Dracula in the original film <u>Dracula</u>?

4. The French philosopher René Descartes wrote the Latin phrase <u>cogito, ergo sum</u> which means "I think, therefore I am."

5. Richard didn't think he would enjoy opera until he saw a production of <u>Carmen</u>.

6. The television program <u>Kung Fu: The Legend Continues</u> is a sequel to the old television show that also starred David Carradine.

7. In 1991, the crew of the submersible vessel <u>Deep See</u> discovered five United States Navy planes from the 1940s.

8. The audience helps decide the ending in the play <u>Shear Madness</u>.

9. All the major articles in an issue of <u>National Geographic</u> are listed on the cover.

10. I was disappointed by the ending of John Grisham's book, <u>The Pelican Brief</u>.

11. Charles Lindbergh titled his Pulitzer Prize–winning book after his plane, the <u>Spirit of St. Louis</u>.

12. Did you see that incredible photograph on the front page of today's <u>Arkansas Gazette</u>?

13. I saw the original painting <u>Woman Doing Beadwork on Buckskin Shirt</u> by the artist Blue Eagle when I visited my grandmother in Santa Fe, New Mexico, last year.

14. Did you notice that every phone number mentioned in that movie began with the numbers <u>555</u>?

15. The music played during dinner was Beethoven's Piano Concerto No. 5.

QUOTATION MARKS

23l Use quotation marks to enclose a *direct quotation*—a person's exact words. A direct quotation always begins with a capital letter.

EXAMPLES   Jon's dad told us, **"**Stay off the phone!**"**

The Declaration of Independence begins, **"**When in the course of human events . . .**"**

Do not use quotations marks for an *indirect quotation.*

DIRECT QUOTATION   Billie asked, **"**May I help?**"** [Billie's exact words]
INDIRECT QUOTATION   Billie asked if she could help. [not Billie's exact words]

23m When an expression such as *he said* divides a quoted sentence into two parts, the second part begins with a small letter.

EXAMPLE   "I believe," Jorge said**,** **"**that that's a dual exhaust."

If the second part of a divided quotation is a new sentence, a period (not a comma) follows the interrupting expression. The second part then begins with a capital letter.

EXAMPLE   "Zack won't be here today," Arnold said**.** **"**He has to take his sister to the doctor."

NOTE   An interrupting expression is not part of a quotation, so it should never be located inside the quotation marks.

INCORRECT   "Davis, Coach said, get in there and play defense."
CORRECT   "Davis**,"** Coach said, **"**get in there and play defense."

23n Separate a direct quotation from the rest of a sentence with a comma, a question mark, or an exclamation point, but not with a period.

EXAMPLES   "Skye, if you're near it**,**" Sam said, "please hand me the hammer."
"Can you come over now**?**" Pearly asked.
"Super!" Stephen exclaimed.

23o Always place commas and periods inside the closing quotation marks.

EXAMPLE   "You know**,"** Shing said, "I'd like a chance, too**."**

23p Always place colons and semicolons outside the closing quotation marks.

EXAMPLES   Sonja listed the extra ingredients in her "Veggie Surprise**":** peas, tomatoes, squash, and mozzarella cheese.
Parthenia said, "I'm not doing anything for my birthday**";** our plans for her surprise party were working.

23q Place question marks and exclamation points inside the closing quotation marks only if the quotation is a question or an exclamation. Otherwise, place them outside the closing quotation marks.

EXAMPLES "How do I get to Route 23**?**" Why did she say, "Synthetic"**?**
She yelled, "Ouch**!**" I hate it when he says, "Okay"**!**

NOTE In a question or an exclamation that ends with a quotation, only the question mark or exclamation point is necessary, and it is placed outside the closing quotation marks.

23r When writing *dialogue* (a conversation), begin a new paragraph each time the speaker changes, and enclose each speaker's words in quotation marks.

EXAMPLE "Dad, can I go with Lok after school?" Winnie asked.
"May I," he answered.
"Dad, may I go with Lok after school?"
"Well," he said, "where were you planning on going?"
"To the marsh," she replied. "Phoebe heard there was a gigantic stork there, and we want to see it."

23s Use single quotation marks to enclose a quotation within a quotation.

EXAMPLE Joel said, "I thought I heard you say, 'There's one more roll left.'"
[Notice that the period is placed inside the single quotation mark.]

23t Use quotation marks to enclose titles of short works, such as short stories, poems, essays, articles, songs, episodes of television series, and chapters and other parts of books.

Type of Name	Examples	
Short Stories	"The Circuit"	"Everybody Knows Tobie"
Poems	"Braly Street"	"The Lesson of Walls"
Essays	"River Notes"	"Rattlesnake Hunt"
Articles	"Strong Medicine"	"Breaking a Sound Barrier"
Songs	"Under African Skies"	"Stardust"
TV Episodes	"Barbara the Mom"	"Shadows in a Desert Sea"
Chapters and Parts of Books	"Drama"	"Historical Introduction"

EXERCISE 4 Correcting Sentences by Adding Quotation Marks and Other Puctuation Marks

In each of the sentences below, add quotation marks and other marks of punctuation where needed. Capital letters may also be needed.

EX. 1. "I have trouble memorizing poetry," Chloe said.

1. Tom said That's probably because you try to learn it line by line instead of sentence by sentence

2. Can you explain that more clearly asked Chloe.

3. Cathy raised her hand and answered I can

4. Do you remember Naoshi's poem that begins She looks to the towering mountains Miss Stuart asked

5. Tom said That's the one in which the list of chores is compared to a mountain range he was obviously familiar with the poem

6. Although there are three stanzas in that poem Cathy said there are only three sentences in the entire poem.

7. So what Chloe questioned

8. Look at each sentence Tom said Think about what each sentence is saying Thinking about each sentence will help you understand the poem. Understanding it should help you memorize it To quote Miss Stuart You have to read poetry on two levels, the figurative and the literal

9. Figurative language uses imagery and other figures of speech to convey meanings Miss Stuart explained

10. What terrific imagery Fred used in his poem that begins with the sentence Dinosaurs are not always prehistoric Cathy exclaimed

11. What two things are compared in that poem asked Tom

12. A comparison is made between a dinosaur and a Model T answered Cathy

13. How wild Chloe said I can't believe that I thought poetry was boring Miss Stuart told me that if I learned how to read poetry, I would enjoy it more

14. Chloe, if you get a chance Tom said read The Fish by Elizabeth Bishop Also you might find it helpful to read the chapter Personal Response to Literature

15. Chloe answered You're right. I thought I heard Miss Stuart say There will be a free-reading period tomorrow

EXERCISE 5 Proofreading Sentences

Proofread the sentences below for correct use of quotation marks, other marks of punctuation, and capitalization. Draw a line through each error, and add any missing punctuation marks or capitalization where needed. Some sentences may be correct.

EX. 1. " I'll give you a clue" Mrs. Spinazola said. "you name the holiday and give me one fact about that holiday."

1. "Will we be graded on this" Art asked.

2. Mrs. Spinazola just smiled and said "a song you might hear on this holiday contains the words "He stuck a feather in his cap"

3. Trina said "Would that happen to be Independence Day she was trying to be funny

4. "Trina, can you give us one interesting fact about that day?" asked Mrs. Spinazola.

5. "You bet she exclaimed!"

6. "I believe, she said "that Independence Day celebrates the day on which the Continental Congress approved the Declaration of Independence."

7. Lynette added John Adams said "It ought to be solemnized with pomp and parade, with shows, games, sports."

8. "Great" Mrs. Spinazola said. Now I'll give you a clue about another holiday."

9. She said "this holiday is celebrated the last week of December by many African American families

10. "Is it Kwanzaa." asked Lloyd?

11. Lloyd said that Kwanzaa is a relatively new holiday, a time for a family to share memories; it was first celebrated in 1966.

12. "Kwanzaa is a seven-day celebration Lloyd added "It is a time for African Americans to focus on their heritage."

13. "Sandra, if you can Mrs. Spinazola said please explain some of the symbols of Kwanzaa."

14. Many of the symbols, like the bowl of fruit, vegetables, and nuts, are similar to those used at harvest festivals Sandra said.

15. As my friend Marissa told me the kikombe, or unity cup, is a special cup that the whole family drinks from each night Sandra added.

CHAPTER REVIEW

A. Correcting Sentences by Adding Punctuation Marks

In the sentences below, add correct punctuation where it is needed.

EX. 1. Lenore sings only when she works outside by herself; she doesn't think anyone else should have to listen.

1. Todd looked around at the nurses and doctors who had come to say good-bye and said I want to thank you for everything you've done. Without your help and your care, I might not be walking out of here today on my own two feet. Thank you so much.

2. Mr. Julius looked toward the back of the room students who arrived late always stood there and said Please stop that commotion right now.

3. I think Annie said that the writings of Dave Barry, a newspaper columnist from Florida are some of the funniest that I have ever read.

4. A series of devastating fires struck the community just as it was recovering from an earlier disaster terrible floods.

5. Students were asked to bring the following items to the school lock-up a sleeping bag, a pillow, a midnight snack, a toothbrush, a change of clothes, and a book or a game.

6. Who would like to volunteer at the senior center after school the principal asked

7. The Emancipation Proclamation begins, Whereas, on the twenty-second day of September, in the year of our Lord one thousand eight hundred and sixty-two . . .

8. A recent television showing of the movie Dances with Wolves included film footage that had not been released before.

9. My older sister is a musician Chan said She just got a job teaching band in a grade school.

10. Yikes Ethan yelled You almost ran over my toe with that thing.

11. Paul asked What did Franco mean when he said Revolutionary

12. How did you like reading Shakespeare's play Much Ado About Nothing Tina asked.

13. Mr. Jensen said, Five years ago today February 6, 1990 we had ten inches of snow.

14. Joanie said My baby brother made us laugh last night when he said Knock, knock, who's there? and then he started to laugh as if he had finished the joke.

15. In his closing remarks, the coach said, Thank you again for this the engraved trophy, and thank you for all the support you have given me.

B. Proofreading a Dialogue for Errors in Punctuation and Capitalization

Correct the punctuation and capitalization errors in the dialogue below. On your own paper, rewrite the dialogue correctly. Remember to begin a new paragraph each time the speaker changes.

EX.   [1] Tomás and I were racing to the train station to catch the

red-eye express ,it was the last train home.

[1] When we had taken our seats on the train we were lucky to find two

together Tomás said, "so what did you think of the movie." [2] We had

just come from seeing The Fugitive, starring Harrison Ford. [3] Terrific I

said However, I'm experiencing various emotions confusion, excitement,

surprise. [4] Did you see that article that was published recently it must

have been in TIME Magazine about the filming of that first scene.

[5] Tomás said. "Wow! that train wreck at the beginning was unbelievable.

[6] I turned to Tomás. [7] "You know, I said they destroyed a real train for

that scene in the beginning of the movie. [8] "Can you imagine, I

continued, how much that must have cost." [9] Filming the scene must

have cost a fortune! [10] Then I added I think I remember reading that

they could only shoot that scene once as a result, it had to be good."

C. Writing a Vacation Journal

During your vacation to Hawaii, you attended a luau. On your own paper, record your impressions and observations, including some of the comments you overheard. You might include statements about clothing, flowers, decorations, food, and entertainment. Before you begin writing, look in encyclopedias and research your topic. Then write at least fifteen sentences using, at least once, each of the punctuation marks discussed in the chapter: semicolons, colons, dashes, parentheses, brackets, italics, quotation marks, and commas and end marks used with quotations.

EX.   July 7, 1995—We dressed in flowered shirts and skirts; we ate tropical fruits and vegetables and sipped sweet juices; then we danced to the music.

THE DICTIONARY

A dictionary entry is divided into several parts. Study the parts of the following sample dictionary entry.

```
     1        2      3        4                    5
  neat (nēt), adj., –er, –est [French net, clean < Latin
                      5                      6
  nitidus, bright, fine] 1. in a well-ordered condition
      7
  [a neat room] 2. having a simple, attractive
  appearance [a neat dresser] 3. clever or appropriate [a
                          8
  neat story] 4. INFORMAL superlative in every way
                                  9
  [What a neat collection!] –neat'•ly, adv. –neat'ness, n.
                          10
  SYN. Neat suggests "order and an absence of
  unnecessary details." Tidy means "orderly." Trim
  suggests "neat and stylish." ANT. disorderly, messy
```

1. **Entry word.** The entry word shows the correct spelling of a word. An alternate spelling may also be shown. The entry word shows how the word should be divided into syllables and may also show whether the word should be capitalized.
2. **Pronunciation.** The pronunciation is shown using accent marks, phonetic symbols, or diacritical marks. Each *phonetic symbol* represents a specific sound. *Diacritical marks* are special symbols placed above letters to show how those letters sound.
3. **Part-of-speech labels.** These labels are usually abbreviated and show how the entry word should be used in a sentence. Some words may be used as more than one part of speech. In such a case, a part-of-speech label is also given before the set of definitions that matches each label.
4. **Other forms.** Sometimes a dictionary shows spellings of plural forms of nouns, tenses of verbs, or the comparative forms of adjectives and adverbs.

5. **Etymology.** The *etymology* tells how a word (or its parts) entered the English language. The etymology also shows how the word has changed over time.
6. **Definitions.** If there is more than one meaning, definitions are numbered or lettered.
7. **Sample usage.** Some dictionaries include sample phrases to illustrate particular meanings of words.
8. **Special usage labels.** These labels identify how a word is used (*Slang*), how common a word is (*Rare*), or how a word is used in a special field, such as botany (*Bot.*).
9. **Related word forms.** These are forms of the entry word created by adding suffixes or prefixes. Sometimes dictionaries also list common phrases in which the word appears.
10. **Synonyms and antonyms.** Words similar in meaning are *synonyms*. Words opposite in meaning are *antonyms*. Many dictionaries list synonyms and antonyms at the ends of some word entries.

EXERCISE 1 Using a Dictionary

Use a dictionary to answer the questions below.

EX.   1. How many syllables are in the word *multiplication*? _five_____

1. How is the word *flirtatious* divided into syllables? _____

2. What is the spelling for the plural form of *echo*? _____

3. Give three different meanings for the word *light*. _____

    _____

4. What is the past tense of *outwit*? _____

5. What is the etymology of the word *Mayday*? _____

    _____

EXERCISE 2 Writing Words with Alternate Spellings

For each of the words below, write the alternate spelling on the line after the word.

EX. 1. dialogue _dialog_

1. rigor   _____   4. calif   _____

2. phoney _____   5. gemology _____

3. litre   _____

SPELLING RULES

ie and *ei*

24a   Write *ie* when the sound is long *e*, except after *c*.

EXAMPLES   achieve, brief, ceiling, priest, receipt, yield
EXCEPTIONS   leisure, neither, seize, weird

24b   Write *ei* when the sound is not long *e*, especially when the sound is long *a*.

EXAMPLES   beige, height, neighbor, reindeer, sleigh
EXCEPTIONS   ancient, friend, pie, quiet, science

–cede, *–ceed*, and *–sede*

24c   The only word ending in *–sede* is *supersede*. The only words ending in *–ceed* are *exceed*, *proceed*, and *succeed*. All other words with this sound end in *–cede*.

EXAMPLES   accede, intercede, precede, recede, secede

EXERCISE 3   Writing Words with *ie* and *ei*

On the line in each word below, write the letters *ie* or *ei* to spell the word correctly. Use a dictionary as needed.

EX.   1. bel __ie__ ve

1. perc _____ ve
2. shr _____ k
3. bes _____ ge
4. pl_____ rs
5. v_____ n
6. br _____ f
7. fr _____ ght
8. h _____ ght
9. n _____ ce
10. counterf _____ t

11. t _____ r
12. cash _____ r
13. ch _____ f
14. dec _____ ve
15. forf _____ t
16. th _____ f
17. f _____ ld
18. v _____ l
19. p _____ ce
20. rec _____ ve

21. r _____ gn
22. rel _____ f
23. th _____ r
24. w _____ ld
25. p _____ rce
26. front _____ r
27. for _____ gn
28. y _____ ld
29. w _____ gh
30. _____ ght

EXERCISE 4   Proofreading a Paragraph to Correct Spelling Errors

The following paragraph contains ten spelling errors. Underline the misspelled words, and write the correct spelling above each misspelled word.

EX.   [1] Bicycle racing first <u>recieved</u> *received* wide notice after the development of the safety bike.

[1] In the United States, enthusiasm for bicycle racing reached a new hieght at the turn of the century. [2] For a breif time, bicycle racing was even more popular than baseball. [3] In 1896, it acheived even higher status by being included in the Olympics. [4] Some of the speed records posted by the first cyclists are unbeleivable. [5] For example, we would have to conceed that for a racer to cover a mile in sixty seconds is amazing. [6] Charles "Mile-a-Minute" Murphy succeded in doing just that in 1889, by riding his bike behind a train. [7] The train was fitted with a large windsheild so that Murphy encountered very little air resistance. [8] Still, no one can say Murphy was moving at a liesurely pace. [9] In 1926, the Belgian cyclist Leon Vanderstuyft siezed a world record by racing over seventy-six miles in one hour. [10] Modern racers would have difficulty superseeding such a feat even in ideal conditions.

PREFIXES AND SUFFIXES

A *prefix* is a letter or a group of letters added to the beginning of a word to change its meaning.

24d   When adding a prefix to a word, do not change the spelling of the word itself.

EXAMPLES   re + write = **re**write   un + natural = **un**natural
in + correct = **in**correct   under + rate = **under**rate

A *suffix* is a letter or a group of letters added to the end of a word to change its meaning.

24e   When adding the suffix –*ness* or –*ly* to a word, do not change the spelling of the word itself.

EXAMPLES   kind + ness = kind**ness**   quick + ness = quick**ness**
bold + ly = bold**ly**   clear + ly = clear**ly**

EXCEPTION   For most words that end in *y*, change the *y* to *i* before adding –*ly* or –*ness*.

EXAMPLES   silly + ness = sill**iness**   merry + ly = merr**ily**

24f   Drop the final silent *e* before a suffix beginning with a vowel.

Vowels are the letters *a, e, i, o, u,* and sometimes *y*. All other letters of the alphabet are *consonants*.

EXAMPLES   vote + er = vot**er**   drive + ing = driv**ing**
note + able = not**able**   dose + age = dos**age**

EXCEPTIONS   Keep the final silent *e*.
• in a word ending in *ce* or *ge* before a suffix beginning with *a* or *o*:
trac**eable**   outrag**eous**
• in *dye* before –*ing*:   dy**eing**
• in *mile* before –*age*:   mil**eage**

24g   Keep the final silent *e* before a suffix beginning with a consonant.

EXAMPLES   love + ly = lov**ely**   time + less = time**less**
pure + ly = pur**ely**   wise + ly = wise**ly**

EXCEPTIONS   true + ly = tru**ly**   judge + ment = judg**ment**
nine + th = nin**th**   argue + ment = argu**ment**
acknowledge + ment = acknowledg**ement** *or* acknolwedg**ment**

315

EXERCISE 5 Spelling Words with Prefixes and Suffixes

On the lines below, complete the word problems by adding the given prefix or suffix to the word.

EX.   1. dis + belief   _disbelief_

1. up + hold   _____   11. mile + age   _____

2. taste + ful   _____   12. fame + ous   _____

3. argue + ment   _____   13. dis + appear   _____

4. im + movable   _____   14. haste + y   _____

5. busy + ly   _____   15. ready + ly   _____

6. re + tell   _____   16. bake + ed   _____

7. simple + er   _____   17. sub + topic   _____

8. mis + spell   _____   18. re + cycle   _____

9. manage + ment   _____   19. nine + ty   _____

10. courage + ous   _____   20. final + ly   _____

EXERCISE 6 Spelling Words with Suffixes

On the lines below, complete the word problems by adding the given suffix to the word.

EX.   1. legal + ly   _legally_

1. normal + ly   _____   11. mere + ly   _____

2. change + ed   _____   12. race + er   _____

3. quote + able   _____   13. messy + ness   _____

4. adventure + ous   _____   14. sure + est   _____

5. loud + ness   _____   15. love + ly   _____

6. believe + ing   _____   16. care + less   _____

7. heavy + ness   _____   17. make + ing   _____

8. simple + est   _____   18. dense + ly   _____

9. notice + able   _____   19. lively + er   _____

10. calculate + or   _____   20. scrape + ing   _____

24h   **For words ending in _y_ preceded by a consonant, change the _y_ to _i_ before any suffix that does not begin with _i_.**

EXAMPLES   carry + ing = carry**ing**
funny + est = funn**iest**

vary + ous = var**ious**
magnify + ing = magnif**ying**

EXCEPTIONS   dry + ness = dry**ness**   sly + ly = sly**ly**

24i   **For words ending in _y_ preceded by a vowel, keep the _y_ when adding a suffix.**

EXAMPLES   play + ed = play**ed**
joy + ful = joy**ful**

enjoy + ment = enjoy**ment**
stay + ed = stay**ed**

EXCEPTIONS   day + ly = dai**ly**   pay + ed = pa**id**

24j   **Double the final consonant before a suffix that begins with a vowel if the word (1) has only one syllable or has the accent on the last syllable _and_ (2) ends in a single consonant preceded by a single vowel.**

EXAMPLES   bat + er = ba**tter**
skip + ing = ski**pping**

concur + ent = concu**rrent**
red + est = re**ddest**

NOTE   The final consonant of some words may or may not be doubled. Either spelling is acceptable.

EXAMPLES   cancel + ed = cance**led** _or_ cance**lled**
travel + er = trave**ler** _or_ trave**ller**

EXERCISE 7   Spelling Words with Suffixes

On your own paper, complete the word problems below by adding the given suffix to the word.

EX.   1. big + est
       1. _biggest_

1. pitch + er
2. ship + ing
3. rely + able
4. boy + hood
5. seem + ed

6. cry + ed
7. wrap + ed
8. sunny + est
9. win + ing
10. crazy + er

11. hurry + ing
12. mystery + ous
13. obey + ing
14. fly + ing
15. refer + ed

16. thin + er
17. begin + er
18. dark + est
19. glory + ous
20. marry + ed

EXERCISE 8   Proofreading to Correct Spelling in a Paragraph

In the paragraph below, underline the twenty spelling errors. Write the correct spelling above each misspelled word.

EX.   [1] Houdini's best trick was his escape from the *packing* packking case.

[1] Harry Houdini, perhaps the most famous magician in history, bafflled everyone with this trick. [2] Handcufed inside a nailed and ropped-up crate, he then had a tugboat lower him by crane deep into the river. [3] The crowd waited and worryed as the minutes pased. [4] But suddenly, he reappearred, having done what everyone thought impossible. [5] The packing case had reemerged with Houdini siting triumphantly on top. [6] The case itself seemmed undamaged. [7] It looked as though Houdini had mysteryously conquerred the laws of nature. [8] But today, we know he had foolled the audience by inventting a clever illusion. [9] Houdini wore fake handcuffs, which he openned with a secret spring. [10] He also had slily tucked away a pair of nail cuters, with which he pried the case apart from inside. [11] Two of his men fixxed the case later. [12] When the tugboat was out of sight, they extractted the broken nails and replaced them with new ones. [13] Still, it was hard to witness the trick and not be impresed. [14] Houdini had to be both highly skiled and quite brave in order to accomplish it. [15] There is no deniing he was one of the greatest entertainers of all time.

PLURALS OF NOUNS

24k Form the plurals of most nouns by adding –s.

SINGULAR	dollar	height	idea	key	rope	mountain
PLURAL	dollars	heights	ideas	keys	ropes	mountains

24l Form the plurals of nouns ending in *s, x, z, ch,* or *sh* by adding –es.

SINGULAR	address	church	ranch	waltz	wish
PLURAL	addresses	churches	ranches	waltzes	wishes

> **NOTE** Proper nouns usually follow these rules, too.
>
> EXAMPLES   the Martins   the Espositos
>   the Rosses   the Goodriches

EXERCISE 9   Spelling the Plurals of Nouns

On the line after each noun below, write the correct plural form.

EX.   1. hunch _hunches_

1. dress _____
2. skier _____
3. sign _____
4. trick _____
5. Burns _____
6. present _____
7. task _____
8. stress _____
9. willow _____
10. six _____
11. lunch _____
12. college _____
13. fez _____

14. arena _____
15. stitch _____
16. fox _____
17. Toscanini _____
18. flash _____
19. wasp _____
20. brush _____
21. López _____
22. fence _____
23. climber _____
24. shoe _____
25. piano _____

24m Form the plurals of nouns ending in *y* preceded by a consonant by changing the *y* to *i* and adding –*es*.

SINGULAR   century   fly   lady   penny   twenty
  PLURAL   centuries   flies   ladies   pennies   twenties

EXCEPTION   With proper nouns, simply add –*s*.

          EXAMPLES   the Bradys, the Olinskys

24n Form the plurals of nouns ending in *y* preceded by a vowel by adding –*s*.

SINGULAR   bay   display   key   Thursday   alley   toy
  PLURAL   bays   displays   keys   Thursdays   alleys   toys

24o Form the plurals of most nouns ending in *f* by adding –*s*. The plurals of some nouns ending in *f* or *fe* are formed by changing the *f* to *v* and adding either –*s* or –*es*.

SINGULAR   belief   gulf   reef   life   shelf   wolf
  PLURAL   beliefs   gulfs   reefs   lives   shelves   wolves

NOTE   When you are not sure how to spell the plural of a noun ending in *f* or *fe*, look in a dictionary.

EXERCISE 10   Spelling the Plurals of Nouns

On the line after each noun below, write the correct plural form.

EX.   1. leaf   *leaves*

1. blueberry _____   11. Kandinsky _____

2. Ripley _____   12. wharf _____

3. thief _____   13. folly _____

4. way _____   14 display _____

5. history _____   15. community _____

6. roof _____   16. story _____

7. country _____   17. knife _____

8. boy _____   18. donkey _____

9. Monday _____   19. Carney _____

10. half _____   20. rally _____

24p Form the plurals of nouns ending in *o* preceded by a vowel by adding –*s*. Form the plurals of nouns ending in *o* preceded by a consonant by adding –*es*.

SINGULAR	barrio	igloo	studio	echo	hero
PLURAL	barrios	igloos	studios	echoes	heroes

EXCEPTIONS	hellos	tuxedos

Form the plurals of most musical terms ending in *o* by adding –*s*.

SINGULAR	alto	cello	solo	soprano
PLURAL	altos	cellos	solos	sopranos

NOTE To form the plurals of some nouns ending in *o* preceded by a consonant, you may add either –*s* or –*es*.

SINGULAR	banjo	tornado	zero
PLURAL	banjos	tornados	zeros
	or	*or*	*or*
	banjoes	tornadoes	zeroes

NOTE If you are ever in doubt about the plural form of a noun ending in *o* preceded by a consonant, check the spelling in a dictionary.

24q The plurals of a few nouns are formed in irregular ways.

SINGULAR	tooth	woman	foot	child	goose
PLURAL	teeth	women	feet	children	geese

24r Form the plural of a compound noun consisting of a noun plus a modifier by making the modified noun plural.

SINGULAR	disc jockey	football	brother-in-law	runner-up
PLURAL	disc jockeys	footballs	brothers-in-law	runners-up

EXERCISE 11   Spelling the Plurals of Nouns

On the line after each noun below, write the correct plural form.

EX. 1. photo _photos_

1. piccolo _____
2. goose _____
3. tomato _____
4. mouse _____
5. flamingo _____

6. man-of-war _____
7. Silvano _____
8. tooth _____
9. stereo _____
10. mother-in-law _____

EXERCISE 12 Proofreading to Correct Spelling in Sentences

In the sentences below, underline all misspelled words. Write the correct spelling above each misspelled word.

EX. 1. All of the <u>childs</u> in the international chorus visited our school.
children

1. Smart drivers fasten their seats belt.

2. In the 1940s, our parents, listening to their radioes, heard singers performing soloes.

3. The President sometimes vetos the bills approved by Congress.

4. During the battle, our torpedos sunk three enemy man-of-wars.

5. Have you ever heard bongoses being played?

6. The mans lined themselves up quickly.

7. Celloes are much larger than piccolos.

8. My sister-in-laws gave me a surprise party.

9. Roberta fed bread crumbs to the gooses on the riverbank.

10. Most recording studioes have pianos.

EXERCISE 13 Using Plurals Correctly

On your own paper, write twenty sentences, using the plural forms of the words below.

EX. 1. ox
  1. We saw oxen pulling carts at the state fair.

1. motto
2. child
3. Navajo
4. seashell
5. eleventh-grader
6. foot
7. contralto
8. taco
9. president-elect
10. sergeant-at-arms
11. zero
12. mambo
13. tooth
14. baby sitter
15. mother-in-law
16. silo
17. mouse
18. rodeo
19. woman
20. patio

CHAPTER REVIEW

A. Correcting Spelling Errors in Sentences

Underline all misspelled words in each sentence below. Then write the correct spelling above each misspelled word.

EX. 1. We were all happy that our team had a *winning* season. *(wining underlined)*

1. Alex openned the drawer and took out two boxs of lightbulbs.

2. The Frederickes took us to see the tennis matchs.

3. Why spend so much money for a car that can excede the speed limit?

4. The raceing boats crosed the finish line.

5. On our block, the Espositoes are fameous for their wonderful partys.

6. During our trip to Hollywood, we toured two film studioes.

7. Betty laughed and said, "I've got the coollest new jacket!"

8. Donald is a duck, but Mickey and Minnie are both mouses.

9. In those dayes, ships entering the harbor had to watch for reeves.

10. Undereporting income on your tax forms is a felony.

11. The nieghborhood committee told us to turn off our stereoes after ten o'clock.

12. Who said the fashions of the seventies were timless?

13. We barly had time to put on our costumes.

14. After sending Roger out to buy three loafs of bread, I waitted for hours.

15. The navigateor usually sits next to the pilot in an airplane.

16. The stars of ice shows have to be gracful dancers as well as excellent skatters.

17. My mother finds amusment parks frivolous.

18. Those boyes ran off with all our blackberrys.

19. Most jurys don't work on Sundays.

20. Triing to guess the right answer all the time won't help you receive the best grade.

B.   Proofreading a Paragraph to Correct Spelling Errors

Underline the misspelled words in the paragraph below, and write the correct spelling above each misspelled word. Some sentences contain more than one error. Some sentences are correct.

EX.   [1] Can you <u>beleive</u> that seashells were once used as currency?
believe

[1] For varyous reasons, money has taken many different forms throughout history. [2] In Asia, bricks of tea were stampped with the name of a bank. [3] The Swedish plate money peice is the largest metal coin in the world. [4] It wieghs forty-four pounds, measureing twenty-four inches long. [5] Ornamental strings of shells were eventually acceptted as money by European colonists and American Indians alike. [6] Perhaps the most unusual type of currency was the stone money used by the people on the island of Yap. [7] These Pacific islandders fashionned huge limestone disks to serve as legal tender. [8] Thier size ranged from nine inches in diameter to as large as twelve foots across. [9] Each coin had a hole in the middle so that it could be carried on a pole. [10] Obviously, any thiefs on Yap had to plan very carefuly.

C.   Writing a Language Workshop Lesson

You have won the district spelling championship and have been selected to teach your own English class a spelling lesson. Pick two of the spelling rules from this chapter to present to your class. On your own paper, write each rule and provide your own examples. Then, for each rule, make up an exercise so that your classmates will have a chance to practice the rule. Each exercise should contain at least five questions or items to complete. For each exercise, create a list of answers on a separate sheet of paper.

EX.   1.   RULE: Words ending in y preceded by a vowel do not change their spelling before a suffix.

EXAMPLES: enjoy + ed = enjoyed   pay + ment = payment
                      gray + est = grayest   relay + ed = relayed

EXERCISE 1   Spelling Words with Suffixes
On your own paper, complete the word problem by adding the given suffix to the word.

EX.   1.   delay + ed   1.   delayed